Gathering
of Strangers

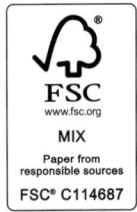

Gathering of Strangers

Why Museums Matter

Maria Balshaw

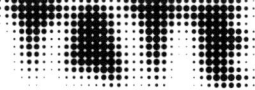

For Colette

Introduction
Museums Now

My first proper encounters with museums were not auspicious. I grew up in the new town of Northampton, part of a large working-class Irish-Catholic family who had settled across the Midlands. Museum-going was not part of my family's habits – nor did the newly built suburban estate I lived on or the local schools I went to foster a sense of curiosity about culture, heritage or art history (though there was a tiny independent cinema, which I shall come to later). The local museum, in the old market town, was old-fashioned though diligently cared for, and featured rather too much on the history of leather and shoes (the local craft practice) to excite a teenager keen on cutting-edge culture. I was encouraged to read, and did so avidly, and my mum harboured a passion for the theatre seeded by teacher nuns who had taken her and her fellow pupils to the Royal Shakespeare Company in the 1960s.

My first encounter with modern art was buying a Penguin edition of Jean-Paul Sartre's *The Age of Reason* from WH Smith at our local shopping centre. I bought the book in a fit of teenage pretension, wanting to demonstrate my intellectual aspirations, but what had really grabbed my attention was the reproduction of Picasso's *Weeping Woman* 1937 on the cover. The original painting now resides at Tate Modern, one of the star pieces of our twentieth-century collection. It was perhaps the thrilling strangeness of that image that compelled me to take the train to London, as soon as I was allowed to make solo trips (aged sixteen), in search of more modern art.

I was not immediately rewarded. My destination was the National Portrait Gallery, where I stood in front of some less than modern-looking portraits of William Shakespeare. The building and collection in the mid-1980s could not be more different from the gallery today, where female sitters and artists, artists of colour, and popular cultural figures take up space on the walls in a broad and varied portrait of the nation. I then made my way next door to the National Gallery, which I found almost too imposing to enter. There was little to make me feel welcome, or to help me read or understand the clearly important 'old master' paintings on the walls. At this point I almost gave up and returned to Northampton. My salvation was realising that the Tate Gallery (there was only one then) was just a short Tube journey away, in Pimlico. There, I thought, I might be able to see *Weeping Woman* in real life.

At that time, Tate presented British and international modern and contemporary art together, along with a selection from the national collection of British art, spanning some 500 years. It was a crush having so many disparate works in one building for sure, but it meant that visitors could see and explore a multitude of great things in one place. In the end it was not Picasso but Bridget Riley that made my London trip worthwhile: there were very few women artists on display, but Riley's swirling, optically agile works captured me instantly. This was the modern that I had been looking for.

Only a couple of years later, in 1988, I moved up to Liverpool as a student and found to my surprise that they had opened a Tate Gallery there. It was the first place I took my parents when they visited, making the gallery part of a story of my newfound independence and my expanded cultural horizons. In the gallery I found more of Riley's work, but also Dalí's *Lobster Telephone* 1938, Rothko's *Seagram Murals* 1958–9 and many other delights that came to shape my way of thinking about art history. I was always welcomed by the gallery staff, even when I was less than a perfect visitor. I remember spending one memorable afternoon with two friends lying on the cool gallery floor looking across at a Richard Long stone circle, resting our sore heads after a night of excess. This, I should add, only speaks to the prescient attitude of the Tate Liverpool visitor attendants, as we would certainly have been asked to leave for inappropriate lounging in most other galleries and museums back then (and perhaps by some today)!

These varied encounters formed the building blocks of my adult fascination with art and, most especially, my love of museums.

•

I share these experiences not simply to anchor this book in my own particular perspective, although this personal connection to museums is one of the main motivations for me in writing this book. Rather, I do it to highlight how much museums have changed in my own lifetime, and how attitudes towards them have shifted even more. We now recognise that museums, as cultural institutions, should strive to engage and consider the thoughts, ideas and interests of the people they are there to serve – you, the general public – and we hold museums to account if they do not. It is this shift in perceived constituency, and the wish to be accountable to a wider range of communities who will necessarily have differing views and attitudes to our museum institutions, that is my primary preoccupation in this book. More than that, it is the central question facing all museums today.

Museums are all, by and large, built on the notion of holding our past in its richness and diversity for our collective pleasure and education. We see this reflected in the mission enshrined in statute at Tate, where I work, to 'increase the public's enjoyment and understanding of British art ... and of international modern and contemporary art' and to hold and grow our collection for the benefit of the public.[1] Simple enough? Not so. This statement of purpose belies the complex and contested history and status of museums in the UK and across the globe.

We might look at this time as perhaps the most dynamic and fast-changing of decades for museums as cultural institutions – certainly, the most challenging. The experience of coping with the impact of the global Covid-19 pandemic between 2020 and 2022 is only the most extreme example of recent challenges to the way museums operate, which together have stretched the capacity of museums beyond our collective imaginings. We should hold in mind that dealing with Covid was, however, only one in a set of dilemmas which have their own long history and which present us with issues and opportunities that continue to affect the global museum ecology.

When Tate closed its doors in March 2020, no one imagined that we would remain closed to the public for the longest period in the history of the museum outside wartime. No one imagined that our ways of working would be tested to such a degree that they might need to be rethought entirely. Yet, as we shall see in the following chapters, every generation of museums has faced its own hurdles, imagining that they were tackling the radical issues or preserving the right objects and ideas. It is all too easy to observe the limitations of the past with the also partial wisdom of hindsight.

It is vital, I think, that we see the challenges museums face today as the necessary correlates of their continued currency and usefulness, rather than as a set of problems that render the institution precarious, or in some way obsolete. More than ever in our culturally contested present we need museums, precisely because of their potential and their constant evolution – they are, as they have always been, spaces where objects and their meanings can be both appreciated and argued over.

Past and Present

Museums are caught within a set of tensions that are bound up with their own history. The wealth and power dynamics that helped to shape the collections and buildings of the world's museums say a lot about their role and purpose in the modern age. It is fair to say that nearly all museums that hold national or regionally specific collections draw on an elitist lineage, sometimes even a royal imperative. Until fairly recently, museums presented history yet were curiously amnesiac about the history of their collections and the sources of the funding that created and supported them. This is no longer tenable for museums if they wish to be active players in the creation and maintenance of an engaged public sphere, as I think they should be. It is not just interesting but useful to note that this is not, as we shall see, a problem unique to today's world, but one that can be traced back to the creation of a network of public museums forged in large part by the forces of a supposed philanthropic good.

At the very least, museums are bound up with the accumulation of power and wealth within systems of capitalism. Still more often, they are bound up with nation- or empire-building. As collections amassed by the powerful are transformed into national museums accessible to the public, they are expected to be for 'everyone', though institutions can be slow to grasp this democratic impulse, and unwilling or unable to address the often painful legacies that led to their creation and are embodied still in their collections.

We can see this in the governing statutes of most major museums, which generally state that objects are held 'for posterity' – interpreted as meaning 'forever'. This leaves us with a sense that it is the task of the museum almost to hold back time and preserve the past through the selection and accrual of rare and important objects. At the same time, the museum is charged with making these objects available and meaningful for people now, in a world where the power dynamics and the local and global demographics that underpinned that original collecting mission have not only changed but have been fundamentally challenged and rejected.

Museums may evolve and change all the time, and indeed they are created and disappear over time, but they are institutions of the long term – designed to fulfil their role for centuries, as a central component of national identity and cultural power. In recent years, however, that long-term thinking has changed.[2] Many museums purport to be about the past, giving us insight into the life, culture and art of bygone times, but in reality they are always about the present – sharing ideas and services with people in the present moment, and irrefutably shaped by that present. The fixed nature of the museum is profoundly at odds with the requirement that it should reflect its own times. Most potently, in a period where there is widespread debate about national heritage and identity, it is, to my mind, the inevitable condition of the modern museum with collections held 'in perpetuity for the public' that our own identity will be riven with contradiction and tension.

It goes without saying that the past is always reshaped in the present – though this is not the way many of the visiting public (nor many politicians) perceive it. Arguments about how we 'interpret' the objects on museum walls or in cases, which have flared up particularly in recent years, are not so much about this political or cultural moment: they go deeper into the productive contradiction of holding objects from the past. This is because we can only ever ascribe meaning after the fact, interpreting meaning through an ever-shifting balance of supposed evidence and our own biases.

This becomes even more apparent if we allow ourselves to challenge the overly determined sense, fostered by museum professionals for much of the history of museums, that these vast storehouses are rational and cool, organised according to dispassionate logic and a strong and consistent evidence base of knowledge. Nothing could be further from the truth. All museums and their collections are shot through with emotions, both internally and externally. Collections are often founded and maintained through the singular enthusiasm of individuals who are very far from dispassionate in their interests: in fact, passion is one of the driving forces for their collecting energies. Even today, the highest regard is paid to the deep subject specialist with the near-encyclopaedic knowledge of 'their' area. We should remember, too, that until really very recently curators of collections were known as their 'keepers', with the concomitant image of their keys keeping the collection not safe *for* the public, but *from* them.

Museum collections, formed with passion as much as precision, are then the subject of interest for those who cross the museum threshold. The ensuing level of dispute encompasses, as we will explore, the current vital and necessary debates about where objects stolen or removed from countries through colonial exploitation should reside now that those systems of oppression have been dismantled. This is a debate that no museum can turn its face away from, whatever its statutes might dictate.

There is another side to this passion, one that speaks to the public's enthusiasm for the things that they know and love in a more prosaic sense. The Horniman Museum in Forest Hill, London is a world collection bringing together nature and culture. The most famous and beloved object in a collection built through the passions of late nineteenth-century tea merchant Frederick Horniman is a very large walrus, which has lived in the natural history galleries for more than a century. We now know that this walrus was dramatically overstuffed by the curators and conservators first responsible for bringing it into the collection, none of whom had ever actually seen a walrus. Any suggestion today that the walrus should be slimmed down to correct anatomical proportions would, I expect, be greeted by a roar of protest. Museums have a responsibility to reflect the world they live in, yet we, the public, do not always want them to be scientifically or historically 'correct', because what drives our connection and enthusiasm is personal, emotional and subjective.

Discussion and Debate

These issues are not new. But we live in a moment when they are becoming more apparent. The museum profession is perhaps more alert than it has ever been to the workings of power, authority and privilege within their institutions. There is still a very long way to go to have a museum workforce that matches the diversity of the public we are tasked with serving. Our public also expect a much greater degree of transparency about the decisions we make, and the power relationships these decisions do or do not invoke. Whether they are very regular visitors or have never crossed our threshold, we live in an age where the general public are rightly active and vocal about what museums should and should not do. The debates play out in the press and, more notably, online – social media has created an exponential expansion in the culture of debate and opinion. Important, too, is the popular success of museums: millions of people visit museums each year in the UK, and in this very popularity we also see political and public resistance to certain kinds of change.

Most significantly, we live in a time where public discourse is peculiarly divided and disputatious. Our current moment is a turbulent one, with economic and political crises, global tensions and conflict, an ongoing climate and nature emergency, a raft of wider social and cultural anxieties, and inter-generational and identity-led clashes of values and mores.

As someone who did not feel a constituent of museums as I was growing up, I feel enormously heartened when I see the active participation and critique offered by the many young adults who now take part in their chosen aspects of museum life – even or sometimes especially when the engagement brings with it criticism and a call for more change. We are seeing proliferating, increasingly confident forms of protest, agency and creative resistance on the part of the many who have not been at the heart of traditional power structures.

•

Rather than thinking that we exist in difficult times, where the liberal values of the arts are being trampled on, I want to reframe our context to suggest that we operate in *sensitive* times, in which we urgently need to cultivate better listening skills and more empathetic codes of engagement. The role, therefore, of the art museum could be to create a space premised on an ethics of care (for people, different views, values and realities) and on expanding the practices by which people can engage with art. If we can do this, we will be doing justice to the nuance and complexity of art practice, and we will also open up our spaces and histories to more than one story, view or idea.

But there are significant challenges here. Creating this kind of space will require us to go to the places and hear the ideas and views of those who do *not* want us, not only those who like us already or are open to the idea that art could mean something to them. We can't only see ourselves as the progressive guardians of all that is good and uplifting in a morally corrupt world. We are, of course, part of the problem. We need to openly explore those profound exclusions and disagreements, because these in part result in the societal polarisation we see in the UK and across the world today. And because now, more than ever, we need to nurture spaces where disagreement, complexity and discomfort can be constructively examined, we need to hear the many other sides of those arguments – all without losing our own values. Otherwise, we fail to hold to the most useful thing about art: that it is subjective and ambiguous. This is as hard for those who identify themselves as progressive change makers within and outside the museum as it is for those 'traditional' visitors who may fear their familiar and known museum is being changed and eroded. Museums, in my formulation, are tasked with bringing together the traditionalists and the reformers and reminding them that we are allowed, as humans and as museum visitors, to disagree with what we see.

The museum as we think of it now has been labelled in multiple ways: elitist, educative, exclusive, inclusive, populist, brutish. It is certainly a space being remade and it is still, most likely, in need of further 'rearrangement'. Many, if not most, museums want to take part in this process. Public institutions do not sit 'outside' society; they are the barometer of time and place. How we open ourselves to change and engage dissenting voices is not obvious or easy. However, as one recent gallery visitor said: 'Art is an invitation to a conversation' – so perhaps the role of the art museum might be to unlock that conversation.

Gathering of Strangers

As someone who went from thinking that museums were not for her, to becoming the director of one of the most influential art museums in the world, I have a particular commitment to making sure museums do the job we need them to. The story of how museums can work – through the collections they hold, the artworks they show, the education they provide and the ideas they promote by means of the artists they collaborate with – is my terrain in this book. It is a personal, partial and largely practical account, and one that is based on my own love of, and ongoing fascination with, these essential, contradictory and inspiring institutions and especially the artists who make ideas manifest within museum spaces.

In autumn 2021, the artist Anicka Yi launched her machine-learning aerobes into the Turbine Hall at Tate Modern. Titled *In Love with the World*, this elegant, playful, otherworldly project captured something unique about that particular moment. The shoal of robotic creatures moved around the vast Turbine Hall space, responding to scents connected to the site, specially created by Anicka, as well as to visitors entering the space: the shoal gathered and congregated where the public did, as if moving to greet them. After the social isolation of three phases of lockdown, the creatures were a loving gift of connection for a city and its people, prompting, as all good art does, not one response, but many.

Nearly twenty years after I had found my cultural home in the galleries of Tate Liverpool, I became the director of the Whitworth Gallery in Manchester, another institution that I had visited, and loved, in my student years. It was my first ever job in a museum, and to say that I had imposter syndrome was an understatement. On top of the daily demands of the role, I was also, alongside my talented colleagues, tasked with reimagining the museum for the twenty-first century. What I learned really underscores everything I explore in this book. The process eventually led to a physical and cultural transformation for the Whitworth, shaped by the relationships we wanted to build with artists, with our collection, and with the communities around us. Working with our architects, we made dedicated spaces for rest, reflection and study, as well as spaces for discussion, disagreement and celebration. A spirit of exchange was made possible by the profile and porosity of the building: we opened up the gallery to both the park it lives within and the people that use it, blurring the boundary between inside and out. This spirit of openness, and reciprocity, was also embodied in the artworks we chose to be integrated into the building, from David Batchelor's *Plato's Disco*, which created a moving colour field for visitors as they made their way in and up the main staircase, to Nathan Coley's light work, *Gathering of Strangers*, which was positioned at the entrance to the gallery, overlooking the park itself. This phrase became the working ethos of the gallery when it reopened in 2015, speaking directly to what we all witnessed on a daily basis, as 440,000 visitors (more than double our initial estimate) walked through our doors.

And it was not just visitors to the gallery who took Nathan's message to heart. Conor Rabone, lead singer of the indie band Gathering of Strangers, has said:

We just cycled past it one day on the way into uni and we loved that phrase. We loved how it tied into us as the boys who came to uni as strangers, and who'd become friends. It also tied into our shows, with all the people in the crowd coming in as strangers, but united in one collective purpose.[3]

The Whitworth, like all museums, continues to offer this powerful experience of conviviality and exchange. Coming together for a collective purpose is the animating spirit of this book. More than a sign of welcome and community, Nathan's work reminds us of the utopian possibility that strangers, however different their views, can unite through the experience of art, and agree that disagreement is valuable, and possibly even world-changing.

1

Museum Origins

'Dingy places with different kinds of bits...'

This dispiriting phrase comes from a survey of attitudes towards museums by people who didn't visit them.[1] The survey was undertaken in the late 1980s, at a point when museums in the UK were really thinking, often for the first time, about the people who walked through their doors. As the first comprehensive study of public attitudes toward museums it painted a picture of a rather gloomy and inward-looking sector, one that I am pleased to say our public would no longer recognise. I am, however, taking this quote as my starting point here, not because I think it still holds true, but because it is part of perceptions that museums still carry forwards, in spite of the remarkable changes of the past few decades.

In order to properly understand the role of museums today – their orientation and disposition as public institutions – we need to understand their past: where they came from, what they did, and why they did it. Tracing the antecedents to the modern museum will reveal the key drivers for the change we have seen in recent years, as well as illuminating why some aspects of museum life have been doggedly resistant to modernisation. Over the past two decades, it is

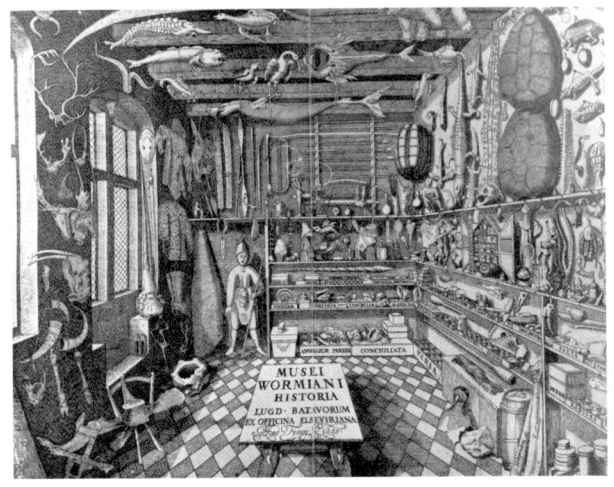

Frontispiece showing the interior of Ole Worm's museum
in Museum Wormianum (1655) (Cole 092F_16)

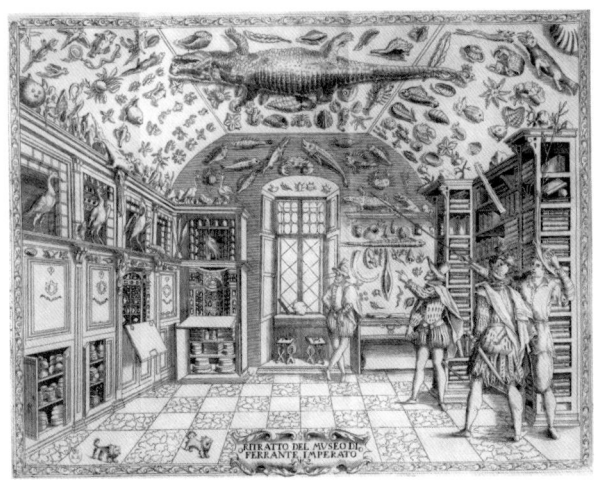

Ferrante Imperato's Dell'historia Naturale. The Natural History
Museum of Emperor Ferdinand III from 'Historia Naturale'
by Ferrante Imperato (1550-1631) pub. in 1672 (engraving)

certainly the case that the museum's image has been transformed from a specialist (even occasionally 'dusty') place for a fairly restricted audience to a more inclusive space where people explore for themselves notions of identity, spirituality, creativity and, I hope, what it means to be human. The transition has been less than smooth, however, and there are still enduring contradictions at the heart of the museum today.

So where does that dusty image come from? There are many tomes of scholarly investigation on the origins of the museum, so I am not going to provide a comprehensive overview.[2] However, it is important to remind ourselves of the basic history of museums and galleries as collections of the elite, and cabinets of curiosity.

The so-called cabinets were essentially private collections for the cognoscenti. Princely collections such as those of the Medici and the Habsburgs were not intended for general consumption, but rather the opposite. In Florence, the Uffizi Gallery, one of the world's most celebrated and popular museums, was originally commissioned by Cosimo I de' Medici as a vast administrative centre ('uffizi' translates as 'offices'), designed to consolidate his hold on Republican Florence. The Habsburg dynasty, who ruled much of Europe from the sixteenth century up to the early twentieth century, amassed such a formidable collection that their particular tastes, and lavish patronage, shaped not only the grand architectural projects they built for themselves, but also many of the great European museums of today. While these collections were certainly intended for looking at, they were really demonstrating the power, influence and wealth of the holders. The invitation to view them also conferred status, and presumed a rarefied sensibility for those who were allowed into this space of privilege.

This desire for the accumulation of objects that demonstrate, often very literally, the extent of royal or state power underpins the

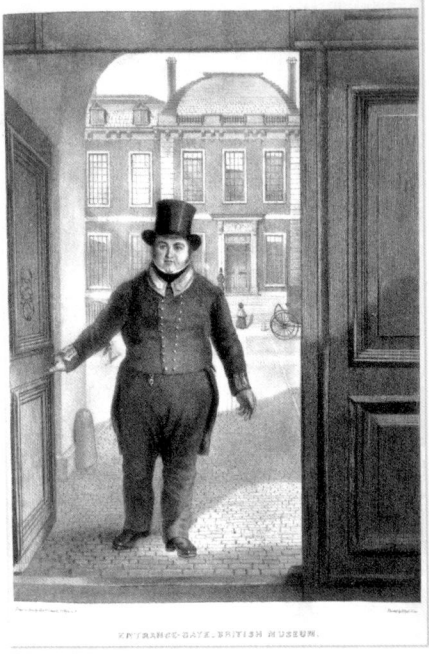

William Sievier, British Museum Porter, at the gate of Montagu House

formation of most national collections, with consequences that live with us to this day. At its most extreme end, the Royal Museum for Central Africa in Tervuren, Belgium holds objects amassed by King Leopold of Belgium, whose exploitation, violence and endemic looting of objects during his personal 'ownership' of the Congo on behalf of the Belgian state is well documented. The museum remains open, but questioning the legitimacy of the collection's provenance given the crimes against humanity that are part of its formation has had to become part of its practice.[3] Although few museums face this degree of challenge, the building of public collections from the private collections of powerful state players means that from their very foundation there is a tension between private pleasure and public accountability.

Class Dynamics

This tension is generally only underscored when these collections make their way into the hands of the state. Most so-called national collections, such as the British Museum, the National Gallery or Tate, began as personal, royal or aristocratic collections that were purchased for the nation through the action of government.[4] Their subsequent expansion came through acquisitions and gifts from collectors keen to see their works in a positively expanding 'national' institution; in turn, this attracted artists to gift or leave works after their death, as J.M.W. Turner did so significantly for the Tate collection. Objects may also find their way into collections by less than savoury means, through the actions of colonisers or from countries ruled by imperial powers.[5]

Although governmental moves to form these collections nearly always came with an aspiration to share great art with a wider public – the National Gallery's Trafalgar Square location was chosen so that the wealthy in their carriages and the working classes walking from the east of London could meet in the common ground of the gallery – the reality was often rather different.[6] The British Museum opened to the public in 1753, but for at least its first century, visitors could only gain admittance upon the recommendation of 'a gentleman or lady of standing', whereupon they had to go to the museum to apply for a ticket via the porter, collect the ticket in advance of their visit, and then return again on the date specified on the ticket for their actual visit. Even when they did get in – which in the late nineteenth century meant passing the armed guards stationed at the museum entrances – it seems that the experience was not a rewarding one. The diary of a Birmingham stationer, William Hutton, describes a visit to the British Museum in the late eighteenth century when, having gone through all the rigmarole of acquiring a ticket, Hutton found the guide completely uninformed and intent on pushing the party through the museum as quickly as possible. He memorably describes being 'hackneyed through the rooms with violence' and coming away from his visit none the wiser.

The early model of public museums was one which distinguished between visitors who had the necessary taste and 'cultural capital' (to use Pierre Bourdieu's useful phrase) to appreciate their treasure, and those who did not.[7] Here we are seeing, again from the very earliest formation of museums, a class distinction that hides within a language of educational requirements. If the princely collections were seen to require the refined or elevated eye of the social elite, then, when these collections became notionally public, there was a sense that a visitor would need a certain degree of education and experience to appreciate them. This sense of elitism was only reinforced when many museums (like the Ashmolean, founded in Oxford in 1683, or the Fitzwilliam, founded in Cambridge in 1816) became associated with, or formally part of, universities. Very rapidly, these museums and collections developed their own research activities, often with deeply focused specialisms, driven in large part by the donor collections that had helped form them in the first place. The focus moved away from the general public.

It is useful to bear in mind that the formation of collections often seen as comprehensive – or, to use the rather more loaded term, 'encyclopaedic' – was mostly a much more idiosyncratic affair.[8] The Manchester Museum's adoption in the 1860s by the then John Owens College, soon to become the University of Manchester, saw an expansive gathering of specialist collections across the natural and human sciences as well as the burgeoning Mancunian interest in the practices of science, with the aim of developing a museum based on 'evolutionary principles' (drawing much on Thomas Henry Huxley's thinking). As well as reflecting local passions, this move also positioned the institution self-consciously in opposition to certain London institutions who still operated according to a Godly order. So, the rich Egyptology collections in Manchester and the academic specialism that follows are born out of the passion and philanthropy of donor Jesse Haworth, who funded a whole new floor to house his collections, and made such substantial subsequent donations that two museum extensions had to be built to accommodate them. With this impetus, Manchester Museum, more rapidly than most, adopted a stance interested in exploring man's scientific mastery over the natural world. It is worth emphasising how much a museum's collection has to do with local donor and academic passions, as it does with any sense of logical or scientific analysis of the world. In the same way, the collection of the British Museum is intrinsically shaped, for good and for bad, by the founding collection of just one man, Sir Hans Sloane.

The sense of the rarity and refinement of some collections and the specialist nature of others reinforces a class dimension to the presumed museum user (when these museums were founded, there were few true 'general visitors' in the sense we would recognise now). These were collections intended for a very special community of informed visitors. Indeed, as many have observed, one of the functions of museums and galleries, historically, was to form part of a constellation of higher cultural activities that served to reinforce class distinctions.[9] Although we might not like to acknowledge it, the sense that a museum visit requires some specialist knowledge still haunts many in our own time and contributes, many would argue, to the low levels of attendance by audiences from lower socio-economic groups.[10] We find traces in most modern museums of a slightly awkward contradiction of the idea of 'open access', with orders of knowledge accessible only to those already well informed.

This unspoken elitism is nicely summarised in an image of the Royal Scottish Museum in the 1880s. In it, we see incredibly complex and densely grouped displays all proudly described as 'open to the public'. Given that the only visitors we see in the picture are the curator and his assistant, however, we might take this to mean that they are the only ones knowledgeable enough to grasp the obscure classificatory principles uniting these disparate objects.

During the first great expansion of museums in the UK, from the 1840s to the turn of the nineteenth and twentieth centuries, this model of exclusivity was overlaid with a somewhat contradictory impulse to improve the manners and taste of British citizens. The supporters of the 1845 Museum Act, which would allow local taxes to be levied to support museums, were strong followers of temperance – the social movement dedicated to educating the public about the many dangers of alcohol – and saw museums as an alternative to the alehouse. The Great Exhibition of 1851 and the subsequent formation of the South Kensington Museums were driven by a desire to improve the quality of manufacturing design, but also to make questions of aesthetics, manners and social mores a matter of wider public interest.

In another contradictory way, museums were also a means of keeping people in their place. Throughout the mid- to late nineteenth century, revolutions were sporadically breaking out over Europe, leading to fears of similar uprisings in Britain. So another impulse behind museum development can be seen in a sometimes covert but often overt wish to instruct the lower classes to accept their position in society. To give just one well-known example, the now not sung (and objectionable) part of the hymn 'All Things Bright and Beautiful' exhorts us to acknowledge the 'rich man in his castle, the poor man at his gate'. The noted museum pioneer General Pitt-Rivers wrote that the purpose of his museum complex at Farnham was to teach people that 'nature makes no jumps' – that 'history teaches that evolution rather than revolution is the proper order of things' – so that working people would 'not listen to scatter-brained revolutionary suggestions'.[11]

Aspiration and Containment: The Whitworth

All of these competing principles – aspirational, educational, democratic, autocratic – were playing out against a backdrop of extraordinary political and societal change. The wealth of industry and Empire were transforming cities and creating new kinds of encounters and opportunities for an improving and growing working and middle class. Modern innovations such as plate glass window technology and gas lighting were revolutionising the streetscape, while the combination of newly created department stores and expanded modes of public transport served to transform urban mobility (and eventually social and gender mobility too).[12] All of these technologies had an effect on museum spaces – the classic large Victorian museum cases utilised the same plate glass technology as shop windows – as well as on those who were able to see and be seen within them.

The new Victorian museum infrastructure had a series of fundamental contradictions at its heart. On the one hand, it wanted to attract a wide audience for purposes of social cohesion; on the other, it could not rid itself of the exclusiveness of its foundation in the collections of the wealthy and the scholarly, which through their reliance on aristocratic traditions and specialist knowledge impelled those who were less well educated to see museums as not for themselves. We can see this in an early plan of the Whitworth, where I began my museum career.

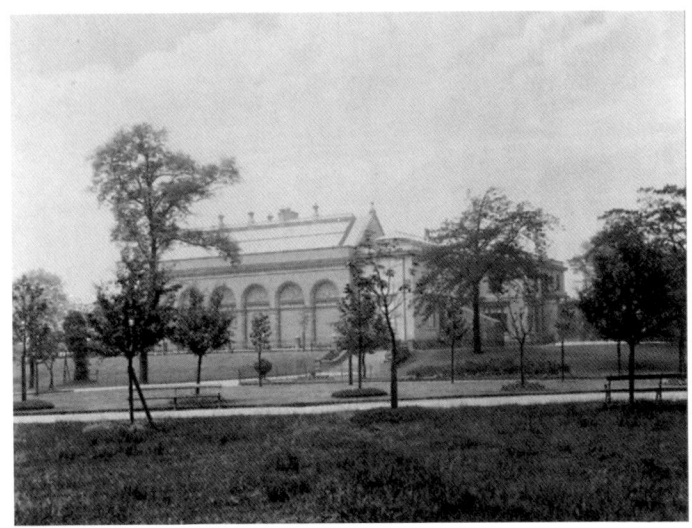

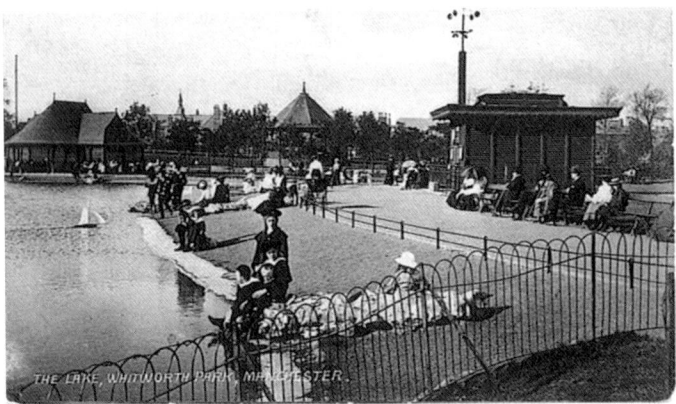

Historical images of Whitworth when it was first built. Museum and park.

The Whitworth gallery and the park around it were created through the fortune of the Stockport-born engineer Joseph Whitworth, who bequeathed a large proportion of his fortune to the city of Manchester following his death in 1887. It was, however, Robert Darbishire, as one of Whitworth's executors, who set out a vision for a gallery in the park as a suitable legacy for his friend. To realise this ambition, he put together a committee of eminent Mancunians – businessmen and art collectors – with the stated aim of:

> Secur[ing] a source of perpetual gratification to the people of Manchester and, at the same time, a permanent influence of the highest character in the directions of commercial and technical instruction and the cultivation of taste and knowledge of the Fine Arts of Painting, Sculpture and Architecture.

A bold plan for the project was set out and quickly realised (the Victorians were speedier with their building initiatives than we now tend to be). As a former Whitworth Director, Charles Reginald Dodwell, observed in the 1980s, the Whitworth was 'a posthumous child Whitworth never saw or imagined'. The park – 'a green and social space in the city', as contemporary reports described it – had a large lake for sailing model boats, a bandstand, pavilion and pleasure gardens; early reports of the gallery committee make much of the fact that these pleasure gardens were 'used by visitors and children of all social classes', and of the frequency and popularity of concerts and other public events hosted in the grounds.[13] The park was clearly constructed and imagined as a space for healthful pursuits to remedy the imagined and actual malaise of inner-city industrial life. Perhaps the most important innovation was the inclusion of a ladies' and gentlemen's 'cloakroom' (or toilet), transforming the gallery and the park into an acceptable social space for gentlewomen to visit during the course of a day in the city.

Yet we also see from the plans of the time that the room for the curator is situated at the very heart of the building. While the wealthy early donors and the committee who governed this gallery – like those behind many late nineteenth-century institutions – proclaimed the Whitworth as a space for everyone, the structures and orders of knowledge they preserved maintained much of their elite lineage.

Take a look at early photographs of the new galleries and you can see dense 'hang' or display of the Whitworth's famed prints and drawings collection, modelled on the classic floor-to-ceiling hang of the country house print room, or the Royal Academy's regular exhibitions. There are so many works on display that it is nearly impossible to appreciate a single one, let alone construct a coherent narrative about what they represent. The story here is more about the importance of the collection (and the wealth and power of those who helped to shape it) than of the artworks. Similarly, the early days of the gallery saw it display a collection of plaster cast copies of classical statuary – not to entice a broader public, but to offer an elevated education in the art of drawing the human figure without the need for naked models. The intention was avowedly instructional, foreshadowing the Whitworth becoming formally part of the University of Manchester, while contemporary committee reports' description of the ambition to 'cultivate taste and knowledge' betrays a desire to elevate and affirm social privilege. All of this speaks to an ever-present contradiction between the wish to engage the growing urban populace while at the same time maintaining long-held modes of display and educational practice drawn from aristocratic traditions.

The Whitworth is an interesting and typical example of this contradictory nineteenth- and early twentieth-century ethos. Similar patterns are to be found across the regional and national museum collections founded and grown in this period: Birmingham, Manchester, Leeds, Liverpool, Newcastle – indeed, all the rapidly expanding northern industrial cities – accrued collections that reflected their industrial and imperial power. One only need look at Sir Charles Barry's Manchester Art Gallery, with its Latin inscription around its ornate roof, or the grand entrances to the Walker Art Gallery in Liverpool or Birmingham Museum and Art Gallery to understand that these institutions were created to entrench cultural ambition and wealth even as they apparently opened their doors to the many.

Imperial Entanglements

The troubling tensions at the heart of the formation of our national and regional museum collections grow only more acute when we consider the relationship between museum-building and empire-building. We cannot talk about the history of the museum without acknowledging the history of trauma and exploitation that is represented by many Western museums in their collections, and in their own actions and activity.

It is telling and embarrassing that open exploration of this has only really taken place in the past two decades. As writers such as Dan Hicks have comprehensively demonstrated, the formation of museums is part of the practice of empire-building, slavery, colonialism and the violent force of industrial extraction and wealth generation.[14] This was argued as early as 1944 by Eric Williams in his book *Capitalism and Slavery*, in which he spelled out the ways in which slavery and the plantation system fuelled the Industrial Revolution in the UK.[15] We can trace, without too much effort, how the wealth generated by Empire and accumulated by a powerful minority actively led to the founding of museums. It is also easy to see how imperial 'exploration' and exploitation formed the bedrock of museum collections across the Western world. This is as true of Vienna and Paris (with their Kunsthistorisches and Naturhistorisches Museums and the Musée de l'Homme respectively) as it is of Manchester, London or Berlin.

While we can find traces of the close associations between colonial and imperial wealth accumulation in almost every museum, some especially egregious examples have come to public attention in recent times. The Geffrye Museum, now renamed the Museum of the Home, took its name from a well-known merchant who built the almshouses that the museum now resides in, and whose fortune was made in part through the forced labour and trading of enslaved African people. Although the London Borough of Hackney consulted and agreed that his name should be removed from the museum and from a number of other locations and buildings in the borough, the decision to move Robert Geffrye's statue from outside the museum caused a great deal of upset and outrage.[16] This only tells us how potent the idea that museums hold a 'never-changing' history remains for those who wish not to acknowledge the uglier side of our complex history. Even when the relationship to the history of enslavement of peoples is not as direct as in the Geffrye example, there are few museums today that do not have a lot to grapple with in terms of their history and its impact on their present practice.

To give an example closer to home, Tate itself carries all kinds of associations through its name and history with sugar, and therefore Empire, and therefore slavery. The truth of those associations is complicated. Henry Tate was a sugar merchant and philanthropist whose collection formed the catalyst for Tate galleries as we know them today. Although Tate began his business as a refiner many years after the abolition of slavery, the Caribbean sugar trade itself, and Tate's subsequent profits, would not have been possible without the slave trade. As a museum that bears his name, we felt that we should have the confidence and fulfil our responsibility to tell those complicated stories. So, several years ago we worked with researchers at UCL's Centre for the Study of the Legacies of British Slavery to explore our history and to share it with the public.[17] Our aim was not to defend Henry Tate, nor to 'cancel' him, but to establish a set of solid facts to turn to when visitors and artists wanted to ask us questions, or when we wanted to ask questions ourselves.

As well as a resistance or reluctance to acknowledge the violence against specific groups and communities embodied in the objects they often hold for, notionally, 'all of the public', museums are also currently struggling to represent the histories of non-white and non-Western peoples within their collections and programmes. That this contributes to the historic lack of engagement by people of colour with the museum complex should therefore also not surprise us.

We can return once again to the Whitworth for a useful example here. Unsurprisingly, paintings and objects that helped found the Whitworth's collection came from direct or indirect connections to the transatlantic slave trade and to the importing and manufacture of cotton. In 2007, curators at the Whitworth embarked on a project to mark the 200th anniversary of the abolition of British slavery, working with artists whose practice and lived experience connected directly to these histories. During the development stages of the exhibition, a wider and more complicated set of relationships were uncovered. A label on the back of one of the Turner works donated in the founding years of the gallery stated: 'When times are good for cotton, times are good for art'. This was a work that had been purchased with wealth generated from the trading and manufacture of cotton goods, whose raw material was slave-grown. Although the early supporters of the Whitworth were certainly philanthropic, one finds nothing in the committee reports to reflect Manchester's position within a colonial trading paradigm, nor in relation to the abolition of slavery – even though the abolitionist movement was strong enough in Manchester for the cotton workers to boycott slave-grown cotton. Nevertheless, the label on the back of a painting remained there, hidden in plain sight, right through to 2007.

Other objects selected by artists Kevin Dalton-Johnson and SuAndi spoke still more powerfully to the way these histories were made manifest beyond the walls of the gallery, and in our nation's collective history. A collection of children's dolls gifted to the collection many decades ago provided an example of textile virtuosity, but also of a painful history of slavery. The dolls were made as keepsakes for the children of an English plantation owner whose business in Brazil relied heavily on the labour of enslaved people, and the dolls themselves were not generic characters but representations of the house slaves whose job it was to care for the children. SuAndi, who grew up as a British-Caribbean child in 1970s Liverpool, firmly described them as Golliwogs, examples of racist children's toys from Britain's past, and was against their display as part of the exhibition. For Kevin Dalton-Johnson and the Learning team working with schools in the predominantly African and African Caribbean area of Moss Side, the dolls were difficult, ambivalent markers of a history that nevertheless needed to be acknowledged and discussed. The artists did not, in the end, attempt to resolve their differing viewpoints, but instead showed the dolls in a way that foregrounded the disagreement: two covered and two uncovered, in the storage box that had concealed them for so many years. With a text on the wall inviting the public to debate and share their views, this partial display became the means to make evident those histories which had always been present but not previously owned or acknowledged by the institution.

The historic links to slavery did not end with individual objects, however. The Whitworth's textile collections, like those of its larger cousin the V&A, were assembled to 'act as a source of help and inspiration for the textiles industry of the North', and to influence and, where possible, improve industrial design. Noted proponents of the arts and crafts movement such as William Morris and Thomas Wardle and designers and collectors alike looked across the British Empire (and beyond) to seek out what they regarded as the greatest examples of artistry in textile form, and the gallery collected extensively from these regions to meet these needs. Closer into the city, a similar thing was happening with the assembling of the ceramic collections at Manchester Art Gallery.

These 'world' collections certainly provided insights into the aesthetic and cultural brilliance of non-Western material culture at a time when 'art' from these countries would not have been regarded as worthy of consideration. The establishment, in these museums' earliest years, of rich holdings of textiles from South and East Asia, from across the African continent and from South America, sets a precedent that endured throughout the twentieth century and continues on to the experiences of visitors to the gallery today. In recent times, the Whitworth has undertaken textile shows that actively rewrite material and textile histories from the perspective of the Global South, because its holdings allow it to do so.[18] Having had such holdings from the Global South from the outset also enabled the museum to continue acquiring textiles from designers and makers from the Caribbean, the African continent and South Asia in subsequent decades, and to establish connections between historic and contemporary practices in ways that interrogate and in some ways undo the historical inequalities of past thinking.[19]

And what of the founders of the Manchester galleries? All were well-established figures in the industrial, metropolitan business elite of Manchester at the time. Many were individuals whose wealth derived from the slave trade, including John Edward Taylor, founder editor of the *Manchester Guardian* (or the *Guardian*, as it is today). We have already met another significant donor to the Whitworth and to the nearby Manchester Museum, the wealthy Bolton-based yarn merchant Jesse Haworth, an avid collector of Turner watercolours, many subsequently donated to the Whitworth, as well as a keen Egyptophile who sponsored Flinders Petrie's archaeological excavations and brought objects from his campaigns back to both Manchester institutions.

While we can certainly see the progressive intentions of Whitworth's initial bequest and the undeniable good work of his executors, who dedicated his fortune to the creation of a public park and art gallery, we cannot deny or erase the complicated histories of these men. We must also remember that Whitworth's own name and fortune were made by his design of the Whitworth rifle, notorious for its deadly accuracy in the American Civil and Boer Wars. Museums today would certainly baulk at taking money from an armament manufacturer.

All this is to make the obvious – but, until recently, little acknowledged – point that the Whitworth, like so many other galleries founded in the era of the Industrial Revolution, was inevitably caught up in forces that pulled powerfully against the idea of the museum as a universal social good. Class dynamics, imperial and colonial dominance, and a patrician (at best) attitude to the 'improving' mission of museums mean they were, from their inception, spaces that invited study and praise, but not questions. This is the case even, or perhaps especially, when the intention behind those museums' missions was a progressive one. As we look from our contemporary position, observing the deficiencies of past thinking, we should always be careful to remember that future generations (perhaps even those travelling with us now) will point to our own power plays, blind spots and deficiencies. There is no such thing as the perfect museum – nor perfected museum practice.

Time for Change

Although I have provided only a potted history, my example of the Whitworth demonstrates the contradictory action of engagement and exclusion which characterises the foundation of most museums and galleries, not just in the UK but around the world. This is, however, a book with some hope in it. Though this difficult museum model persisted for a good part of the twentieth century (and some might argue persists too much still today), we can trace the emergence of a different museum model – more open, more inclusive, more critical – to the early part of the last century. There are heartening stories of women moving wholesale into the running and protection of museums during the Second World War (women sadly deemed dispensable again once the war ended). Ideas about 'opening up' museums to raise people's spirits in the challenging wartime period saw piano recitals in the National Gallery, while museums sent their precious collections off to safety to such unlikely (but very environmentally stable) places as the Cheshire salt mines. When Tate's collection was threatened by the Blitz, artworks and objects found themselves carried down into Tube stations by diligent staff members.

The 1950s and 1960s saw accelerated change in the museum sector as part of the powerful social movements – around citizenship, rights and equity – that rippled across the globe. At the same time, the expansion of mass media and the subsequent democratising of taste that came about through the global expansion of mass market capitalism began to make itself felt in the museum and art gallery world. As we will see, the creation of the welfare state – including the formation

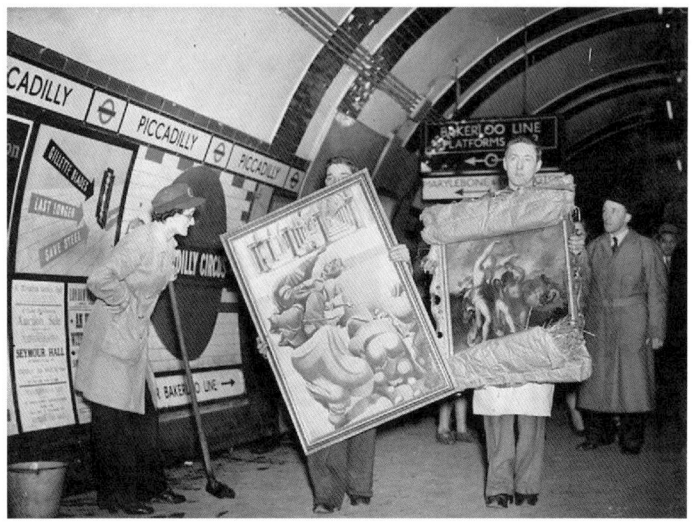

Protecting Works of Art during the Second World War 80 feet below the surface of Piccadilly Circus, art treasures from the Tate Gallery, London Museum and other collections have been stored during the war in a disused part of the Underground line, which was sealed off for their safekeeping. Photo shows: Works of art being brought out of storage along the platform at Piccadilly Underground Station, to be returned to their usual resting places.

of an Arts Council tasked with connecting a wider public with the arts – also introduced a sense of a public good, supported by taxes, being part of the operation and purpose of museums.

It is at this historical point that museums begin to be seen as something that can be popular with larger numbers of visitors. The social changes that went hand in hand with civil rights, women's liberation debates, and the move to 'comprehensive education' and the expansion of higher education all speak to a growing lower- and middle-class audience interested in museums, and the beginning of a call for museums to genuinely represent the people they were ostensibly built to reach. Within the labour movement, the student movement and across countercultural popular movements, questions of individual rights and individual representation came to the fore in new and forceful ways.[20] For the first time, the voices of those unrepresented in museums began to be heard, and museums began to change.

Although it's difficult to pinpoint the exact moment when that change began, there are some notable examples – and personal favourites indeed – that for me point to these new ways of working, and to the future.

The first of these is the Anacostia Community Museum in Washington, DC, established in the early 1960s as – rather remarkably – a branch of the otherwise firmly establishment Smithsonian Institution in an all-Black part of the city. The Anacostia didn't have a collection; it didn't even look like a museum. In fact, it looked more like a shop. Its exhibitions were developed and designed to be of direct interest and relevance to local communities above all else. One of its most popular exhibitions was about the history and habits of the rat, a particularly troublesome and ubiquitous pest in the neighbourhood. The Anacostia promoted an art that was rooted in its locality, providing visitors with practical, insightful and useful art about their environment and their own lives. In this respect, the Anacostia was way ahead of its time.

Today, we can see the ideas of Arte Útil, or Useful Museum Practice, at play in many major museums around the world. Fostered in the last decade by curators and directors within previously quite elitist contemporary art institutions, Useful Museum Practice typically works with socially engaged artists to redefine the museum as a space of co-production, with the promotion of social good their primary outcome.[21]

The influence of radical social thinking on art practice also began to make itself felt on the art museum spaces themselves. It is instructive to note that our contemporary questioning of the art museum's use and purpose began much earlier than we like to think; its roots are often embedded in the practice of individual artists whose work did not find a happy home in the art museum until much later. Skipping forward a decade to 1973, then, we find the artist Lynn Hershman Leeson developing the first documented example of a site-specific work, *The Dante Hotel*, a project which ran for nine months in the San Francisco Bay area. Hershman Leeson's ideas were spurred in part by the social protest movements in and around the Bay Area at the time, and their impact (or lack of it) on the museum there. Indeed, at the time, the University Art Museum in Berkeley had recently risked losing its funding and reputation because of its failure to exhibit work by women artists.

Hershman's initial approach was to create a simulation of a hotel room within the gallery, complete with found objects, sheets, and a soundtrack of breathing and other everyday noises which was activated as visitors approached. Not long after the work opened, however, curators insisted that the sound element was inappropriately noisy, and the exhibition was closed.[22] Rather than continue to fight to be in the gallery, Hershman Leeson took the radical step to move her work beyond the gallery walls. As she said:

> I realised that instead of bringing the hotel room to the museum, it might be more appropriate to simply work in the context of a 'real' hotel room. Similar in spirit to Duchamp's ready-mades, *The Dante Hotel* functioned as a 'found' environment.

A suitable hotel was duly found, the exhibition environment was recreated, and *The Dante Hotel* opened its doors to visitors again. The project was an enormous success: hundreds of people 'trespassed' in the rooms in the months that they were open, twenty-four hours a day, and the *San Francisco Chronicle* ranked Hershman Leeson's work as one of the Bay Area's ten most important fine-art exhibitions of 1973.

Alongside this radical rethinking of museum and gallery practice we began to see new kinds of museums being established in the 1960s and 1970s, as a heritage and nostalgia boom developed in response to the closure of traditional manufacturing industries and the decline of traditional ways of life. Ironbridge Gorge Museum in Shropshire, for example, was established in 1968 as a museum of a whole industrial landscape, with open-air spaces and enclosed buildings. The Museum of Science and Industry in Manchester was created on the site of both the first cotton warehouse and George Stephenson's first railway station and bridge; in many ways, it was and is an homage to the very industrial might that fuelled the growth of museums as a whole in the UK, and across much of the world, as much as it is a museum about science and engineering. As Robert Hewison has written, much of this 'growth' in museums can be seen as a commodification of these institutions toward becoming a 'heritage industry', part of the post-industrial decline and then later cultural regeneration of industrial cities across the UK, Europe and North America.[23]

The traditional museum, of the type that I outlined at the beginning of the chapter, was beginning to crumble. New ones began to take their place (over half of the UK's approximately 2,000 museums and galleries have been established since the 1970s), and the well established had to evolve. As a result – the commodification of our museum sector notwithstanding – we now have museums devoted to many subjects, and the voices of previously marginalised groups and those entirely omitted are heard more clearly. I would note, however, that not as much has changed as we might imagine.

Anya Gallaccio's exhibition at Ikon Gallery, Birmingham in 2003 was a sensorial assault, with real apples rotting on cast bronze trees and a whole room covered in chocolate.[24] Visitors were instructed not to touch the walls, though this was a signal failure in my family at least, as my two-year-old headed in one direction and the four-year-old in another, each licking a wall despite my best efforts to stop them. While the gallery walls can be covered in chocolate, there are as many rules dictating access and enjoyment as Charlie encountered in Willy Wonka's fabled Chocolate Factory. More recently, at Tate Modern, we asked visitors to 'try on' some of Franz West's Body Sculptures, while making it very clear that they needed to stay behind the barriers for the rest of the exhibition. The resulting confusion felt like an illustration of the broader uncertainty visitors might feel around whether galleries really want to 'make people feel at home' or make them stand up and pay attention.[25]

Vulnerability or Certainty

Museums tend to be slow-moving creatures – but, as a colleague recently said to me: 'These past two years, it's as if someone has had their finger on the fast forward button.' We in the cultural sector have no other option but to be in this turbulence. It is our terrain. And imagining a 'fast forward' button is also, of course, a gorgeously analogue metaphor for our times (you have to be of a certain age to recall the speeded-up sound of fast forwarding through a song you don't like on your tape recorder).

As much as I welcome the radical shifts in cultural authority and want to support them, I have to acknowledge that they have also been immensely challenging for Tate and, in one way or another, for all museums today. It's hard because it means putting one's head above the parapet and really beginning to address issues of power, privilege and control. Most leaders of national cultural institutions just now, however radical their own background and however sincere their commitment to changing who these organisations speak for or to, have to engage in this contradictory debate. Vulnerability is more powerful than certainty in this context: vulnerability allows space for accepting that any organisation might not have all the right answers, nor will it always do the right things, but that stepping into an uncomfortable, risky place, where failure is embraced as part of learning how to be different, is not only important but non-negotiable if we are to be of our times.

Within my own career span I can see how slow museums have been to openly acknowledge their deep implication in the histories of colonialism and imperialism. For too long, these remained 'special projects' or moments rather than the main business of the museum. The work that is still needed across the museum world to address these histories remains immense, and has powerful implications for how we see museums now.

Most museums and galleries today embrace new subjects, new forms of art practice, new voices, wider audiences, and better methods of interpretation. They have, in turn, benefited from much greater public and political support because they are seen to have a strong social purpose. At the same time, they have also become highly adept at earning their own income as powerful visitor attractions generating jobs and adding value to the economy, and securing the support of private philanthropy and corporate largesse. All of this has introduced further tensions which pull our museums in multiple directions at once: the tension between being a large-scale tourist attraction and providing a space for contemplation of art; the tension between commercialism and public service; the ethics or otherwise of corporate and private sponsorship. And behind all this remains the ever-present historical tension between the desire to include and the exclusionary foundations of museum culture.

2

Whose Museum?

In Trust

We are now aware of some of the shaping antecedents and tensions held within the space and the institution of the museum. There is, however, some additional history to uncover, in terms of the extraordinary cultural and economic challenges faced by museums in the past few years, including the national lockdowns from March 2020 onwards as Covid-19 spread across the globe. The lockdowns and subsequent social distancing rules pushed most major museums to the brink of collapse, compounding many years of dwindling public investment and rising expectations and costs. It was not all doom and gloom: the value of arts and culture to the public was undoubtedly affirmed in many ways, from the appetite for live streamed and digital arts content during lockdowns to, once restrictions had been lifted, the emotional responses of visitors online and in person, grateful for access to culture and creativity in daily life.

Normality has now (we hope) resumed. We cannot assume, however, that it will be back to business as usual for cultural institutions. The sector has shifted in profound ways, and the prolonged period of closure – during a time of already more than usually turbulent cultural and political conditions – trained a spotlight on many difficult ongoing questions about how museums operate, including who museums are really for, and how they can change their ways of working to reach a wider audience.

These are questions that have preoccupied me for as long as I've been working in museums, as I'm sure they have many of my colleagues. I was trained at a time when the arguments for the wider social benefits of museum participation had largely been made, and the arguments and tensions I mapped out in the previous chapter might have been thought to be largely of the past. Yet, as I survey the museum landscape now and follow the larger cultural and political debates about the purpose of our institutions, I sometimes feel like my own wish to make change has achieved very little.

My first role in the cultural sector, as Director of Creative Partnerships in Birmingham in 2002, was an action research project tasked with building the evidence base for the value that artists and creative learning approaches bring to an educational setting. I was motivated in large part by the wish to see my own children, then entering nursery and primary education, experience an arts-rich education. The body of research gathered across sixteen pilot areas demonstrated emphatically that children and teachers had a better learning experience, and were happier and more committed to school, when the arts was valued in the school, when artists were a regular part of school life, and when cultural experiences both in schools and, crucially, out in the world were the norm. Nonetheless, the initial research for Steve McQueen's *Year 3* project at Tate Britain undertaken eighteen years later by A New Direction – an arts education organisation that grew out of one of the London Creative Partnerships pilot schemes

– found that nearly sixty per cent of the schools that participated in the project had never visited either Tate Britain or Tate Modern. Most schools, in the crowded and highly exam- and test-focused curriculum that has become the norm in UK schools, were unable to offer regular cultural experiences or visits to cultural institutions.

Our museums are well visited, but the large majority of visitors are still well educated and affluent audiences from the cities and towns Tate now operates in. That, in itself, is no bad thing – no museum director wishes to exclude those who are already motivated to come and who enjoy what we offer – but we are clearly some way away from having a visitor base that accurately represents the population at large. I do not wish to presume to fail so early in this text, and I don't think I will ever abandon my ambition to widen our reach. What we need if we are to see real change in our sector, I feel, is a better sense of the journey we have made already, what we have accomplished along the way, the distance still to travel and the inherent resistances we must counter.

For the Public

If collections within museums were once assembled for the pleasure and prestige of the wealthy, or to inform the specialist work of the scholar, they have, since the 1960s at least, come to be understood as for the people. In the language of the National Museums Act in the UK, formulated originally in 1954 and redrawn in 1992, our collections are held for exhibition and for study, 'to promote the public's enjoyment and understanding of art' (or science, or history, depending on the type of collection). We can trace this developing awareness of the public benefit and the public good associated with museums back to the larger political and cultural discourse that emerged with the establishment of public services such as the National Health Service in 1948. Among them was, of course, the creation of the Arts Council which was tasked, for the first time, with using public money – people's taxes – to support an arts infrastructure across the UK. This was a momentous step, as it established the principle that the state *should* have a formal role in supporting the arts, for the benefit of a wider public (even if, in 1951, the Head of the Arts Council famously stated their role was to support 'few, but roses' – so primarily a small number of recognisably elite organisations).[1]

It is this pioneering spirit that was captured, in terms that still inspire today, by the arts minister Jennie Lee, whose 1965 white paper *A Policy for the Arts: The First Steps* still makes a brilliant read (and remains one of only two governmental policy papers published in the UK on the arts in one hundred years!). Lee's paper echoes some of the perceptions of dusty, unwelcoming museums we examined in the first chapter when it chides those museums who have failed to move with the times, retaining a 'cheerless unwelcoming air to all but the specialist and the dedicated.[2] No greater disservice can be done to the serious artist, she states, than to present his [*sic*] work in an atmosphere of old-fashioned gloom and undue solemnity'.

The democratic cultural optimism of the 1960s and 1970s was also embodied in the proliferation of new art spaces and community-based art projects that connected artists' ideas to the experience and aspirations of a wider and more diverse public. During this time, our understanding of the power of culture as a tool for social or political liberation changed. If this felt like a social revolution, that was because it was often intended to be so: public art projects frequently went hand-in-hand with new forms of creative, collective action. Feminist communes, working-class art movements, and art activism on a large scale really began to take hold. Often the impetus came from public intellectuals like Paulo Freire, Antonio Gramsci and Augusto Boal, who were enormously influential in forging grounded cultural and political action that became recognised as the community arts movement, and slowly found its way into museums.[3] In the academic world, the Centre for Contemporary Cultural Studies in the West Midlands – led eventually by the great writer and thinker Stuart Hall – began to develop an intellectual approach to culture that was founded on dissident, culturally diverse forms of popular cultural activities, profoundly challenging and reshaping the old orthodoxies about high and popular culture.

Other examples from this period, including collectives such as Jubilee Arts in West Bromwich and Arts Lab in Birmingham, fostered a radical multi-artform practice that included artists (especially artists of colour) who are only today receiving the recognition they deserve.[4] Individual artists working far outside the establishment structures of the art schools and the museum space – and, even more potently, feminist and Black collectives who seeded thinking and creative actions around gender and sexuality – form a vital antecedent to the critical experimentation of today's generation of artists. These individuals and groups, more than any other, prefigure the challenges to the canon and the institutional critique of museums that we ordinarily regard as solely of the present moment; they viewed art and artmaking not simply as for the people, but made *by* and *with* the people as a tool for constructive social change. But much of this work remained firmly outside the field of art history, or the remit of the art museum.

Perhaps my favourite example of the work done by these groups is the Tipton Playbus *Museum on Wheels* of 1978–83. Devised and supported by Jubilee Arts (there is a personal link here, as my aunt, Sylvia King, who sadly died in early 2022, was the organisation's brilliant director at the time), the bus took creative activities into the heart of communities that did not find culture on their doorstep.[5]

Organisations such as Jubilee Arts and many other locally based, practice- and politics-entwined groups were committed to giving people creative tools to tell their own stories – stories that were often excluded from other history- and story-holding institutions, including museums and archives. The legacy of this work can still be felt in the socially engaged art practice of our own time.[6] It is also seen more tangibly in the continued work of organisations like Multistory in the West Midlands borough of Sandwell.

Thankfully, we are embracing these radical beginnings a bit more nowadays. In 2023, a group exhibition of British feminist, activist art, *Women in Revolt!*, opened in Tate Britain's main exhibition galleries. Curators Linsey Young, Zuzana Flaskova, Hannah Marsh and Amy Emmerson Martin worked in collaboration with some of the leading thinkers and change makers from the 1970s and 1980s – those artists and activists who shaped my own political and cultural thinking – to forge an exhibition made by women who, at the time they were originally working, never found a space or even a foothold in the museum or gallery world.[7] The enthusiastic response, with nearly 140,000 people visiting the show, suggests that this kind of radicalism is of strong, popular interest to an inter-generational public.

The changes are global. Curated and co-produced by Indonesian collective ruangrupa, *Documenta XV*, the 2022 iteration of the international contemporary art exhibition in Kassel generally recognised as the bellwether event of the visual art world, featured a collective of collectives. Much of the practice, which focused on creative engagement and the cultures and habits of daily life (market stalls, eating, performance, and interventions in social situations fostered by groups such as the Bangladesh-based Britto Arts Trust), was designed to raise awareness of critical social and environmental issues. It demonstrated my earlier point that we should not see art world practice as separate from global questions of power and conflict, as multiple accusations of racism and antisemitism caused considerable controversy and debate about artistic freedom of expression.[8] While it will certainly continue to be challenging, for me, these 'new' movements within the contemporary art world are a refreshing echo of some of the powerful social movements of my own youth.

To go back to the 1980s for a moment: that period saw the governments of the day, in the UK and across much of Europe, move strongly to the right. As a result there was a very significant ideological shift within the traditional museum space away from cultural experiments that challenged the social order. Rather perversely, radical spaces nonetheless continued to prosper as they took on a more overtly oppositional or campaigning role: it is in this period, for example, that we see the emergence of ACT UP, born out of the anger and consequent campaigning for rights and support for the gay community facing the HIV/AIDS epidemic and the social and cultural prejudice fostered in its wake.

Looking back, we also see 'cultural campaigning' in support of the Miners' Strike and the Campaign for Nuclear Disarmament, especially by women artists associated with Greenham Common and by artists who actively campaigned about and around specific political or social issues. I still remember being shocked seeing Peter Kennard's *Haywain with Cruise Missiles* 1980, not long after having gone with my aunts to an anti-nuclear demonstration at the US airbase at RAF Molesworth. At the same time, the fight against racism and racial inequality was playing out through practices of resistance, often collective, by groups such as Black Audio Film Collective, and the early years of television's young upstart Channel 4 (which began broadcasting in 1982) providing a platform for Black, queer, working-class and feminist artists.[9]

Our larger museums, operating on a national or a regional scale, by and large did not engage with these forms of social practice. There are, however, some notable exceptions, such as the People's Palace museum in Glasgow and activities coordinated by museum workers and arts services within local councils like Walsall, Sandwell and Birmingham. For many, especially regional museums, the 1980s were a challenging time, when government disinclination to fund cultural institutions from the public purse – the Thatcher government cut funding for the arts throughout the 1980s, seeing arts organisations as a political nuisance and a drain on public finances – was combined with a political directive to move firmly into a market economy. Notions of the 'leisure economy' took firm hold in political and wider public discourse, along with the rising expectations of a public that had an increasingly wide menu of other cultural activities to engage with. Visitors were increasingly seen as customers who could and should pay to see the collections held by museums; by the end of the 1980s, only a handful of museums – Tate, the National Gallery and the British Museum – had managed to resist the relentless pressure on budgets and maintained free entry, which was seen, and is still broadly understood, as the critical factor in being able to attract a socio-economically diverse audience. Trustee roles were also seen in a new way – as political appointments or even rewards for loyal service – and there were numerous spats and disputes between a government that was giving less money but wished to maintain ideological control, and those institutions and trustees who had been used to operating at quite a far remove from government. As we shall see in the next chapter, these shifts in relations between the arts and government provoked critique from more radical elements of the artist and curatorial community.

Things Can Only Get Better

In the UK, two changes in the 1990s reignited museum visiting and a wider debate about who museums were really for. The establishment of the National Lottery under John Major's government, with arts and museums designated as one of the 'good causes' eligible to receive lottery funding, saw a Conservative administration become the sponsor of the large-scale renewal and expansion of the UK's museum and arts infrastructure. Meanwhile, the Millennium Commission capital programme, supported by the Arts Council and the then Department for National Heritage (DNH, which became the Department for Culture, Media and Sport [DCMS] in the late 1990s), created a roster of new museums across the UK, including Tate Modern, as well as offering a lifeline to the country's Victorian museum infrastructure, in which leaking roofs and outdated buildings were holding back the museums' potential to be part of the post-industrial renewal of northern cities.

The other critical issue at the time that remains pertinent today was the political and cultural campaign for free museum entry. Securing this was part of a wide-ranging set of cultural policy commitments made as part of the manifesto that secured the landslide Labour victory in 1997. It was a sea-change from the long period of Conservative government during which, as John Holden observed, the arts and museum sectors were undermined and demoralised by the attrition of negative attitudes to the arts.[10] The new Labour government made a commitment to reinstate free entry in order to increase both the number and the diversity of museum visitors. It was noted that those museums that had managed to remain free through the late 1980s and 1990s had seen visitor numbers increase hugely, and there was a further belief (sadly not entirely borne out in practice), in line with the social policy framework adopted by the incoming Labour government, that making all museums free would see a more diverse museum demographic in socio-economic terms. Not all charging museums were in favour of the change, with the Natural History Museum and the National Maritime Museum holding out until the bitter end. Ultimately, it took until the second Labour victory in 2001 for free admission to be agreed, thanks in part to focused campaigning led by the Art Fund and other sector bodies, as well as to chancellor Gordon Brown's introduction of a change to the VAT arrangements for free museums that made free entry impossible to argue against. Entry charges were dropped in stages: for children in 1999, the over sixties in 2000 and finally for all visitors from 1 December 2001. The impact was immediate: when the V&A removed its £5 ticket charge in 2001 its visitor numbers rose from 1.1 million to 2.3 million in the first year – an increase calculated at 111%. In the first fifteen years of free entry, UK museum visits went on to more than double, from broadly 7.2 million in 2001 to over 16 million in 2015, and continued to grow to just over 40 million in the 'peak' pre-pandemic year of 2019.[11]

The removal of an entry charge wasn't the only factor, however, in shifting perceptions of who the museum, especially the art museum, was for. The wish not only to grow overall museum visits but also to serve a more diverse range of visitors was part of a much wider set of actions to address social inequalities through programmes of cultural support and empowerment, sponsored by the Secretary of State for DCMS, Chris Smith. These ideas were not a million miles away from the forms of community engagement and support seen in the late 1960s and 1970s, and arose from the dedicated work of the Social Policy Units which had helped shape Labour policy in the run up to the 1997 election (these units included such figures as Ed and David Miliband, Ed Balls, Andy Burnham and James Purnell). They included programmes like Sure Start, designed to address social inequality in the earliest years of children's lives; a programme to tackle homelessness; and Creative Partnerships, an action research programme (which I worked on for four years) to support schools in the most economically challenged areas of the country to work directly with artists to foster a creative and arts-rich curriculum.[12]

In retrospect, the cultural policy initiatives brought in after 1997 seem remarkably prescient and important even now.[13] Research undertaken in subsequent years, however (and indeed examination of visitor demographics now), suggests that museums simply being free to enter does not change the visitor profile, and that there are significant additional economic as well as cultural barriers to participation. Furthermore, programmes such as Creative Partnerships were founded on principles drawn from academic studies into creative learning. These pointed to the twin benefits of broad cultural participation for children and young people as a factor in social and personal wellbeing as well as academic success, citing the open-ended, risk-taking, problem-solving learning approaches that are seen often in the so-called creative subjects (drama, dance, visual and practice-based work). The core text underpinning this thinking was (and probably still is) the inspiringly titled 'All Our Futures' by Professor Ken Robinson.[14]

Creative Partnerships in Birmingham co-produced some extraordinary projects, including a full-length ballet, *Safahr,* choreographed by the Birmingham Royal Ballet (BRB) artistic director, David Bintley, with BRB's Learning team and the active creative input of children aged three to eighteen from five Birmingham schools: a secondary, a primary, a nursery school, and two schools for children with physical and educational additional learning needs. Other projects, planned through close collaboration between teachers, children and artists to co-design activities that aided the learning outcomes of the children, included a series of short films devised by young people with Birmingham-based Maverick TV, and an extraordinary edible playground and plant- and food-based creative curriculum at Handsworth's George Dixon secondary school, fostered by none other than Anya Gallaccio. The programme was based on the principle that if artists and arts organisations could become partnered with schools and made part of daily school life, then the result would be a creative curriculum and improved outcomes for pupils across the board. This was seen to be particularly impactful if the schools and communities represented had previously felt unable to engage meaningfully with the arts.

Creative Partnerships, along with other social provisions such as Sure Start which used culture as a grounded tool to empower and engage with people, set out a framework addressing social isolation and economic challenge that drew greatly on the positive lessons of the 1970s community arts movement we have noted. Indeed, most museum and arts organisations' Learning teams still draw on this legacy.[15] The movement gives us an evidence base for a curriculum fit for the twenty-first century – one that would equip young people to work in a knowledge-driven economy and to survive the strains of the social media universe we now inhabit. We would be wise to look back and bring these creative lessons to the fore again.

The 1990s and early 2000s period was, in retrospect, a golden era for the arts in the UK, with a renewed focus on the museum visitor, of every age.

Palaces for the People

Tate Modern is a working example of a change in public attitude and behaviour towards art, and especially contemporary art. Throughout the 1990s, Tate's then director Nick Serota and his colleagues made a powerful and prescient argument that London and the UK needed a museum of international modern and contemporary art. The art market was also expanding and globalising, with the creation of catalytic events like Frieze Art Fair, the consequent movement of many of the major commercial art dealers, and the boom in young artists settling in what were then the less popular and more affordable sectors of east and southeast London. These forces of cultural and creative change – alongside the powerful arguments of Serota and his colleagues – would eventually create the right conditions for the creation of Tate Modern itself, supported in good part by lottery funds. London became an art-world mecca – a leading art centre and the hub of an expanded global arts network. This was transformative for the capital.

Tate Modern opened in 2000 to widespread acclaim. The arrival of Louise Bourgeois's *Maman* transformed more than just thinking about the art historical canon. Hand in hand with the argument that women artists making feminine and feminist work at scale should be part of the canon of international art was a contention that contemporary art could be for everyone, whether they came from Southwark or Seoul. The more than four million visitors to Tate Modern in its first year established Bankside-to-Southbank as one of the busiest pedestrian thoroughfares in London.

Inside the gallery, changes in behaviour were also taking place. Olafur Eliasson's *The weather project* 2003 brought an unprecedented audience to bathe in the glow of the 'sun' suspended in the Turbine Hall. Olafur's project was a lovely example of engagement by stealth with an extended public: he spent a year consulting people on their feelings about the weather (that favourite British topic), and from this forged an experience that invited people to get comfortable and observe the 'weather' and themselves. In a stroke of genius, the ceiling was mirrored so that people could see their reflections, and the response was phenomenal. Strangers took it upon themselves to collaborate to spell out names and messages, and a spirit of playfulness presided. It is a great example of the connecting power of art, that 'gathering of strangers'.

I remember taking my own children, then aged five and three, to London to see *The weather project*. They spent a good hour rolling around and laughing at themselves reflected in the mirrored ceiling as they tried to spell their initials with their bodies (and inveigle their tired mother to join in). Fifteen years on, when Tate colleagues conducted market research ahead of Olafur's solo show in 2018, we found that although few people recognised the artist's name, once the word 'sun' was mentioned people remembered precisely the transformative experience of the display. For many years afterwards, my own daughter referred to Tate Modern as the 'sun gallery'.

We use the shorthand 'immersive' to describe this kind of work, often a bit dismissively, and certainly museums around the world find this kind of experiential contemporary art very attractive to audiences, particularly families and younger adults. It's easy to understand why: these works tend to be visually and physically compelling (and highly Instagrammable), thus driven by massive word of mouth recommendation.[16] But *The weather project* and Yayoi Kusama's *Infinity Rooms* – the most recent, and wildly successful, example of this kind of work – are characterised by something else: a connection established between the visitor's own body and emotional state, and the people (sometimes known, sometimes unknown) they experience the work with.[17] It is also, it's worth saying, an experience that visitors are able to understand with relatively little mediation, direction or explanation from the museum.

My daughter wasn't looking at me for direction about what to do with Olafur's sun, nor was she reading a museum text panel or a leaflet. She was looking herself, observing what others around her were doing and finding her own way to engage with the artwork. All Tate colleagues really had to do was not intervene. Sometimes museums have been too quick to stop visitor 'mischief' in the name of protecting the art, when really it's more that visitors' behaviour doesn't conform to museum expectations. One colleague shared that Olafur himself was none too pleased about the visitor response initially, as it took the work into realms of play he had not envisaged – thankfully, once he appreciated the depth of visitor engagement and feeling, he relaxed. His work offered visitors the space and agency to find meaning in it in their own way, whatever their age and background. Likewise, Kusama's singular 'cosmic' vision, and the efforts she makes to allow us to share in that vision, mean that people forge very strong emotional connections to her work, in its simple but profound infinite formulation. It is perhaps helpful if we see this kind of immersive work in galleries not so much as part of current commercial experiments with high-end VR or AR (as seen in the virtual Van Gogh experience and its ilk) but rather intrinsically connected to the radical gatherings or happenings of the 1960s, of which Kusama herself – along with artists such as Allan Kaprow – was a noted pioneer, and which were developed to resist the pressures of the market-driven art world and to harness the power of human connection for social change.

There are, of course, many ways in which we can read the popularity of this kind of experience in the gallery or the museum, but for the purposes of this strand of my argument, I want to highlight again three critical elements. Firstly, the experience welcomes people to take part, without the need for specialist knowledge, or initiation; secondly, it invites a personal playfulness or creative action on the part of the visitor; and finally it requires a public, these being experiences that take place only when the individual is part of a crowd.

There have been many other examples of such playful abandon at Tate and many other museums in the past twenty years – Carsten Höller's slides at Tate Modern, or the swings of SUPERFLEX, for example. Each experience captured the popular imagination; each, too, brooked a certain amount of critical disdain and even unease – a mildly snooty anxiety that all this fun was no good for museums. We might do well to remember the lesson from another 1960s radical, Cedric Price, whose utopian idea for museums as 'fun palaces' counsels wisely that 'there should be a fast lane and a slow lane' within any truly liberating space, so that many moods and attitudes can be embraced and catered for.[18] What these large-scale, playful, immersive, often celebratory experiences certainly do is reduce the threshold anxiety for those who are visiting our galleries for the first time.

Shifts in the nature of art practice – in this case, taking place within the relatively large space of a national museum, rather than on the radical edges of the cultural sphere – also definitely start to break down the sense of the rarefied and 'niche' appeal of contemporary art. By the early 2000s, there was extraordinary growth in the popularity and, we might argue, the success of museums. If we read back through the annual Association of Leading Visitor Attractions (ALVA) reports we see that until 2007 the most visited attraction in the UK was Blackpool Pleasure Beach. From 2008 onwards it is an annual battle for top spot between Tate Modern, the British Museum and the National Gallery. This is not a point against the popularity of the beach and the amusements: I'm a massive fan of Blackpool Pleasure Beach, myself. Rather, it is to say that museums (and indeed art itself) have become popular – in ways that we do not always appreciate. The fact is that art these days is definitely not a minority sport: through the work of artists, the government and the institu-

Gathering of Strangers

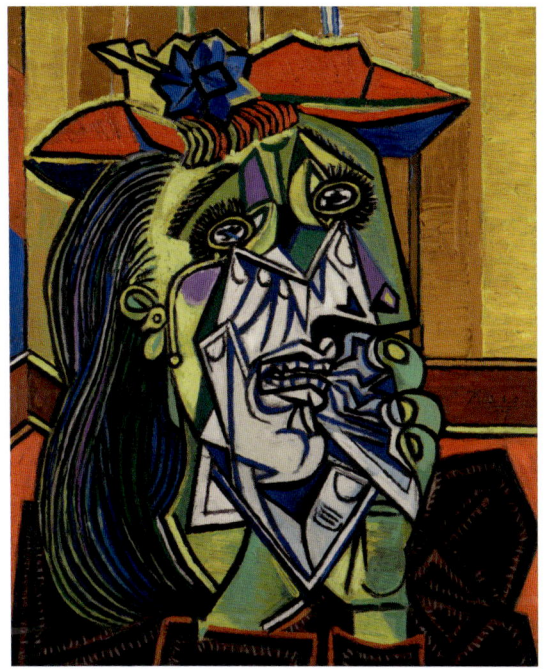

Pablo Picasso *Weeping Woman* 1937 p.10

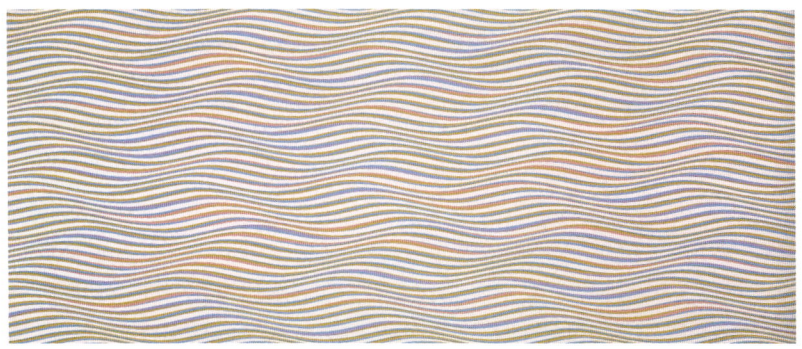

Bridget Riley *To a Summer's Day 2* 1980 p.10

Gathering of Strangers

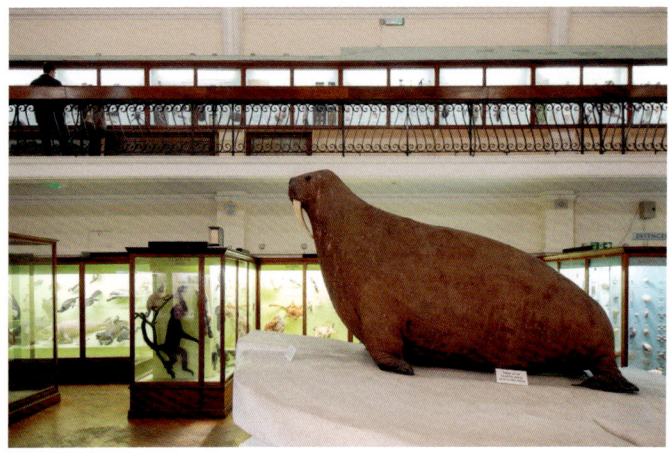

Taxidermy mount of a Walrus from the Horniman Collection p.16

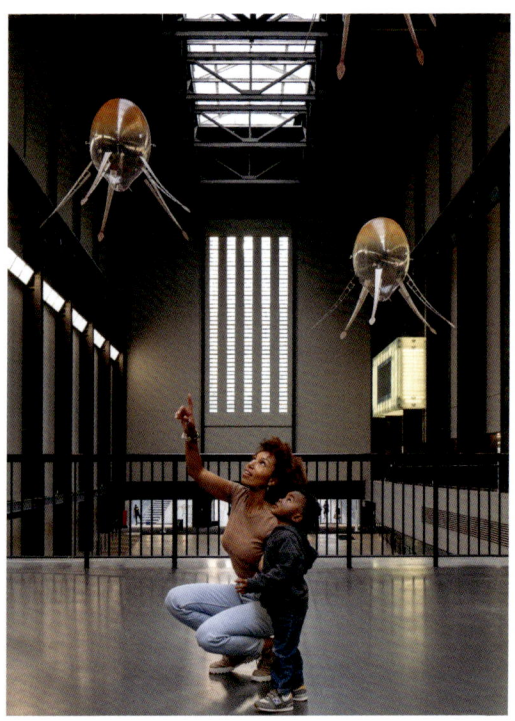

Anicka Yi *In Love with the World* 2021 p.19

Gathering of Strangers

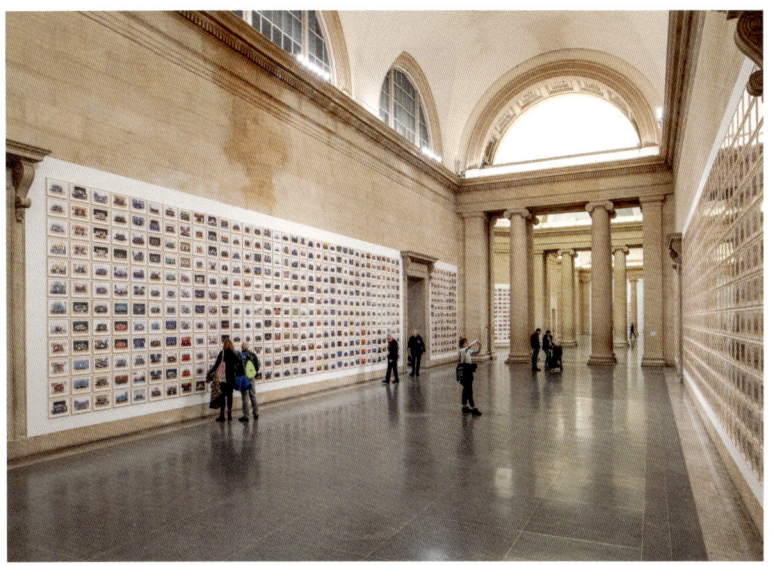

Steve McQueen *Year 3* 2019 p.50

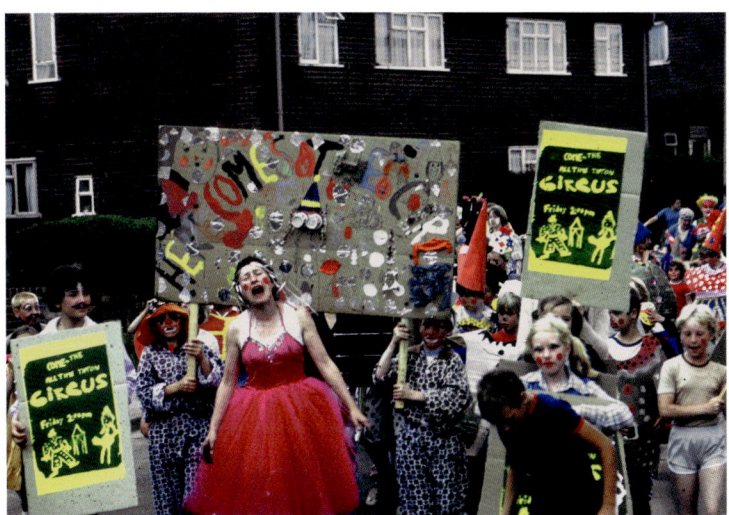

Sylvia King *Circus Week Tipton* 1980 p.53

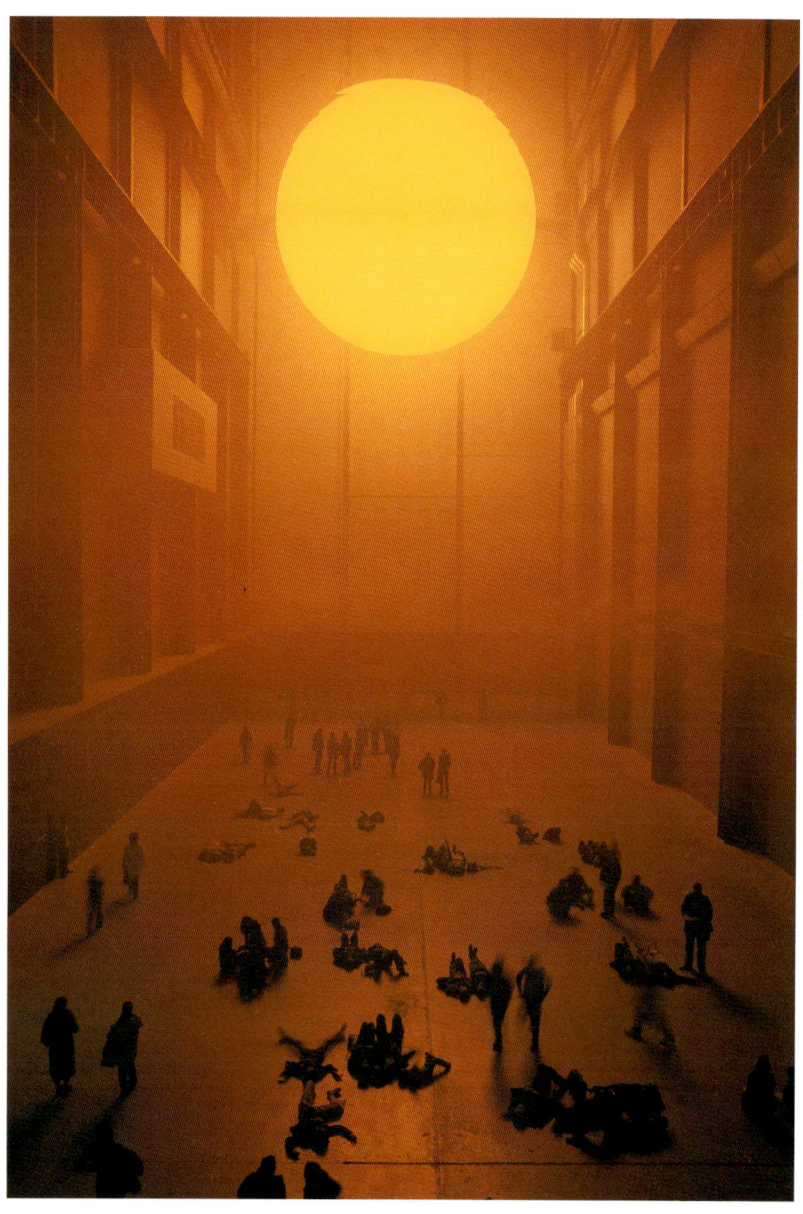

Olafur Eliasson *The weather project* 2003 p.61

Gathering of Strangers

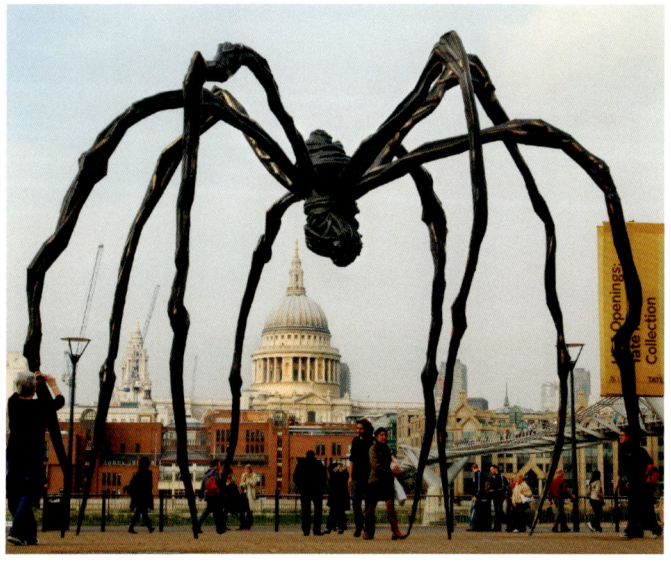

Louise Bourgeois *Maman* 1999 p.61

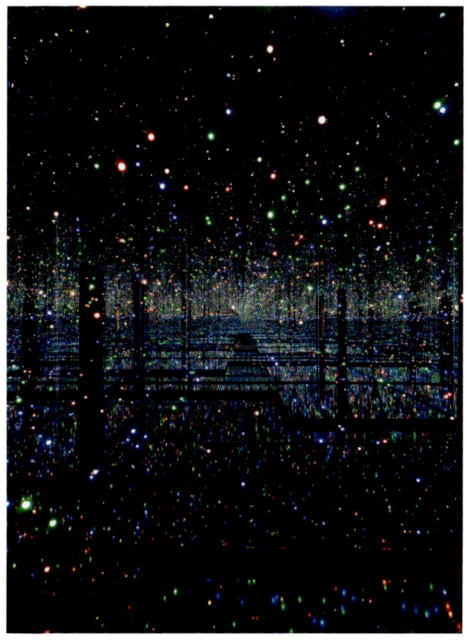

Yayoi Kusama *Infinity Mirrored Room* 2011 p.62

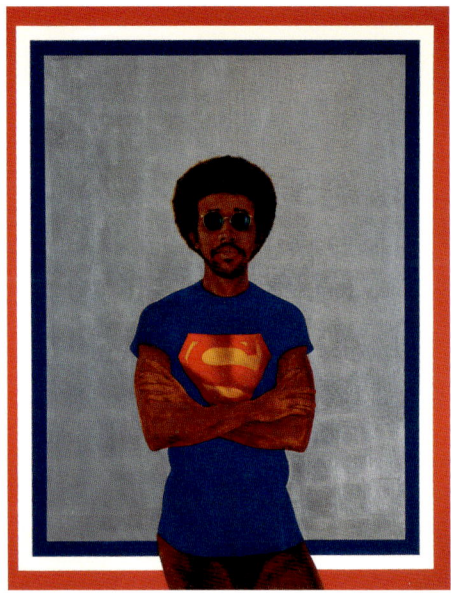

Barkley L.Hendricks *Icon for my Superman* 1969 p.68

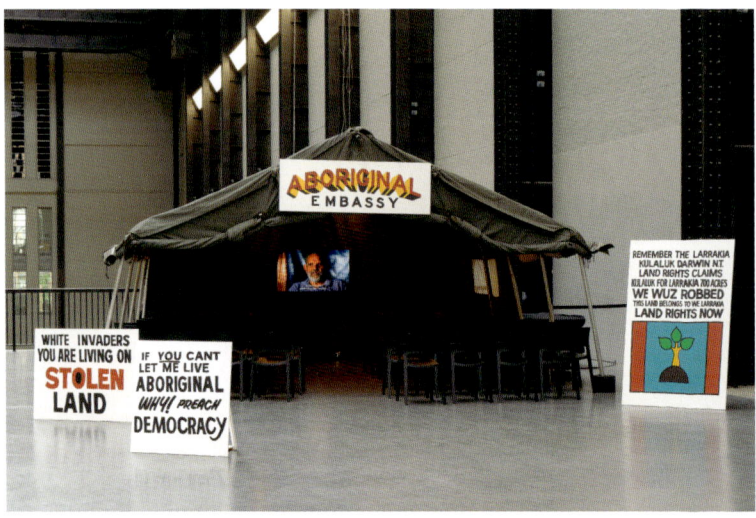

Richard Bell *Embassy* 2023 p.75

Gathering of Strangers

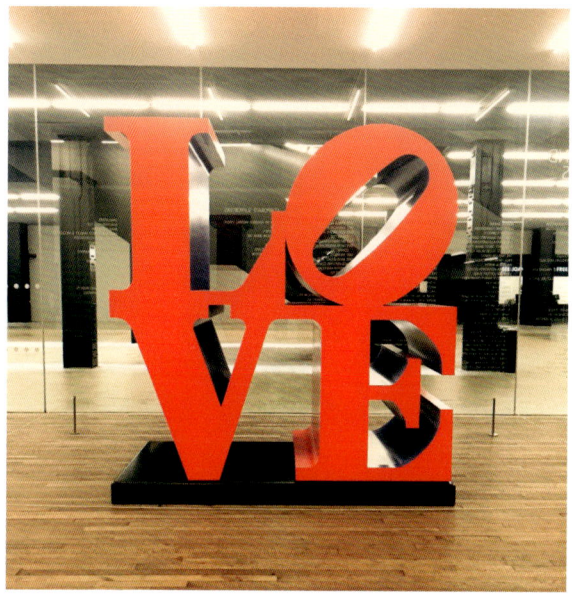

Robert Indiana *Love* 2021 p.76

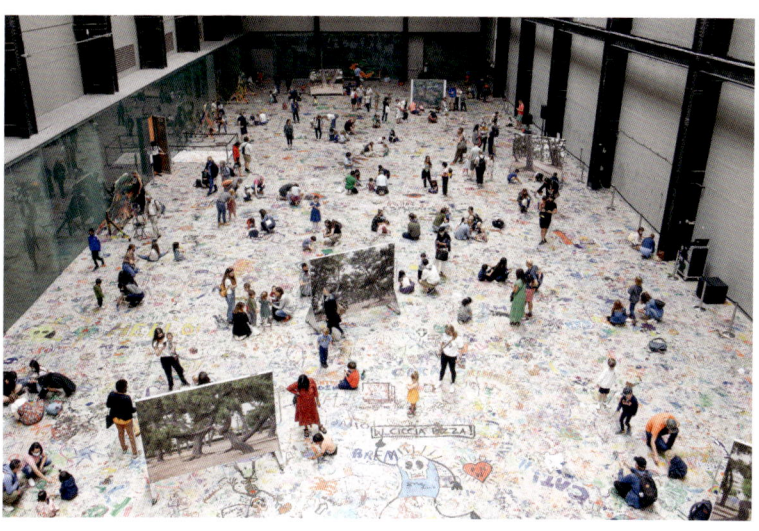

Ei Arakawa-Nash *Mega Please Draw Freely* 2021 p.78

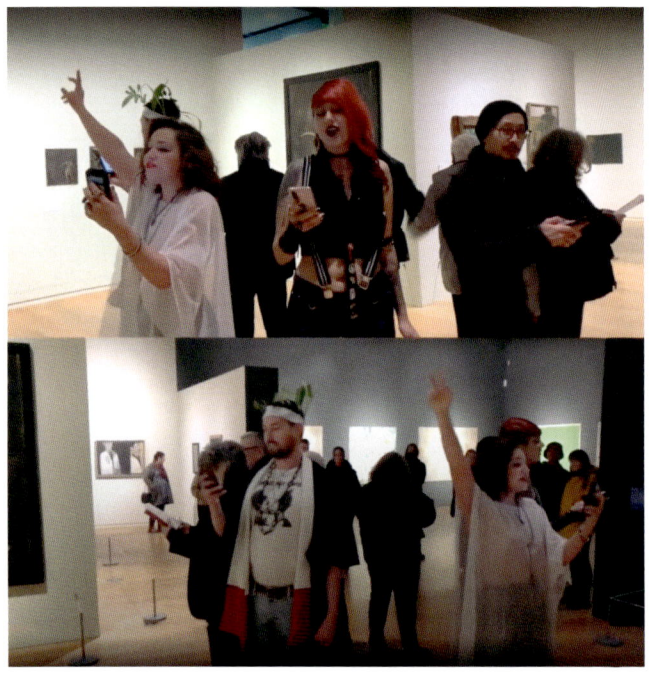

Greg Thorpe *A Minute's Violence for Derek Jarman* 2022
(with: Ally Davies, Anne Louise Kershaw, Greg Thorpe, Tony Openshaw,
David Hon Ma Chu, Norman Goodman, Monica Pearl, Ruth McCarthy) p.82

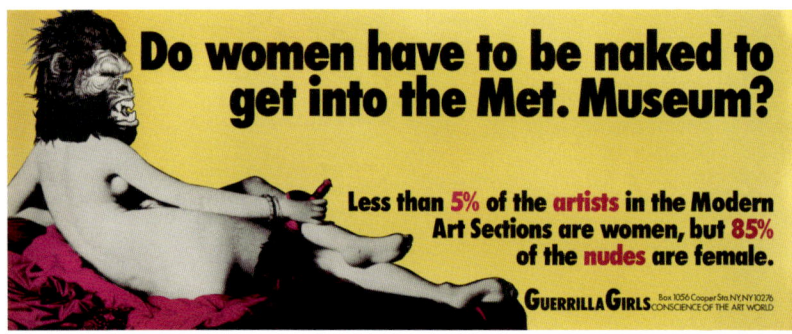

Guerrilla Girls *Do Women Have to be Naked to get into the Met. Museum?* 1989 p.85

tions themselves, museums have moved from being like fencing at the Olympics – appreciated by a small, specialist minority, late at night – to the 100 metres final. And for museum professionals like me, that is a wonderful thing.

The Question of Diversity

Despite this success, the question of who the museum is for is still relevant, and still urgent. As I noted earlier, audience behaviours are complex and not necessarily influenced by free entry alone.[19] As we also see from our own visitor perception surveys, audiences from marginalised backgrounds, and especially from lower socio-economic groups, still report that they feel less comfortable in museums – or even actively uncomfortable. When other socio-economic factors such as the price of travel and accommodation, and taking time off work or using up a busy weekend, are taken into consideration, it is clear that there remain significant barriers to visiting for a great proportion of our local and national audiences.

In addition, a lack of knowledge about the art on display and a feeling of intimidation about the buildings themselves can still make people feel that they are unqualified to appreciate the art held for their benefit. Recent survey responses by people who don't visit our museums explain that they are fearful of being turned away, of being asked to pay, of not understanding the art on display and – more deeply felt – that they just don't belong. Without meaning to, the language of the museum or art world can exclude, and the longer we reside within our institutions, the less our ear is attuned to this form of exclusion. This builds on my earlier point about immersive exhibitions, which are there to be experienced, rather than explained.

Anyone who has worked in museums over the past decade will be well aware of these challenges, which are the subject of numerous museum conferences and policy debates. As I set out in my introduction, my background, my intellectual foundations and my own experiences as a parent as well as a museum professional all anchor my vision for the museum as a shared, if contested, terrain for the widest possible public. The history I have been tracing across these first two chapters means that we have to be explicit and active in making this more real in our institutions – because, to date, mere good intentions haven't carried us far enough. So, like many public museums, and despite the challenges inherent in the project, Tate's vision is to make our public, our programme and our own organisation more reflective of the cities and towns our museums are in, as well as reflecting the global reach that a museum such as ours can and should have.

To date, as I mentioned earlier, our efforts have seen some positive change: the demographics of our audience are now close to 20% Black and Minority Ethnic and programmes explicitly speaking to the art and social history of specific communities see significant shifts; nearly 50% of ticketed visitors to Tate Britain's *Life Between Islands: Caribbean-British Art 1950s–Now* in 2022 were of Black British origin. This is good for a national museum – but as one of my colleagues said: 'I don't want us to compare ourselves with the past, nor only with other museums. We should compare ourselves with the London we are in today!' Although we are approaching the point where 50% of London's population identifies as not White British, we are nowhere near seeing that reflected in our overall audiences. Nor do visitors to Tate Liverpool or Tate St Ives – two very different cultural settings – reflect their own socio-economic locations. I'm interested in how an institution like Tate, which has always tried to be ground-breaking and radical but is also large and definitely an 'institution', can be nimble and responsive enough to take up the call to action to connect to different people and connect in new and different ways that we see from younger generations of visitors – and indeed from our own staff and the artists we work with.

What we have learned at Tate is that, while the diversification of artists and programmes is important, it does not necessarily translate into diversification of audiences. Solo exhibitions by artists of colour or women artists are very much welcomed and land well with the press, with peers, and with certain audiences. These tend to be the most arts-engaged – a cosmopolitan audience looking for new experiences and happy to be challenged. This group can be quite diverse but is also heavily skewed toward more affluent, usually university-educated audiences. Furthermore, it takes time and the building of trust to ensure that these exhibitions connect to visitors with shared lived experience who are not regular museum visitors. That is usually done by word of mouth or social media connection, either through peer networks or trusted advocates. We have seen that if we want these shows to have the impact they deserve (and we need), we have to leave them running for longer to allow this word of mouth to spread. We also need to actively market and promote them differently, through different means. Our research shows that big well-known 'name' exhibitions, rather than shows targeted at specific communities, are actually more likely to attract a truly diverse audience. Within the art museum, we might rightly see it as necessary to challenge and rewrite the art historical canon, but for the non-specialist audience this is not an initial motivating factor – though seeing a spectrum of work that reflects the world in terms of gender, race, ethnicity, disability, class and sexuality is certainly key to retaining a broad audience (and ought to be a given in the 2020s). There remain only a few 'universal' known names, or topics – Picasso, Van Gogh, the Terracotta Warriors – that can be relied upon to attract large audiences across a very wide demographic. Although we are working to expand that list, only time will tell if the actions of my generation of curators will bear fruit. There are some signs that public appetites are changing: the global enthusiasm for Yayoi Kusama and the acclaim for Hilma Af Klint speak to a shifting cultural climate that sits alongside the now rapid improvement in representation in film, fashion and TV.

Another key driver in terms of audience diversity is exhibitions or displays which tell a powerful story, or capture a sense of real social and political change, sometimes characterised as 'Zeitgeist' exhibitions. I don't think this term, with its connotations of a fashionable and fleeting moment, really fits: 'Storytelling' shows might be a better characterisation for such exhibitions, which often succeed because they relate the story of a particular community of interest in a way which speaks to us all about who we are, helping to shape new thinking about society and history through cultural objects. These are moments that last.

Soul of a Nation: Art in the Age of Black Power, presented at Tate Modern in 2017, is a good example of this kind of show. The exhibition traced the story of Black art from 1963 to 1983 in America, in so doing providing a new perspective on American culture as well as a platform for an often overlooked generation of American artists, among them David Hammons, Barkley L. Hendricks, Romare Bearden, and other stars of the post-1960s African American scene. The exhibition was a huge success – one, in fact, that Tate was slightly unprepared for. The exhibition was intended to travel to one venue only after Tate, Arkansas's Crystal Bridges Museum of American Art. Instead, its initial success in London instigated a long journey across the US, taking in Brooklyn, Los Angeles, San Francisco and finally Dallas. Tate had begun the work to reflect African American artists in its collection well before this moment, but *Soul of a Nation* accelerated this project considerably, not least because collectors who were also supporters gifted works to the collection. Beyond its simply being a well-curated and well-told exhibition, its popularity came from a shared desire on the part of the audience to see art that was politically urgent, and from the way it spoke to the wider cultural mood of the time.

Soul of a Nation opened at a moment of real political turbulence in the UK and around the world, following the Brexit debate and referendum and the 2016 election of Donald Trump. It also presented a complex, nuanced view about African American art as part of wider discussions about Black art. Taxing the mind as well as appealing to the emotions, it was no easy blockbuster. Black and Minority Ethnic audiences accounted for 38% of all visitors to the show, more than double the percentage that we had previously seen for a ticketed Tate Modern exhibition, and the vast majority of visitors were under the age of thirty-five. The exhibitions team worked with prominent figures such as Jay-Z, Solange Knowles, Will Smith, Spike Lee and Laura Mvula to get people talking about it. Solange, inspired by a photograph of artist Betye Saar (whose work featured in the exhibition), created an interactive work launched at a Tate Late event where the exhibition was also free for under twenty-fives. But Jay-Z tweeting the exhibition to his millions of Twitter followers was one of the biggest factors in connecting the show to a much wider global, as well as local, audience. The exhibition culminated with a Lates Weekend during which the galleries stayed open until midnight, with long queues of visitors enjoying being part of a public spectacle of waiting with friends and family for a last glimpse of a once-in-a-generation show.

This popularity with intergenerational and much more diverse audiences was also seen in Tate Britain's *Life Between Islands* five years later. Like *Soul of a Nation*, this show offered a revised cultural narrative, with a wide-ranging selection of works by known and lesser-known artists firmly shifting not just the art historical canon but also broader public understanding of these important cultural figures. It also told an explicitly London story, which spoke to communities a short walk or public transport journey from the gallery – Brixton, New Cross, Notting Hill, Deptford.

Both shows used powerful visual storytelling in their marketing and presentation. In addition, they looked to other popular forms of culture – music, fashion, domestic design – to connect to a wider and more expansive sense of culture. Both exhibitions had superb soundtracks, and *Soul of a Nation* cut a very cool vinyl album. There is a critical factor here about strong storytelling built around a core community of interest but taking a non-didactic approach forged with a larger general audience in mind.

Another significant shift in museum practice in recent years is the move towards accommodating families. The family unit is an easy win for museums: parents simply want reassurance that their kids will be made welcome and – very importantly – might be able to learn something while they play. Non-arts-attending, often lower-income, families have a much higher threshold anxiety, because the codes of welcome are not always in place or easily evident. For a few months in 2017 the SUPERFLEX commission at Tate Modern, which saw swings and a colourful carpet installed in the Turbine Hall, became a mecca for young families, offering stimulation for children, space to rest, relax and explore for parents, and some assurance for our less frequent visitors about the welcome they could expect to receive.

Engaging with and actively targeting families does change, as well as grow, your visitor base; Tate's recent summer season, the Uniqlo-funded Tate Play series, has done this in an intelligent and imaginative way, with three large-scale family participation projects drawn from art and artists embedded in our own collection and often taking the radical practice of conceptual artists as the foundation for creative learning and play. Kusama's *Obliteration Room*, the Gutai-inspired *Mega Please Draw Freely* by Ei Arakawa-Nash (to which I shall return below) and Rasheed Araeen's *Zero to Infinity* 2023 all derive their energy and radicalism from the same sources as the community arts of the 1970s described above. Each work wears its radicalism lightly but offers a dismantling of hierarchy and an invitation to (art) practice and play that has attracted a significantly younger and more diverse audience.[20]

It has become a truism at Tate that the younger your audience, the more your locality is reflected, and therefore for much of the UK, the more diversity you see. If this can be handled with care and forethought regarding intergenerational appeal as well as provision for the quiet and the noisy, the young and the old alike, with options and experiences spread across the day and into the night, then we will start to see an audience that looks more like the cities, and the country, we serve.

Doors of Relevance

One way of expressing this is found in US museum educator and director Nina Simon's writing on relevance, which she imagines as a key that unlocks meaning and the potential of the museum for 'them'. In order to bring in the people who do not choose to pass through your doors, museums have to open new doors, to new people seeking new meanings. As Simon reminds us, this can be uncomfortable, and it may initially startle existing visitors, but exploring this discomfort can be a positive driver for change for everyone.

Queer British Art, shown at Tate Britain in 2017, unlocked fresh relevance for some of the most traditional parts of our nineteenth-century and early twentieth-century collections. Marking the fiftieth anniversary of the 1967 decriminalisation in England and Wales of sex between consenting male adults, the exhibition was an experiment in how relevant and emancipatory our relationship with the art of the past can be.

The exhibition's historical starting point was the point at which 'acts of sodomy' ceased to be a capital crime – meaning the death sentence – in 1861, although sex between men remained illegal until 1967. The opening room featured a portrait of a young Oscar Wilde at the height of his creative powers, hung next to his actual prison door from Reading Gaol.

The initial idea for the exhibition was a suggestion from our LGBTQ+ network, following remarks from colleagues who had looked for 'their' history in our collection databases and the narratives we hold only to find none, or no one – even though they were certain there was an important, if difficult, story to be told. The exhibition had strong champions on the board, with its chair acting as an advocate for the exhibition, and was supported by a carefully developed set of partnerships with community organisations and public figures. These actors and writers became spokespeople for the exhibition on radio, in press and on television. Throughout the summer, we flew the rainbow flag from Tate Britain, and in July 2017 Pride London was launched at the gallery, alongside a sustained public programme developed in partnership with the BBC (radio was particularly important). 60% of visitors to *Queer British Art* self-declared as LGBTQ+, and it had the widest age demographic of any Tate Britain exhibition.

The most powerful aspect of the exhibition, I would argue, was the space created at its end, where visitors were encouraged to record their thoughts and ideas about the issues raised. There were many more comments than we had expected, most speaking about the visibility and profile the exhibition gave to a community that still had strong memories of prejudice, violence and exclusion. One comment that stayed with me read: 'I think it might be safe to come out now.' Another said: 'This is the first time I have found myself and my history in a museum.'

The creation of a space for comment and conversation – a space for active engagement with the audience – was repeated with equal success in Zanele Muholi's 2020–1 exhibition at Tate Modern. The point is not simply to ask visitors 'Did you like it?', but to create an active place for sharing connection, and building solidarity with fellow visitors and with the organisation itself.

Both of these examples make concrete a process of 'opening doors of relevance', to use Simon's term. Furthermore, they speak *from* as well as *to* subject positions that are, at the moment, still largely absent from the museum workforce and the art historical framework within which museum personnel are trained. *Queer British Art* was developed with a strong internal steering group who worked hard to build connections with the wide range of LGBTQ+ networks across London, particularly working across generations, in order that those who are not yet part of the museum workforce could help shape these new stories. The intention was to develop a polyphony of voices and ideas that we hope will continue to expand both knowledge and points of connection to the work of the museum, the exhibitions and displays that we present and the works we hold in our collections.

This sees art history not as a story set in stone, but as an ongoing conversation in which multiple points of view are not marshalled to be a single narrative; rather, we take responsibility for the way prior histories were shaped by Tate and other institutions like us as well as the world around us. This process then offers different points of connection for the visitors who come to the exhibition – meaning we begin, in a relatively straightforward way, to foreground the different perspectives of people who better reflect the diversity of the Britain we live in now.

These examples, and many others that I might cite, give us cause for optimism. Certainly the visitor demographics for all three exhibitions mentioned above came much nearer to achieving our goal of more closely reflecting the demographic make-up of London. But there is greater challenge in achieving long-term change, and it comes back to some of those inherent tensions I outlined in my Introduction. Once these exhibitions move on, our audience demographic tends to return to prior levels. These levels are steadily improving – moving from 11% Black and Minority Ethnic visitors to 20% over the past seven years – but this includes periods of really significant difference in visitors (like those seen for SUPERFLEX) and includes late night events targeted at younger people, where a 12,000-strong crowd might enjoy the museum equivalent of a club night, and where the audience more closely matches London's diverse demographic. So the composition of visitors on a 'normal day' has not shifted much. This is depressing and vexing for those of us who work in public museums.

What do I think is going on here? As much as I am drawn to the integrity of building in relevance, I am not yet sure how we achieve it. We can imagine creating new doors into our institutions, with all the radical energy of the community arts movement I saw at first hand in the 1970s and 1980s; however, it is this work that often dispenses with the objects in our collections as retrograde items in favour of more radical actions. What happens to a museum's collection in this model?

Furthermore, it is sometimes the case that this new usefulness becomes itself a very didactic format indeed, and one that requires a certain amount of ideological buy-in from the visitor.[21] Usefulness is often not entertaining – and I very much wish to hold on to Cedric Price's revolutionary idea of fun. I want to embrace the necessity of allowing museums to be in conversation with different communities of interest, but I would also like Tate still to be a museum that keeps objects and artworks of many useful and also useless forms, which I see as the fundamental aspect of being a museum. If we are to cater to a really wide range of people, we need sites of Sunday sauntering as well as sites of radical action. We ought to be broad enough to house a display like Richard Bell's *Embassy*, which offers space for the discussion of land rights and migrant experiences, and also to be at ease with kids cartwheeling down the Turbine Hall slope.

If we return to the exhibitions and events that engage some of our largest and most diverse audiences, they are those featuring art and artists to which people feel an *emotional* as well as an intellectual connection. This fact does not condemn us to an endless cycle of overfamiliar blockbusters, however: once they feel comfortable inside our walls, visitors are curious for the new as well as the known, especially if they feel they are discovering a new or little-known story.

There is a further issue that we should consider. As I noted above, museum learning practice has evolved over the past three decades into a specialised and deeply effective mode of sparking engagement between people and art. Often beginning with the school visit, but going far beyond this, the deep impact of creative learning has been demonstrated again and again in studies that illuminate the different kinds of non-didactic, open-ended learning journey that can be fostered within the art or museum space. As many of my colleagues would argue, this offers an ever more needed opportunity for young visitors to experiment and learn how to fail, creatively and constructively. At a time when the overburdened school curriculum has less space than ever for the arts, this a vital part of the museum's role in contemporary society. However, like much of the excellent community arts practice I mentioned earlier, this kind of work requires intensive engagement: it is rooted in a sustained encounter or exploration, as much community arts practice was. It is also rooted in a very particular locale, and therefore brings profound benefit to a small number of people at a time. I like to think that these deep, close engagements gain momentum and scale over time, but this is slow work.

To achieve real change returns us to the idea of an ethics of care across the whole museum organisation. This is found par excellence in many, many learning encounters in museums – but we need to think through how this is manifested in our whole museum experience. We must think of the whole museum as a space of welcome and connectedness, and we need to invite people to find their own space within our buildings. Those people, in turn, might reasonably expect to see some of their histories, ideas and thinking reflected in the stories we choose to tell through our displays, our exhibitions, our public programmes, even our shops, food, escalators and entrance halls. We need mass participation from colleagues across our organisations toward the goal of wider participation in our public: sustained change in who comes to the museum will only emerge through a long-term commitment to collaboration between parts of the organisation that might previously have felt they had different motivations.

Sometimes these changes can be very light, as in the case of Robert Indiana's *LOVE*, which has become the Instagram anchor point at Tate Modern for a new generation dating in London. I think we are either slow to notice these phenomena or embarrassed because we think they are a bit superficial – but this example shows that the changes we are seeking need not always be deep and meaningful. We need to challenge our own prejudices here. Museums like Tate have been successful in building audiences within a 'cosmopolitan' framework made up of culture-hungry tourists and an expanded 'arts-engaged' audience. We have moved far beyond the dusty stereotypes – but if we return to my belief that the modern museum is in a state of potentially productive tension, then it's clear that we need to take fun as seriously as anything else we do. We need a spectrum of enjoyment for a wider range of people as part of our theory of deeper social change. This is really difficult when we are also balancing the necessary wish to retain our scholarly integrity, a passion for social equity, and the needs and wishes of a wider spectrum of visitors.

Playing Differently

Before we leave the subject of the museum visitor, let's briefly return to the post-Covid moment for museums globally. The grand growth curve of museum visitors recorded in the ALVA stats or the annual *Art Newspaper* visitor numbers was abruptly halted by the pandemic.

Tate Modern was still the most visited museum in 2020, but it saw 1.2 million visitors, rather than the 6.4 million of the previous year. That is a catastrophic collapse. Beyond the lockdown periods, nearly all London museums are still seeing depressed visitor numbers, a consequence of the absence of the international tourists who typically accounted for 50% of annual visits for the British Museum and Tate Modern. The post-Covid recovery period saw a non-negotiable experiment in deepening our relevance with a local audience far more diverse than any we have seen in the history of museums. This might have been the liberating learning curve we all needed, since deepening the connection to a hyper-local audience does not have to be at odds with international visitors enjoying themselves also. Certainly, the meaning and pleasure of seeing things alongside strangers, the pleasure in the physical encounter with an object, and the profound wellbeing benefits of learning socially in the shared museum space have only been underscored by our collective experience of isolation and anxiety during the pandemic period. Moreover, the rapid switch to digital that museums and audiences effected during lockdown meant that we have genuinely engaged new and different people, both locally and globally. This has been particularly potent when it has connected to a desire to learn and self-educate. The audience for the Tate Kids website, for example, grew exponentially in the first lockdown, as tired parents looked for high-quality resources to help educate their kids at home. Our challenge now is to capitalise on these new contacts even as we note the after-effects of pandemic isolation and too much screentime for many people.

As we reflect on the massive societal challenges of the recent years, I think museums must stop themselves looking backwards – hard as this is for us as repositories of the past – and stop seeing the largest number of visitors as the best criterion for success. It is a performance measure that has actually got in the way of achieving that bold aspiration set out in the early 2000s, to see a *different* public in our museums. There are many factors to balance and challenges that need to be addressed.

A recent large-scale experiment in 'radical play' at Tate Modern neatly underlines some of the history and arguments I have set out. Based on the Japanese Gutai performance practice of the 1950s and 1960s, which sought to break with the rigid conventions of post-war Japan, the work is part of our global collection and carries with it all the radical questioning of avant-garde artist practice and the desire to question and effect social change. *Mega Please Draw Freely* was reformulated by artist Ei Arakawa-Nash as a giant-sized experience of drawing in the Turbine Hall for families throughout the 2021 summer holidays. Deliberately seeking to break down the museum walls while still leaving them standing, it drew some of the most socio-economically diverse audiences Tate Modern has ever seen, and helped us recover our sense of the museum as a space where people come together.

The choices we have to make now are related directly to this project: sustaining a connection with our local communities and building a wider relevance for audiences worldwide, rooted, above all else, in the art we hold for the public.

3

The Museum in the World

A Minute's Violence

Within the expanded public and social realm where museums now exist, the level of noise about our activities can sometimes feel overwhelming. I think it is important to remember that the level of passion people feel for museums stands as evidence that museums matter, and that the public want a stake in what they say and do. This is a good thing.

And I want to repeat here that the challenges every museum faces today – the probity of donors, the politics of influence and reputation, the questionable sources of funding, the direct criticisms and public debates – are not simply the stuff of our time, but go all the way back to the Medici, or that grand nineteenth-century art baron and philanthropist Joseph Duveen, still honoured in Tate Britain's main halls, none of whom would have an easy time in a present-day museum ethics committee discussion.

But before I get into the detail of these challenges, a little bit of action. On Saturday 5 February 2022, a group of friends gathered at

Manchester Art Gallery's exhibition of Derek Jarman's art, *Protest!*, to stage what they called *A Minute's Violence for Derek Jarman*. Unlike some recent examples of museum activism we might bring to mind, such as bouts of Just Stop Oil paint-throwing, this was a gathering that served to amplify the mission of the museum and to occupy space in the spirit of the queer artist and activist Derek Jarman – perhaps the best known, and still best loved, of a generation of artists galvanised to cultural action by the impact of HIV and AIDS and the rapid demonisation of queer communities by governments in the UK and across the world. The way that Jarman and his friends used the locus of the gallery and the museum, as well as film and other media, to construct a positive space of resistance against a mainstream society that felt overwhelmingly hostile is key to my argument in this chapter.[1]

Notably, however, this minute of violence was not organised by the museum. Rather, as the performers said, 'a gang/coven of us queer folk did an unofficial zap'. They went on:

> The exhibition opening [in December 2021] held a minute's silence for World Aids Day. We wanted to offer A Minute's Violence to centre the fact that queer protest is not just historical, it is still vital, as Jarman always knew it was. The 'violence' of the title comes from the intensity and urgency of the texts and the things we are protesting ... summoning Derek's fighting spirit and resisting gentrification with politics and sass.[2]

I like the idea of resisting with sass very much indeed. I also know that this performance was thoroughly welcomed by the gallery, even though it took no part in coordinating it. In fact, it had more potency – 'good magick', to use the performers' description – because it was the action of a community finding space within the galleries as part of the public life of that museum. The performance is entirely congruent with the long history Manchester had with Jarman – who had staged an exhibition called *Queer* at Manchester Art Gallery in 1992, and another at the Whitworth Gallery, *Evil Queen*, in 1994 – as well as with the *Protest!* exhibition of which the performers made themselves a temporary part.

Both those earlier shows by Jarman likely caused more trouble – in the context of the then in-force Section 28 prohibitions against the 'promotion of homosexuality' by local authorities – than this performance in 2022 (although Manchester as a city had long been for queer politics and against Section 28). It is interesting to note that what the actors claim here – rather like Jarman and his collaborators in their day, who frequently flaunted the fact of getting arrested for their protests – is the wilfully disruptive power of their unofficial minute. A certain frisson of lawlessness is needed in order to highlight the continued battle facing many LGBTQ+ communities, particularly queer people of colour. This energetic hijack of the exhibition on a busy Saturday centres our attention on one of the critical features of contemporary museum life: that we are ever more part of the world, and the debates about the world are part of our remit, whether or not we organise them – and even if we do not truly wish to welcome them.

Megaphones

As one of my colleagues says, a space like Tate Modern's Turbine Hall is effectively a building-sized megaphone for anyone with an idea to share.[3] Whether we invite people to 'protest' or not, our spaces are public. As long as 'protest' or 'performance' is not endangering or impeding our other visitors, or damaging the objects in our care, it would be difficult for us to stop people using the galleries in these ways, even if we wanted to. Of course, in recent times we have seen climate activists like Just Stop Oil take actions that move perilously close to the destructive and illegal. But even as we might be appalled at throwing paint or tomato soup on a painting, we should not take these extreme actions as reasons for forbidding dissent, complaint or protest in our museum spaces. And it is worth noting that even these acts of damage are (so far) well researched to ensure maximum impact without permanently damaging the works.[4] Stifling protest would also run counter to the arguments I have been laying out in this book about the importance of engaging with and listening to a public whose wide-ranging views we might not always agree with but who we are bound to serve. It would also be flying in the face of much socially engaged practice in contemporary art for us to do so.

The term 'socially engaged practice' has emerged to describe work by artists that needs or engages with a public, or directly addresses public debate or social issues as a fundamental aspect of its realisation. A powerful recent example would be Iraqi-American artist Michael Rakowitz's *Waiting Gardens of the North*, staged at the Baltic in 2023. The exhibition was a garden, kitchen, food laboratory and eating space within the gallery rooms, developed in collaboration with people living in Newcastle and Gateshead who had experience of forced migration. The garden acted as a vehicle for exploring histories of displacement, war, trauma and adaptation. Six organisations that support displaced peoples through gardening, food and language support were the active partners in conceiving, implementing and continuing to activate the garden for its lifespan in the gallery, tasks which included tending the plants and making food from the participants' home countries to share with visitors and to take home as recipes. Gently held and imagined by the artist and the gallery, Rakowitz's work gave agency to visitors, asking us to help create a sense of place and home and also to imagine a different, better future. Given the so-called 'hostile environment' policy prevailing in the UK in 2023, this is certainly activist, socially engaged work by an artist collaborating with a diverse local community. The work makes its political arguments through the shared plates of different food cultures, but for it truly to succeed it requires a public that feel they too have a stake in the gallery, can share their views and participate. This requires a gallery space that is open and relaxed about allowing questions and dissent.

This kind of practice is now widely accepted as part of the contemporary art world. The Turner Prize nominations in 2021, after the profound social challenges of the pandemic, consisted only of socially engaged collectives.[5] If we are to respond both to the wish for the public to be genuinely engaged (as the actors in Manchester Art Gallery clearly were) and to the direction in which artists as agents of positive social change (as many now actively choose to be) are taking us, then we have to ensure we cultivate porous relationships with the world beyond our walls. The lines between artists, audiences and activists are increasingly blurred, and museums need to embrace this ambiguity, rather than resist it. We are public institutions, and the public have every right to hold us to account. I would argue that, even if the arguments sometimes have a high temperature, it is proof of a museum's relevance if the public care about what we do, not a sign of failure.

So that's my happy start. There is so much to love about the co-option and adoption of museum spaces for dissident social purposes. For my generation of feminist curators, the Guerrilla Girls spoke for many of us as they protested at the gender and racial exclusions of the museum world.

The Guerrilla Girls' unrepentant rudeness, humour and visual dynamism – as well as their mask-wearing anonymity and their use of irrefutable statistics – meant that their message landed with a wider public as well as an engaged arts audience. Their campaigns remain ongoing, and as their 2017 residency at Tate Modern revealed there is much work that still needs to be done.[6] Indeed, it is depressing how little shift there has been in terms of the representation of women across major collections, the art market, and even the exhibition programmes at major museums. More than this, even when we see brilliant examples like Cecilia Alemani's 2022 Venice Biennale – which did not make a 'thing' of focusing largely on women and gender non-conforming artists, preferring rather to emphasise the brilliance of the art and new forms of historic and contemporary storytelling about art through works that simply happened to be by women and gender fluid artists – there is still a remarkable amount of huffing and puffing from (usually male) critics, and some art world figures, about the 'exclusion' of the male artist. In my view, after countless centuries of male domination, the art world can afford a few years when the gender balance is the other way around.[7] The Guerrilla Girls were needed then, and they're needed still, and I'm glad there is a growing space for their brand of art activism in the UK and around the world.

There is also a long tradition of artist protest making its point within rather than outside of the museum: one only need think of Mark Wallinger's *State Britain* 2007, a recreation from scratch of Brian Haw's protest against the UK government's actions in Iraq, initially established outside the Houses of Parliament in 2001 and eventually confiscated by the police five years later. In recreating Haw's protest in Tate Britain, a short walk from the seat of national power, Wallinger's installation amplified and expanded the message, providing a direct and resounding rebuke to a sitting government's foreign policy. It is testament to the strength of the 'arm's length' principle at that time, whereby institutions like museums are funded by government but not absolutely directed by the policies of said government – answering rather to an independent Board of Trustees – that the work was not only tolerated but became perhaps the leading artwork of its moment, eventually winning the Turner Prize. Examples of government response in recent times to the perceived activism of museums have been rather different, and have placed museums – and the 'megaphones' their spaces provide – in a rather trickier place.

Money, Money, Money

Sometimes the complexity of the funding and organisational structures of the museum mean that one can see and read a cognitive dissonance between the stated goals of the museum, the views and ideas of those artists it shows, an interested public keen to see positive social change, and the means by which the museum is funded. Whether this funding comes largely from the state (as in much of Europe), from the private pockets of donors and corporations (the US situation) or from the combined (sometimes characterised as neo-liberal) compromise of public money plus private funding plus earned income that is the UK model, the tension between what the museum does and where its money comes from has never been higher.

An uncomfortable, though ultimately productive, example of this unfolded as part of a 2018 Tate Lates event. Organised by colleagues within Tate, in collaboration with cultural collective gal-dem and others, the event marked the hundredth anniversary of the Representation of the People Act 1918 that gave adult women in the UK the vote for the first time. Sponsored by Uniqlo, the Lates series very often works through a takeover mode, in which the Tate Modern building and platform is given over to other groups or collectives to create and curate for audiences that they are connected to and who might not otherwise connect to Tate. It's a constructive, generative and generally very productive way of opening different doors within the museum complex, and fostering the kind of constructive disagreements that I believe are an essential mode for the museum today. On this particular occasion, however, we became aware that cleanclothes.org, an organisation campaigning for workers' rights and more ethical practices in the garment manufacturing supply chain, were planning a projection on the outside of the Tate Modern building to highlight Uniqlo's lack of action in investigating the mistreatment of workers by some of its suppliers (the company has subsequently addressed this situation).

What is fascinating about this example is that the activist group didn't critique the events organised within Tate Modern. Indeed, they seemed to want a certain proximity to them. As one of the organisers, Thulsi Narayanasamy, then Senior Programme Officer for War on Want, said:

> Tonight's Tate Late rightly celebrates the amazing activism that women engage in, by [showcasing] creative and inspiring methods that [women] have used to demand their rights and raise their voice. We absolutely support the event itself and the organisations involved, however we believe Uniqlo should not be able to buy credibility through sponsorship while simultaneously ignoring the voice of thousands of women workers whose labour made them rich enough to do so.[8]

What is rather beautiful is that the forms of cultural activism in relation to museums often closely resemble the modes of artistic expression that we and the artists we work with also employ. This was Tate Modern, on the eve of the COP26 summit, giving artistic voice to the urgency around the climate emergency as part of the organisation's ongoing work.[9]

I sometimes wonder what the average evening walker makes of the various things projected on our buildings, sometimes by Tate and sometimes through the actions of others. I'm pretty certain they just read them all as 'Tate', whether they actually belong to us, and even when they are also campaigning against us. It would require more vigilance and hysterical policing of the outside of our public buildings to stop this happening, and I fervently believe that if we are of the public sphere, we have to accept that we are in it, for good and ill.

This also holds for our supporters, individual as well as corporate – even though this may not always be comfortable for them. They, too, step into a world, the museum, which is not entirely under their control. Of course, they gain credibility by doing so (this is at the heart of the 'artwashing' critiques), but neither they nor the museum itself are able to dictate the range of views – including disagreement – that might be occasioned by corporate support of museum work or culture more widely. In the current climate, we should perhaps also note that corporate partners have to take this on the chin when they choose to operate in a public sphere where a great deal of information (and opinion) is readily to hand, and where social media means that the space of the gallery is not the only place brand positioning will be debated.

If we hold the concept of the free-to-access public museum as our central goal then we have to accept that an interested public, with a wide range of views, *will* make themselves heard in relation to our actions. This might sometimes be uncomfortable for museums, their directors, their trustees and their sponsors, but it is an essential measure of our public value.

Liberate Tate

There are still more tricky examples where the actions of the museum itself become the focus of activist attention, and the museum and its works find themselves in a position where protest against its actions becomes part of an institution's life. The museum has to expect that ever deeper public interrogation of decision making, through Freedom of Information requests, social media debates and protest in the museum space, is and will continue to be a means by which larger social issues are debated and fought over. The best example I can point to here, and one that sits within the written and digitally documented history of my own museum, is the long history of Liberate Tate.[10]

Liberate Tate was founded during a workshop in art and activism, commissioned by Tate itself, in January 2010. The informal but well organised campaign group aimed to invoke creative disobedience against Tate until it dropped its sponsorship by BP. This was a particularly difficult and sensitive reputational issue for Tate, given that its chairman at this time was Lord Browne, a former CEO of BP. As might be imagined, internal and external recollections of the events leading to the formation of the six-year campaign (2010–16) against Tate differ. I was not working at Tate during this period – although there have been other such campaigns during my time as Director – and so this account is a summary analysis, after the fact, from a reasonably dispassionate observer interested in understanding how these critiques actually become part of the daily life of any museum, and not, I would stress, a criticism of any of the actors involved.

The power of the campaign came from the closeness between the institution itself and those who were leading the campaign, the form the campaign took, and the fact that its subject – the (in)actions of the oil and gas industry in relation to the climate emergency – was one about which the museum itself, and certainly the contemporary artists showing there, had very strong feelings.

On the tenth birthday of Tate Modern, Liberate Tate offered the following statement:

A birthday present, a gift to liberate Tate from its old-fashioned fossil fuel addiction – a gift for the future. Beginning during your 10th anniversary party and continuing until you drop the sponsorship deal, we will be commissioning a series of art interventions in Tate buildings across the country. Already commissioned are Art Action collective, with a birthday surprise at this weekend's No Soul For Sale event, and The Invisible Committee, who will infiltrate every corner of Tate across the country in the coming months. We invite artists to join us and act to liberate Tate. Free art from oil.

By this stage, Tate Modern had made a compelling case for performance art within the art world and across the wider public, so the campaign was using Tate Modern's by then highly admired efforts as its mode of engagement. The museum was also forging ahead with embracing work by artists addressing the climate emergency. Having commissioned the workshop that gave birth to Liberate Tate, however, it found itself caught in a problem of its own creation when there was the suggestion that, although the issues around oil and gas 'artwashing' could be discussed, no criticism of Tate's donors and sponsors could be made. It was this that effectively handed the public galleries over to campaigners. A series of increasingly inventive, large-scale, often humorous and always disruptive performance art actions unfolded across Tate's sites. These were targeted with deadly accuracy to chime with the art, the calendar and the interests of the museum – generally because it was drawing on internal knowledge and information to structure its campaign.

Liberate Tate gained powerful traction through the media: certainly, the gallery gained almost as much photo coverage for the protests as it did for the art on show.

Similar protests have occurred in museums across the globe. At the Louvre, where the institution and the police were rather less accommodating than Tate chose to be, one actor recalls:

> I joined hundreds of people to demand that the gallery sever ties with oil company sponsors Total and Eni. We were gathered out of concern both for the climate as well as the contaminating presence of the oil company in the gallery, and its potential to toxify the community of artistic practice of which we are part. When oil companies enter the gallery, all our ethics are at stake.
>
> 10 performers (myself included) launched an intervention in which, barefooted, we slowly walked outwards from a pool of oil-like molasses, spreading the imprint of the oil sponsors more visibly through the gallery space, beyond their crisp logos engraved on the walls. Following the performance, police arrested all 10 of us, and from inside jail in Paris, we sneakily uploaded a video to YouTube explaining our actions.[11]

The fact that the Louvre action made its way into the public realm, despite the arrests, points up the always on/always seen nature of working in a public institution in the context of an expanded highly contested social media sphere. No amount of asserting that activists do not have permission to be in the space or to film is likely to stop these events unfolding. In the context of the climate and nature emergency, it is not so difficult to agree with the contention that 'when oil companies enter the gallery, all our ethics are at stake'. But the ongoing protests in relation to the Science Museum have adapted the performative tactics of Liberate Tate into a new and still more disruptive form.

The Science Museum, active itself in helping to shape science-based solutions to climate change and nature collapse, maintains that its sponsorship money comes from the extractive industries that need to be part of the solution to the climate emergency. That this has made no difference to the campaigning shows that nuance and complexity is often lost in an argument that is about public opinion and advocacy, and when being seen to be on the right side of history is what is asked of the museum.

The headache for any museum director is that the pressure to raise money has probably never been greater. Museum boards are independent from government, but also come with their own business, life and cultural allegiances; these are rarely aligned with one another, and even more rarely aligned with those of the artists and actors who have recognised that the museum is a very effective platform for amplifying debate. Colleagues internally, spanning different generations and a wide spectrum of political and cultural opinion, are also likely to have very strongly held views and to want their organisation to stand for their values, even though these might not all be the same. Add to this varied governmental preferences – here I am thinking of issues such as former Brazilian president Jair Bolsonaro's attempts to prevent museums exploring LGBTQ+ issues, of right-wing administrations in Poland and Hungary sacking museum directors who deviate from the government agenda, to the discomfort most liberal US museums felt with the views of the Trump administration, to various recent interventions by our own government into matters relating to culture – and you have what is, essentially, a minefield to navigate, in terms of securing necessary funding and simultaneously adhering to the values of your community.

Some controversies are complex and nuanced. Here, I am thinking of the protests at the Whitney Museum of American Art by groups denouncing featured artist Laura Owens for contributing to gentrification through the presence of her studio and gallery in a diverse, working-class neighbourhood in Los Angeles – which demonstrated that even artists themselves are not beyond criticism of the complicity between the museum, the art market and the commercial forces that might displace communities. Other controversies are, with the benefit of hindsight, far more straightforward. The campaign against Sackler family philanthropy due to their involvement with opioid addiction in the US and elsewhere, which spanned major museums across the globe, only scaled new heights of artistic inventiveness when artist Nan Goldin – herself previously addicted after having been prescribed OxyContin for a wrist injury – created performance interventions that made the most of museum spaces, as she also galvanised artists to be lobbyists toward the organisations to which they had powerful connections.

This long-running campaign has now resulted in virtually all museums removing the Sackler donor title. That so many lives were damaged or lost through the inappropriate prescribing of OxyContin might have made this a relatively clear decision for museum boards, but there is and will continue to be ever greater scrutiny of the potential for dissonance between the museum mission and the business activities and ethics of those who give large donations to museums.

Most public institutions now rely on ethics committees to help them navigate the hard place they find themselves in. The constitution of these committees, as well as the nature of the boards that govern institutions, then becomes the subject of debate. It should not surprise us that an independently elected ethics committee or board of trustees, who are meant to represent a wide range of views, skills and experience, might themselves disagree about matters as contentious as repatriation, colonial histories or the politics of gender and sexuality, nor that sections of the public might disagree with them – or might not even recognise their right to decide about the 'shared' space of the public museum.

The critical challenge in the UK is enshrined in the Charity Commission guidance for public museums. We are supposed to accept money *unless* it actively contravenes our mission (and most museums have a very wide mission), or if it comes from illegal actions. Fairly straightforward? If only. What constitutes 'against our mission' is perilously subjective. Even demonstrating convincing illegality is far from easy for a museum, big or small – and this before we even get to types of activity that are legal but not so fragrant in the minds of the interested visiting public (gambling, for example, or perhaps alcohol companies). Where public ethics and appetite sit – never mind the ethics and feelings of artists – may be very different from where governments, boards of trustees or the ethics committee locate themselves.

The contemporary art museum finds itself in a particularly volatile space: living artists, after all, may simply choose not to show in places supported by causes they personally don't agree with. More than this, art practice these days is very often engaged in forms of cultural critique such that the artists will not simply withdraw their own work and labour, but may advocate for others to do so. When Hito Steyerl withdrew from her proposed exhibition at the Serpentine Gallery in London because of the Sackler name on the gallery's North building, she memorably described the association as 'like being married to a serial killer'. In her book of essays *Duty Free Art*, Steyerl points to the other, subtler ways in which art is used and instrumentalised as a 'fig leaf' for the questionable morals and motives of powerful corporates and individuals.[12]

For any museum that has to raise money from private sources, the charge from some artists (and a portion of our public) is that we simply do not wish to look hard enough at the systems of influence and control that patronage entails. As many of these instances are highly sensitive and deeply contested, I shall again use one from my own experience. In selecting a group of collectives for the shortlist for the Turner Prize in 2021, we also selected their political beliefs and tactics. We should not have been that surprised, therefore, when nominees Black Obsidian Sound System felt it necessary to make a statement critiquing Tate's handling of sensitive issues around race and artistic freedom.[13] Even as they agreed to be part of the process and platform that the Turner Prize represents, the collective were not able to accept without comment our decisions on matters that were not part of the Turner Prize, but which nonetheless had some impact on our reputation. Two years earlier, the four artists nominated for the Turner Prize 2019 decided that they did not wish to see a winner, asking the judges instead to recognise all four artists as a collective winner, and remarking that the pressure on artists to make work and survive in an increasingly precarious market system was only exacerbated by the requirement to compete against each other.

Both of these examples show that the museum operates in a constantly shifting worldly position, whether or not it wishes to. It is fair and honest to say that in 2019 the Tate Trustees were not initially overly keen to see the rules of the long-established art prize change. In the end, Tate and the artists were able to reach agreement because we had to remind everyone that the Turner Prize was formulated to reflect the nature of the artistic ecology at each given moment, and that a questioning of neo-liberal economics and a turn toward greater collectivism was certainly characteristic of the 2020s. This was not appreciated by many members of the establishment art press, but then part of their role is to howl at the contemporary choices made each year for the Turner Prize. The public who came, as ever, to see what all the fuss was about were a rather more open-minded jury: they, at least, mostly embrace the idea that in the space of the museum we will find some things that we like and others things that we really don't.

I can't conclude this section without mentioning the vexed idea of 'balance'. This issue – which troubles almost every major museum – is what we in the UK might call 'the BBC question': the notion that our public organisations should be politically neutral, or 'balanced', to reflect the views of the widest possible public. This has never been easy, particularly since, as a critical discipline, we are mostly all schooled in the awareness that institutions like our national museums are institutions of state, even if they act at arm's length, and have always, even with the best intentions, mostly reflected the views, ideas and interests of a dominant cultural elite. But the question of balance has grown acutely difficult in a post-Brexit world, especially for those of us engaged with the ideas and beliefs of living artists who are more than happy not just to let their political views be known, but to make them the stuff of their art. Jeremy Deller takes an open-minded approach and is a passionate defender of the importance of museums – and he has been a trustee of Tate and a number of other museums and arts organisations – but I am certain he would be decidedly unhappy if his 'Fuck Brexit' T-shirt work was presented alongside an 'I love Brexit' banner simply for the sake of 'balance'.

Change from Within

We are not always balanced, then – and nor should we be. At the same time, and even taking into consideration the personal and political position of its leadership (in my case: feminist, left of centre, mother, menopausal, from a working-class family), the museum carries with it its own power and its own particular privileges. It is never neutral, nor can it be, in relation to its present, nor, indeed, its past. We hide, to be honest, behind a liberal notion of artistic freedom, and freedom from censorship, to give us protection in difficult times. And it's probably fair to say that protests like *A Minute's Violence* and Liberate Tate are manageable for us because they are framed within an art practice that we recognise, and present a political position we feel we can align with. Long live the dissident artists, I say – but this freedom does not work the same way everywhere in the world, as recent arguments about showing artists such as Ai Weiwei in Hong Kong and China remind us.

There has now been an extended period of activism and challenge from the public, as well as from artists working within museums, in relation to climate campaigning. For the most part, museums have been able to adapt and divest themselves of associations that produce the kind of cognitive dissonance I outlined a moment ago. At Tate it was possible to move with some integrity from being the target of sustained action demanding change to actually becoming an organisation prepared to declare a climate emergency and to work with a wide coalition of artists and museum professionals to use the amplifying force of our spaces to advocate for positive cultural change.

The leadership and advocacy of former Tate Modern director Frances Morris demonstrated that activism can, and should, be embraced for the good of the organisation, as well as for the world. As we shall see in Chapter 6, this has aligned with the practical actions of workers across the whole field of museum practice, who are now working towards achieving a lower carbon future for the sector.

There has been, and remains, one much deeper challenge to the functioning of the museum in the world – one which, if it goes unaddressed, poses a fundamental challenge to the values of the sector as a whole. The way in which museums deal with race and racism, both within their own organisations and in the wider culture, has long been an issue of tension and challenge. In the terms that I have been exploring in this book so far, the museum sector has not adequately served or engaged with people of colour, at least since the 1960s, and, more accurately, since their very foundation as institutions bound up with the operation of colonialism and Empire. People of colour are significantly underrepresented in the museum workforce and in the demographics of those who visit. Until the last decade, too, art, history and cultural materials from the Global South, or work by artists of colour, were also significantly underrepresented in the programmes and activities of most museums. There is a long history of critique of this failure in representation, and constructive engagement by museums and the sector bodies has helped shape museum policy in the UK and globally. However, in the span of my own twenty years working in museums, I have noticed that there seems to have been an ability to diagnose the issue but not to change the outcome.

In the summer of 2020, with the global outrage at the murder of George Floyd as well as other acts of violence by the police against people of colour, there came internal (staff-led) and external (public-led) recognition that the museum as a space and a set of practices had not changed enough. As my colleague Michael Govan, Director of Los Angeles County Museum of Art (LACMA), commented, 'The Black Lives Matter movement has touched museums very deeply ... The calls to rethink museums have come very broadly and particularly generationally – even in my own staff, among younger curators, [the call is to] not just rethink the museum, [but] almost tear it down and rebuild it again'.[14]

Recently, then, museums have seen greater debate about their mission and structures than perhaps ever before. Protest and activism around gender or sexual representation, or about art and the climate emergency, encompass a range of concerns shared by most of those working in the cultural sector: they are, if you like, reflective of the broad constituencies working inside the museum and, in large part, of our visiting public, too. Among the issues in museums that the Black Lives Matter movement highlights are racism, colonial and imperial legacies, and the continued lack of representation of narratives and perspectives of non-white people, even when collections or artist shows are global. These are all issues that have long been debated within museums, but these debates have failed to bring about change significant enough to be evident to those inside and outside institutions.

What was fundamental about the powerful critique of museums and arts organisations across the globe in 2020, then, was not the issues raised, but the fact that the voices of those routinely excluded from the museum were finally being listened to. They asked us to look at ourselves and at the way in which our structures and processes contribute to the lack of representation in our workforce. It is true that museums are still, almost exclusively, led and staffed by white people. This challenge to museums has taken many forms, from open letters and social media debate, to publications critiquing the thinking and behaviour of the institution and embodied protests that draw on the long history of activism outlined earlier.[15] It is clear that we as institutions have to take action to accelerate change in terms of equity, diversity and inclusion. Belated though it may be, this change is non-negotiable if we are to serve, represent and reflect a wide and diverse public.

Many museum professionals of my generation thought such action was about changing representation in and through our museums' practice. It is true that some progress has been made in this regard: in collecting policies, in exhibition programmes, and in the issues and debates that museums now explore. The deeper issue is that the structures and processes that are routinely used to define and run our profession contribute to the lack of representation in our workforce.

This, in turn, points to how much structural change is required if we are to begin to challenge the racism that makes our institutions unreflective of the social world.

In the wake of global Black Lives Matter protests, most museums found themselves ill-equipped and lagging far behind where many of their own colleagues and artists – especially the younger generations working in museums, as well as significant portions of their public – wanted to see them. We tell ourselves that one of the reasons museums and galleries have survived for well over two centuries is because they are able to flex and bend to accommodate the kinds of tensions I have been sketching out, adopting new shapes to accommodate new circumstances. Over the past two or three years, we have been challenged to make more profound changes. Sometimes these tensions seem so strong that museums have not been able to flex far or fast enough, and may be on the point of snapping – because the forces causing these tensions seem irreconcilable. We have felt this most acutely, I think, when museums have been criticised simultaneously by younger politically engaged generations who want to see faster change and by those at the other end of the political spectrum for changing too much, too swiftly and acting only in the interest of a so-called activist minority (I am not even going to give the 'w*** word' the dignity of repetition here).

However, I want to believe that the museum as a space and as a concept is equipped to navigate this terrain. As examples across the globe demonstrate, the changes needed now are to finally address the issues I identified earlier: the barriers to entry for too large a proportion of the population, and the still evident traces of an elitist or scholarly mode that presumes a shared cultural knowledge and a shared view on the world. Still more significant is the impact of having very few people of colour within museums, especially at a leadership level. Museums need to change how they recruit, who they recruit and how they act as a social player in the world, in order to be part of making change through doing. This requires us to place equity issues at the heart of our organisations, so that they define our essential policies, so that they are reflected in who sits in decision-making positions, so that they inform who we consult and engage with when we formulate the work we share with the public. Equality should define who we take money from, how we generate our resources and what we use these funds to do. The answer here has also been stated in plainer terms: simply put, it means seeing people of colour in leadership positions across our sector, all the way up to executive or CEO level. To use the US terminology, and in the words of the African American collector and philanthropist Pamela Joyner, there has to be a focus 'on who sits in the boardroom and who sits in the C-suite'.[16]

The importance of thinking through the resourcing of equity within the sector has been championed in valuable and uncompromising ways by philanthropic foundations in the US and the UK. The Ford and Mellon Foundations in the US, both led by people of colour who are highly influential thinkers in the sector and more broadly across the cultural field, have effectively reset their criteria so that it is now a requirement across all their grantmaking that their funds be used to address racial, ethnic and class inequalities.[17] At the Mellon Foundation, this has included tackling some of the most contentious issues relating to the history of slavery, through their Monuments research and funding programme which deals head-on with public campaigns to remove Confederate statues and the dogged resistance to doing so that is still in evidence in some quarters.[18] In the UK, Esmée Fairbairn, the Art Fund and the Paul Hamlyn Foundation have also adopted similar tactics to make it a given that museums in the 2020s must act to address social and cultural inequalities in their very organisational structures and their thinking. What is notable across these different trusts and foundations is that they have taken an active role as advocates for change, and have then made access to resources dependent on recipients demonstrating active change in addressing racial inequalities.

This is beginning to make change happen faster across the museum world. In the past few years we have seen more people of colour take up leadership roles in the UK and elsewhere. Indigenous communities are reshaping the practice and holdings of museums that hold objects and materials relating to their culture and belief systems, and holding positions of authority within institutions so that changes are structural rather than just in terms of temporary programmes. Recent biennials in Gwangju and Liverpool, whose radical thinking and practices so often presage larger changes the art ecology needs, have been formulated to centre practices of First Nation peoples. These have brilliantly brought forward a new ethics-based consciousness that unites ecological concerns and equity questions with an exploration of different modalities of time and space – often slowing down thinking and practice in ways that resist global economic systems and, in turn, proposing less exploitative power dynamics for culture.[19]

What I'm saying here is that providing a megaphone is not enough; we also need to think about who has access to that megaphone. We in the 'old world' of museums should listen and lean in to the change that is needed from us. It's time to admit that making change is difficult, and that we have not done enough yet. This means long-term action to shift the composition of our profession, and the creation of different entry routes into our profession – through apprenticeships, paid internships, supporting career development, building staff support networks, and developing partnerships with people and organisations who are leading the field in this area and advocating for these changes across our sector.

The work also needs to be evident and actively supported by museums' executive or 'C-Suite' leadership, and within their governing bodies. We have to make a long-term commitment to expanding our field of knowledge, our networks, and our connections to communities whose experience has either not been included within the museum space or has been misrepresented. We must be aware that this learning, indeed, not only can but *should* change the way a museum chooses to operate in the world. It also means understanding that we have a very long way to go: this is long-term, uncomfortable, but necessary work.

There is no doubt that Tate, like many museums around the world, has been too slow to address the continued racism within our own practices and processes, and slow, too, to put in place the actions needed to improve social equity. Colleagues of colour across the museum sector have highlighted these issues, but it should not have needed this kind of internal activism for us to take these issues seriously. As our colleagues raise legitimate criticism, we should be aware that the debates about these issues should happen in public: if we are willing to be honest and take action in this area, doing so will only expand the important convening role the museum can have for the wider public. The responsibility sits with us. At Tate, this means that organisation-wide work on race equality issues and anti-racist actions forms part of our daily operations. While essential, this is not easy, especially when we hold in our collections objects and histories that are racist and offend people internally and externally. The Rex Whistler mural at Tate Britain is a case in point. Finding a way to address a racist work painted on the very walls of our building, after a very long history of not wishing to look at this difficult problem, has been an object lesson in how we, as national cultural institutions, can and should function (in the next chapter, I explore in more detail how we tackled this particular case). If we cannot learn how to do this then, as we shall soon see, museums will not be able to act as institutions that can live in constructive tension with the pasts we are tasked with holding.

For Tate Britain right now, this has meant creating a dialogue and an interpretative context in which a Black British artist of our own time, Keith Piper, can reframe the ways in which the public sees and understands Rex Whistler's mural. Keith's own work gives us some different tools to address the offence inherent in the work of the past.[20]

In My (Humble) Opinion...

It may come as no surprise that I welcome these debates. If there was no controversy, paradoxically, I would think something was obviously wrong. As my earlier examples suggest, the shared, public nature of the museum space means people care about what happens within it. In addition to providing a plurality of views, we also have the opportunity to model behaviour that is less divisive and more constructive than that we currently see in social media, in the media, or indeed in government. This really means not telling people what to think. So although I see the museum as a hopefully educative space, I think we have to work hard not to be too didactic or preachy. We should try to model tolerance of multiple points of view. We also need to work with a sense of humility and acknowledge that we don't have all the answers. This would allow us to concede that museums have made mistakes in the past and will inevitably make mistakes as they test new ways of working. I believe this is part of how we steer a different course for the future, and how we make our museums more equitable and inclusive in the present. We also need to operate with a due sense of what we do not yet know – about practices that will emerge as we expand both the remit of our collections and the nature of the exhibitions or programmes we create with and through the knowledge of others. This flexibility is essential if the museum is to continue to evolve.

My example at the beginning, a 'zap' in the museum space, is a very good place to return. *A Minute's Violence* was intended as a jolt to our thinking; as the world around us polarises, we would do well to remember that protest is needed for change to happen. As museums and institutions, we have not always managed to keep up with the world we find ourselves in, but we stand a better chance of doing so in future if we hold a space for protest, as and when it is needed, to remind us that we want a world where dispute is allowed and does not have to be weaponised, except with love in the name of a good cause.

4

Living with the Past

The Past in the Present

In this chapter I arrive at one of the weightiest and most disputatious issues confronting museums today: the problem of how we, as museum professionals now, can and should present our shared histories, both good and bad. We might set this out as a question:

> How do public institutions present their ideas and collections, both past and present, in a way that resonates with the expanded audience that we wish to see in museums, in an era of increasingly sensitive identity politics?

Not catchy at all – but perhaps that is appropriate. Because, despite the best efforts of some of those parties polarising cultural discourse on these issues, there is nothing neat, easy to resolve or evenly balanced about them.

As I hope I have made clear in earlier chapters, the profile of museums today is intrinsically linked with the systems of power and influence that prevailed when they were founded. This persists not just in the provenance of the institution and the collection or collections it may hold today, but also in certain modes of thinking and behaviours that govern its actions today – and even, you could argue, in the physical form that museums take. There is often an inherent contradiction between the origins and evolution of any given museum and their stated aims and ambitions, which shows as they seek to open up dialogue with a wider range of communities and histories.

For historians such as Dan Hicks, the violence associated with the establishment of the so-called encyclopaedic museum in the colonial period, and the continued assertion of absolute rights of ownership over objects obtained under duress from other countries and continents, means that the modern museum is condemned as brutish, then and now.[1] I have some sympathy with his impatience at the apparent lack of generosity or humility from some Western museums, especially in relation to objects whose provenance is demonstrably problematic, like the very well-known Benin materials.[2] As you might expect, I do not wish to tear down the museum institution altogether: rather than seeing these contradictions as fatal, I believe they can offer museums a way to frame their future, if they are honest and brave enough to do so. Museums must also accept that decisions about their collections, and their use and display, need to be negotiated through dialogue with a wider range of stakeholders. This must be a prerequisite if we want our museums to be alive to the ideas and histories of the people we claim to be for.

Since museums have actively courted a wider constituency of visitors, researchers, artists and peer professionals, as I have been tracing in this book, it is inevitable that the nature of the collections we hold should come in for increased questioning. We know this intellectually, and indeed often welcome these questions. Lubaina Himid's exhibition *The Thin Black Line,* made originally at the ICA in 1985, took on a different resonance when shown at Tate Britain in 2011 (as *Thin Black Line(s)*), at a time when most of the Black women artists she selected were still unrepresented within Tate's own permanent collection. It took nearly thirty-five years for that situation to shift significantly, but the point was well made immediately for the public who came to see the exhibition in both its iterations.[3] Although the long-standing absence of British artists of colour from its collections is being addressed now at Tate, we cannot disown the part we played in maintaining an unequal status quo for so long.

More challenging still for museums beyond the art field has been the critique of museum collecting itself, posed by indigenous communities from across a variety of First Nations whose claims to ownership of objects for spiritual and cultural purposes need to supersede any legal title claim the institution may have. Partnerships have been built in good faith between indigenous communities and museums so that the wider public (and the museum itself) can better understand the objects these institutions hold. Ultimately, however, if the museum answer is 'But we still own them', the power dynamic underpinning the relationship does not shift and the relationship will likely founder.

What we need to hold on to, as I hope my discussions in previous chapters will have made clear, is the fact that museums have always been in motion, as sites and spaces that are constructed by their age and by the needs of that particular age. What this means in practice that within any collection, and certainly within any of the ways in which that collection has been thought about and written about, one will encounter objects and ideas that are abhorrent to our current cultural frameworks, whether for reasons of racism, classism, homophobia or sexism. This does not mean – despite what a relativist right-wing press might sometimes claim – that things we now think are racist or sexist were not thought of in this way at the time: even cursory analysis reveals that the objects and ideas were generally recognised by the subjects and by some viewers as derogatory and hostile in their own time as well as our own.[4] What has changed is that, as museums seek to engage a much wider constituency of people, their ability to ignore the deplorable aspects of their history becomes yet another contradiction to navigate.

We cannot say that we welcome all people if some of the objects and ideas living within our collections are actively hostile to particular groups. At the same time, as museums have been taking active steps to own their difficult histories or to challenge the thinking and habits of their colonial inheritances, there has been a rising complaint – from the press, but also from some of our most familiar audiences – that we are destroying what museums are supposed to be: the guardians of a shared past. This is particularly vexing for museums which, as I observed above, are places where objects and their interpretation change all the time.[5] Against this, the pithy but deeply unhelpful slogan coined by the then Secretary of State for Culture, Oliver Dowden, 'Retain and explain' – intended as an instruction to museums in terms of dealing with objects from the past – undermines the evolving cultural narration that is the practice of museums.[6]

Underneath this slogan and the thinking that goes with it is a powerful animating idea: that history cannot be rewritten, and any attempt to do so is against the facts, or at least the common good. This flies in the face of the actual fact that, as all historians are aware, the past is never fixed, but is rewritten by every generation, every new school of thought. It also leads logically to a very basic question: if you do subscribe to the notion of history as only having one author, who should it be?

Outrage

These issues, complex and much debated, get packaged far too neatly under the heading of 'culture wars'. This phrase, which has a long and unedifying lineage, has seen activation in the past few years as something like a banner for collective outrage, rather than a way to explore the complicated, nuanced and ultimately fascinating questions outlined above. By sketching out the nature of what gets polarised in these culture war debates, we can perhaps see a clearer way through them.

First of all, I want to resist the very language of war – be it real or phoney. Apart from the obvious incongruity, museums should be spaces to hold and promote constructive debate and argument. Dispute is what makes us what we are, so it should never be fatal to us, personally, professionally or institutionally. Furthermore, these arguments do, and should, lead to positive change, and an opening up rather than a closing down of debate. In the face of an actively created cultural opposition cast too often in the hostile language of assault, public institutions (museums, but also libraries, heritage sites, theatres and other bodies) find themselves caught between populists on the right, who will defend the immutable truths of our history as they see them, and the liberal left, who are set on examining or re-examining these perceived truths in an attempt to promote the voices and stories of the marginalised. In this view, one side is determined to protect our past and one to destroy it. Keeping a beady eye on proceedings, and occasionally flexing a muscle, we have governments – in the UK and elsewhere – that champion the idea of firmly retaining *our* history, *our* objects and *our* global identity, often as onetime leaders of Empire, in the face of a dramatically altered global world order.

So where does the museum sit in all of this? The Design Museum curator Danielle Thom said: 'If we are actually embroiled in a "culture war", even a manufactured one, then museums are battlegrounds, because they shape and reflect cultural contexts.'[7] I agree with the last part of Thom's sentiment, but we must, I think, resist battlefield analogies: it is more useful, in my opinion, to see museums as holding a responsibility to respond to, and ideally to defuse, the polarised terms of debate. We therefore cannot entirely disentangle the beloved Victoria and Albert Museum from its origins as – at least partly – the East India Company's repository, a location for much of the 'collecting' (sometimes gifts, often loot) carried out in South Asia by agents of British colonialism. Kew Gardens, seemingly one of the most virtuous green stretches of London, played an integral part in the redistribution of thousands of rubber seeds from Brazil to the British colonies, a significant act of biopiracy that broke Brazil's monopoly on the rubber industry. And, as I said in Chapter 1, we cannot deny the fact that Tate was established on the back of an industry that would not have existed in the form and scale that it did without slavery. Nor should we want to turn our faces away from this history, for we would be turning away from the art that needs to be made today – like the work by Guyanese British artist Hew Locke recently on display in our Duveen Galleries.

Locke's installation *The Procession* 2022 takes as its starting point the history and character of the Tate Britain building and of its original benefactor, the sugar refining magnate Henry Tate. As the introductory panel to Locke's commission stated: 'As we join *The Procession*, and Locke's artistic imagination begins to work on us, the figures invite us to walk alongside them for a while, into an enlarged vision of an imagined future.'

Ultimately, museums are civic spaces, and it would be disingenuous to suggest that we have arrived at a point where we are always doing the best or right thing. We can never be neutral or apolitical, even if boards of trustees would like us to be, or politicians direct us to be. What I wish to keep emphasising is that the very contentiousness of these issues, and the way in which flames are deliberately fanned to divide us into factions, is the reason we need to do our utmost to provide a safe environment for the exploration of difficult issues, in ways that do not intimidate or alienate the visitors we have the honour of hosting.

So, at the risk of offending those who think that all aspects of our past need retaining and explaining 'as is', I want to touch on that most problematic of past objects: the statue of Edward Colston, the philanthropist and slave trader, which stood near Bristol Harbour until June 2020 when, following widespread anti-racist and Black Lives Matter protests in the wake of the murder of George Floyd, it was toppled by demonstrators and cast into the water.

What to do about Colston's statue, and indeed the places and streets in Bristol named after him, had been the subject of long-running, angry debates in the city and beyond. Like many examples of this type, it was delay and indecision – by heritage professionals, planners, historians and local leaders – that in the end spurred protestors to action, when they surrounded the statue, pulled it from its plinth, and pitched it into the harbour.

This spontaneous action provoked a widespread response across the globe, as well as strong pushback from a government anxious to insist on a more benign conception of British colonial and imperial history. Historian David Olusoga argued it was correct to remove statues commemorating slave owners from plinths in public spaces where, he argued, they sit largely 'mute', shorn of appropriate context and the possibility of debate, their oppressive histories instead appearing as part of the furniture of daily life.[8] Instead, he suggested the museum would make a better home. Thanks a lot, might have been the response from some in museums struggling painfully to contend with their own contested objects and histories.

The statue was eventually rescued from the water, and was indeed put on display in the city museum, M Shed, in a display that has attempted, in an extraordinarily balanced way, to engage with and stay true to the very divergent views about what happened and what should now happen with the statue itself.

In February 2022 the We Are Bristol History Commission published a report sharing recommendations about the future for the statue.[9] 80% of Bristolians consulted felt it should continue to be displayed in the city museum, on its side and daubed with protestors' paint. Its former plinth, ran the consensus, should become the locus for artworks that would explore the history of the trade in enslaved people in Bristol and challenge the ways in which these histories have been told. Though there were some more radical suggestions from a small minority of people – dividing the statue in two, for instance, to represent divided opinion in the city – the overwhelming feeling expressed by respondents was a desire to acknowledge the difficult past and, in fact, know more about it.

The removal of Colston's statue also prompted a call for a new public monument. Many who had long campaigned to have the statue removed had a strong wish to see a dedicated space in Bristol where the history of enslaved peoples of African descent could be explored. Getting to this place of consensus was not easy, and the group charged with arriving at a decision experienced ugly moments of racism, including death threats. But the public wish to know and to understand ultimately won out, which can only be a good thing.

Between 2020 and 2023, museum investigations into colonial provenance and histories, although undertaken in scholarly and thoughtful ways, and with the object of expanding the field of knowledge about the objects in collections, have come under increasing scrutiny and hostility. In 2020, the Dresden State Art Collection undertook the project of reviewing and amending the titles of any of the 1.5 million objects in its collection (note just how many objects!) that were discriminatory or inaccurate. The reaction from the right wing in Germany was immense, with political parties accusing museum leaders of being speech police, politically motivated and – the greatest of all evils – 'woke'. It didn't matter to these groups that, as the Collection's director patiently explained, titles of works are rarely bequeathed by the artists, and are often changed several times over generations. Nor did it matter that the Collection had, in the end, amended the names of a mere 143 objects – less than 0.01% of the collection. The Collection was defended in parliament by Andreas Nowak, a lawmaker for the conservative Christian Democratic Union, who accused the right-wing parties of 'trying to attack museums' freedom to research and teach'. He also said, however, that the museum had made an error by inadequately explaining the title changes to the public and leaving scope for what he described as a tabloid 'shitstorm'.

There is a lesson here. The Dresden State Art Collection was unprepared for, and genuinely surprised by, the reaction it received, having initiated the exercise as a seemingly innocuous part of the ongoing research work of any museum to update the information held about its objects in the light of new scholarly approaches. Within the museum field, the information used to describe an object to the public is usually referred to as 'interpretation'. This is an illuminating term, as it makes us aware that the knowledge and language used about the object is subjective, and liable to change over time. Some very interesting work is currently underway in the UK, across a group of arts and heritage organisations, to look at how one can trace these shifts in language over time and how one might wish to retain previous, potentially objectionable terminology as part of the object history, precisely so that we can record those various cultural and political meanings as part of the history of the object, rather than erasing them altogether.[10]

That the Collection was unprepared for the hostile response its project received is also true of many cultural institutions attempting to make their way across this slippery terrain, even as this kind of work becomes much more commonplace. At the same time the work in Dresden was taking place, many other international institutions were pursuing similar programmes of investigation, with the Musée d'Orsay, under the leadership of Laurence des Cars, expanding understanding and challenging stereotypes through its *Black Models: from Géricault to Matisse* exhibition of 2019. At the Rijksmuseum, an even more thoroughgoing programme of research has led to questioning of the phrase 'the Dutch Golden Age' to describe the period of Amsterdam's commercial heyday from the 1580s to the 1670s, given that this wealth and 'golden' time was underpinned by holding and trading enslaved peoples, and by the commercial exploitation of the Dutch colonies. In each case, these programmes of research were initiated by curators and researchers, sometimes arising directly from engagement with a wider community of scholars in the field, as well as the interested public. Such initiatives are then generally supported by the museum leadership and boards as part of what is regarded as progressive museological practice. What boards and executive leadership are rarely prepared for is the way in which issues and questions rise up and change shape so swiftly, from ministerial debates to mercurial social media platforms, from activist circles to student forums, even to public protest. In the face of this rapid and heightened response, which can often feel like an attack on the museum's very legitimacy, the traditional decision-making mechanisms are not always capable of allowing museums to reflect and respond in a timely and appropriate manner.

I will give you another example. In 2018, ahead of her major exhibition at Manchester Art Gallery, the artist Sonia Boyce collaborated with a group of drag artists and a queer actor to reframe some of the works hung in one of the galleries within the building. This was a gallery focused on (very traditional) ideals of beauty, which had not been rehung in nearly twenty years. The performance sought to explore and explode some of the gender stereotypes and myths that underpinned not just the works themselves but the way in which they had been chosen and displayed, structured around the celebration of largely passive and entirely white naked or near-naked female figures.

The culmination of the performance, which took place on a Friday night, was the removal of the John William Waterhouse painting *Hylas and the Nymphs* 1896 from the gallery for forty-eight hours, with the public encouraged to share what they thought should be on display in its place. The space on the wall where Waterhouse's painting had hung was left empty for visitors to post up notices of agreement or disagreement with the topics in the painting, its display, its temporary removal, or indeed anything else in the gallery they wished to comment on. Sadly, in the end, the public barely got a moment to have a view. In an interview ahead of the performance, the gallery's curator Clare Gannaway described the thinking behind the performance and the temporary removal of the work, explaining that in 2018, as questions about gender and power were being raised by the #MeToo movement, it felt an appropriate moment to explore the way in which women were portrayed in these historic works.[11] By invoking the MeToo hashtag as a shorthand for describing a cultural moment, the curator unleashed an onslaught on social media, and then across the press.

I am not going to give more space to what we would now recognise as a classic Twitter pile-on, but suffice it to say it was of such violence and volume that one might have thought that the artist and the gallery had taken down all the paintings and put them on a bonfire, rather than removing a single work for two days to create a space for debate. The gallery and the curatorial colleagues concerned were subject to often violent abuse, and were pilloried as 'woke curators' determined to censor historic art and undermine the very foundations of civilisation as we know it. The removal of a single painting for a short period, something that happens practically every day in an art gallery, became national news – and Sonia Boyce's name practically disappeared in the coverage. The sentimental idealisation of the naked female form, and the easy sexism of these temptress nymphs, got entirely lost in a vitriolic narrative that portrayed the female curators leading the gallery as feminist fun-spoilers. As Boyce herself said in the aftermath: 'Some museums – I suppose the type I am most interested in – consider the museum as a place to explore new meanings and to forge new relationships between people and art. In my mind, the past never sits still and contemporary art's job is increasingly about exploring how art intersects with civic life.'[12] In all the noise about the painting's removal – noise which ran along very well-worn and gendered lines of power – that simple point was lost.

A Question of Interpretation

As we have seen, it is not always easy for museums to present new views about a familiar past. This poses a real challenge for national museums that hold collections shaped by and representing difficult histories.

Tate Britain is the home of the national collection of British art, spanning some 500 years. In 2023, it completed a multi-year project to rehang its collection displays, organising works according to three core pillars – 'The Past and the Present', 'Britain and the World' and 'Art and Society' – as well as a more familiar chronology. This rehang has been largely well received by the public, with increased visitor numbers happy to see a much wider representation of Britain's diverse art history, as well as the more direct approach of locating the works both in their time and in our present moment. Interviews with a cross-section of new visitors to the collection at Tate Britain reported that they had not previously viewed the collection because they assumed it would not be for them, and that they would not find a history relevant to them. There was surprise and appreciation when they found points of connection to their own histories and lived experience. The press response, however, has been typically divided, and not even along political lines, with castigation for the rehang being 'too political' and also for being not political or radical enough! Yet all of this sits within an overall appreciation for the new works and new stories being shared. As the chair of Tate ruefully commented, such rehangs are always high stakes for not always clear returns.

In the context of the argument of this book, such points of renewal and reflection matter because they actively seek to renegotiate the museum's relationship with an expanded public: those who already visit, and those who might previously have not. But before I reflect more on this moment of inflection, it is worth exploring an example that ruffled a few more feathers.

Tate Britain's 2021–2 exhibition *Hogarth and Europe* took an approach intended to open new doors to meaning to an artist whose position in British art history is unquestioned. It would have been easy enough to give people the Hogarth they know – the prolific printmaker and painter, the scurrilous social commentator – without significantly deepening visitors' understanding of the rich complexity of his work and his time. Setting aside for a moment the fact that I happen to think doing so would have meant failing in our mission to promote the public's understanding as well as enjoyment of British art, it has become clear over recent years that 'sticking with the paintings' doesn't really cut it any longer in terms of meeting the needs of a wider public. In particular, the team working on *Hogarth and Europe* wanted to see if they could appeal to a younger, more diverse audience less likely to engage with the historic fine art shows at Tate Britain. A major premise of the exhibition was that we can, and should, expand the voices, the expertise and the orders of knowledge brought into the exhibition, to meet the diversity of subject and people in Hogarth's expansive oeuvre; this, it was hoped, would bring a wider diversity of visitors to the show. This 'expansion' work was undertaken by two Tate curators and by our Interpretation team, who have long been advocating for and forging more inclusive and nuanced ways of offering points of engagement with the history of our collection. They recruited a wide group of advisors – artists, designers, academics, historians, visitor guides – whose different lived experience contributed to offering varied views on the paintings and on the exhibition as a whole. Their interpretations were shared with the public in shortened form as part of the wall texts in the exhibition, while longer essays could be found in the exhibition publication.

These voices spoke from subject positions that were – and still are, at the moment –largely absent from the museum workforce and the art historical framework within which museum personnel are trained. For me, one of the most arresting interventions was the text by contemporary artist Lubaina Himid, who won the Turner Prize in 2017. Himid has long cited Hogarth as a major influence on her work, and indeed her celebrated version of his *Marriage A-la-Mode, A Fashionable Marriage* was on display in her solo exhibition at Tate Modern at the same moment *Hogarth in Europe* opened its doors at Tate Britain.

Himid's contribution offers a commentary on the fourth painting in the *Marriage* series, in which a recently titled countess holds a social reception at her daily toilette, echoing an ancient royal ritual. Himid's text gives voice to some of the characters who are marginalised in the painting, 'speaking' first as Oumar – the Malian butler in the middle background of the scene – and then as Adeban, the Black child in the image's right foreground. The first disruption comes with the use of first person, the voice and the 'I' of Oumar: 'My name is Oumar and I am a butler-cum-manservant from Mali.' The incongruity and surprise of encountering the character speaking to us implicates us immediately as viewers of this scene, something Himid intends and underlines when Oumar places the viewer, too, as a visitor to this gathering: 'The invitees to our breakfast gathering (including you) pale into insignificance next to the guest of honour ...' While Oumar's dialogue is with the viewer, giving us his perspective on the scene we have chosen to look at, it is delivered back to us in the spirit of Hogarth's dissecting eye. Oumar's frank assessment of the scene helps us read it more easily and incisively, and is certainly one of the more engaging ways of delivering the details to a contemporary viewer who may have neither the history, nor perhaps the habits, to appreciate the nuance of this satirical scene at a glance.

Having grasped Oumar's view of the drama, we are then wrong-footed again by the voice of Adeban: 'The butler Oumar can be bitter, I know, but you must forgive him.' Adeban – 'the cleverest person in the room', according to Oumar – reminds us that a singular perspective is unreliable, drawn from the particular sensibility of one actor in this drama of many. In speaking to this instability, Himid achieves several things. The distinctive voices reaching us from the painting bring figures from its background – the people of colour – into the foreground, reshaping the Eurocentric framing of Hogarth's time and our own. In addition, Himid's words 'straight to the visitor' are scathing and frequently funny – just as Hogarth so often is – and act as a wake-up call to the visitor expecting to be given a 'neutral' or 'objective' account of what takes place in the scene. Certainly, I felt myself being given a good poke in the ribs and reminded to look harder at what I *thought* I was seeing as I made my way around the rest of the exhibition.

Some visitors, however, did not appreciate this perspective. Some felt we had dragged Hogarth inappropriately into the twenty-first century, projecting the concerns of today's society on an artist and a period of history that should be judged by its own mores. Others criticised what they saw as an attempt to diminish Hogarth, in an age of political correctness. Given that Tate went to considerable trouble to assemble a truly remarkable group of paintings, prints and drawings, and to solicit deep thinking and research from a much larger body of thinkers than we would typically use in making a historic British art show, this was obviously not what we intended. But, as with my earlier example from Manchester, we touched a cultural nerve. Rather than expanding the range of views and voices on a foundational figure in British art history, we were accused by some of telling people what to think about Hogarth. Worst of all, we were telling them that he – like so many figures from our conflicted past – was a bad 'un.

With the lovely benefit of hindsight, it is clear that we could have done more to bring general visitors on the journey with us. There is truth in the charge that we veer towards a didactic tone sometimes, especially when we are attempting to rewrite histories or critique embedded ways of seeing and thinking. No one much likes being told what to think, and the reactions by some to the approach we took in that instance remind us that we should err towards giving people the tools to think rather than telling them *what* to think. In my view, an artist of Hogarth's stature is more than up for this challenge. We can also take heart from the fact that the debate took place at all – and without it, we might not have heard the sentiments voiced by press and public.

Sacred Ground

There are two interesting points for me here. The first is that there is, for museums and heritage bodies alike, a perception of sacred ground that we should *not* tread on. If and when we do, the reaction will be intemperate, and often unconstrained in its language and passion. A recent furore focused on the National Trust which prompted agitation at the AGM and vocal calls for the resignation of its leadership was occasioned, we should remember, by a thorough, scholarly and mostly unremarkable report about the obvious colonial and imperial histories of the houses in the Trust's care.[13] Along with the public outcry, many staff at the National Trust and the author of the report received extreme harassment in person and online. We should not let this pass lightly, and it goes without saying that public organisations, let alone individual staff members, do not have the means or the power to defend themselves from the violence of such attacks.

These sacred territories are nearly always bound up with the social, economic and cultural power relations of the past. Great spleen is vented when the gender or sexual dynamics of nineteenth-century art are questioned, as we again saw in the Manchester example above. Critique of the racial or ethnic beliefs of the past almost always occasions hyperbolic condemnation of the credentials of the person or persons making comment; this is combined frequently with an invocation of a green and pleasant land of the past, which the writer or speaker's critique is supposed to be destroying. This idea of a bucolic past reveals much about anxieties concerning change and, I would argue, about the perceived losses – by an also imagined dominant culture – that the expansion of equity for all will entail. This requires, of course, both an imagined past *and* an imagined present. This perhaps tells us why museums, whose rationale and mission task us with imagining the past and shaping the present, have so often found themselves caught in this cultural crossfire. The volume of current complaints from certain quarters might even suggest we are making some progress.

The second point, and the one that is most important to repeat, is that we are seeing again that pervasive notion that history cannot be rewritten, when in fact it is recast by every generation, every new school of thought. To cite a figure routinely invoked in 'culture war' skirmishes, we should remember that Winston Churchill, far from thinking that history was objective, was alleged to have said: 'History will be kind to me, for I shall write it.' Whether or not Churchill actually said this, it requires its own riposte, offered by the Nigerian writer Chinua Achebe – 'Until the lions have their own historians, the history of the hunt will always glorify the hunter'.[14] The writer Afua Hirsch takes a small leap in applying this notion to the arts: 'If history is written by the victor, then art – throughout the history of modern European traditions – has been commissioned by the oppressor.'[15]

The question has been asked. Museums are now beginning to find ways to answer: centring other narratives in ways that address previous exclusion, but are not only defined by this fact. In the past few years there have been some brilliant examples: to cite a few just from my own experience, the Rijksmuseum's *Slavery* exhibition; the National Gallery of Victoria's (NGV) dual exhibition *Colony: Australia 1770–1861 / Frontier Wars*; and the *Afro-Atlantic Histories* exhibition conceived and staged by São Paulo Museum of Art (MASP) in 2018 and later represented at the National Gallery of Art in Washington.[16] In 2017, the Rijksmuseum announced it would present an exhibition about slavery for the first time in its history. As curators Eveline Sint Nicolaas and Valika Smeulders explained, a vital first step in the development of their show was identifying gaps in the museum's knowledge and experience, and recruiting a wide group of individuals to help steer and shape the show. New staff members with relevant professional as well as personal backgrounds were hired, a think tank was assembled, and there was an extensive exchange of ideas with national and international experts on the history of slavery. The exhibition was developed over a four-year period via a consultative process that sought input from descendants of enslaved people as well as scholars and activists across the globe. It was a completely new way for a national, historic museum to develop an exhibition, and one that put the idea of 'many voices' at the heart of the process from the very start. While the rationale for working this way drew the usual criticisms from some quarters of the press, the public's response to the Rijksmuseum exhibition was resoundingly positive.

A related example in the US is *Mayflower 400: Legend and Legacy*, an exhibition which The Box in Plymouth, UK, shaped drawing on ideas from both sides of the Atlantic. The exhibition was created in partnership with the Wampanoag Advisory Committee to Plymouth 400 in Massachusetts. It drew help from over one hundred museums and archives in the UK, US and the Netherlands. The 400th anniversary of the Mayflower landing presented a huge challenge for the only recently formed organisation, as the brutal history of violence associated with the colonial conquest of the USA meant the anniversary felt far from celebratory for many communities. Following months of exchanges, a partnership was established with an indigenous group called SmokeSygnals in order to 'develop a foundation of a shared history between our people'. SmokeSygnals challenged the curators' aspirations, understanding and outlook for what the exhibition could be, allowing them to learn and live with the past through the practice and objects of contemporary indigenous artists and artisans, and together turning a seventeenth-century moment into a meaningful twenty-first-century exchange of ideas and practices. Together, the two communities realised they could shape a new interpretation of a shared past, even a brutal one – an interpretation which included the indigenous communities at its heart.

As I mentioned, in 2018 I was privileged to see the dual exhibition at the NGV in Melbourne, *Colony: Australia 1770–1861 / Frontier Wars*, which took a challenging revisionist approach to a contested national history. The history of English 'arrival' in, or colonial imposition on, Australia was expanded and critiqued with care and respect, in ways that resonated powerfully with the challenges we face in examining British history here in the UK. The exhibition began simultaneously in the past and the present – a continual 'duality' of focus reflected in the exhibition's double title, in its presence across two floors of the museum itself, and in the fact that it examined the moment of 'arrival' from the perspectives of those who were there already as well as those newly landed. Aboriginal communities played an active role not just in interpreting the objects from the past but in what was and was not included, making a complete review of all the objects proposed by the museum team. This was a simple and powerful change in museum practice, one which allowed generative engagement between those working within the museum and the indigenous communities whose lands had been colonised and who, until recently, have rarely been present or welcomed within the heritage space. Alongside this, the work of contemporary artists – such as Yhonnie Scarce, whose *Blood on the*

Wattle (Elliston, South Australia 1849) 2013 commemorates a bloody clash between settlers and indigenous peoples – provided alternative framings of how the past presented in the exhibition might be read and understood. The foreword to the exhibition catalogue includes a powerful statement by Aboriginal Elder Joy Murphy Wandin:

> Seen from the heart, this exhibition should remind all people of their right to agree or disagree. Remembering respect for each other should be at the forefront of all discussions.[17]

Afro-Atlantic Histories, held at MASP, São Paulo in 2018, examined the visual cultures of Afro-Atlantic territories, responding to Brazil's own history in receiving approximately 46% of the 11 million Africans transported against their will across the Atlantic over a 300-year period. Featuring over 450 works by 214 artists from the sixteenth to the twenty-first century, the exhibition explored the rich and lasting legacy of African cultures on Brazil, and reshaped a known history by juxtaposing multiple representations of Brazilians of African descent with as many representations by them.[18] By doing so, it was able to disrupt dominant colonial narratives, and also to construct a new and powerful paradigm for understanding the interchange between contemporary art practice and the revision of a history of the nation. Like the NGV example, the exhibition adopted a polyphonic approach to the renarration of national identity – most especially in the interplay between the views and ideas of the past – offering not only a long lineage, but also a powerful legitimacy for artists of the present.

A final example underscores the shift I am noting here: the extraordinary exhibition *Mixpantli: Space, Time, and the Indigenous Origins of Mexico*, organised at LACMA in 2021. The exhibition broke with tradition by presenting its significant selection of materials from its own collection in such a way as to counter widely held notions of the colonial conquest of Mexico City. Rather, it centred the creative resilience of indigenous artists, mapmakers and storytellers, highlighting their active role in shaping the narratives of the future through artistic practice. The exhibition placed early colonial art in conversation with pre-Columbian artefacts to demonstrate how the Nahua (indigenous Mexican) and Christian world views evolved alongside each other, and how deeply indigenous world views shaped Mexico itself. In offering this new story, the museum had to question its own prior narratives about the objects it held, as well as conceive of the exhibition within a different time, space and world view. By concentrating on a non-Western, indigenous-centred approach, the museum fulfilled its stated aim of engaging more fully with the majority Hispanic communities that constitute greater Los Angeles today. What I witnessed in this exhibition, as well as in the examples above, was a simple but powerful determination to hold more than one position in view – two different world views, not in conflict, but illuminating each other.

If we take one thing from these examples, it should be that telling a more equitable story of the past nearly always means complicating the story, rather than simplifying it. The exhibitions I describe also all point to the necessary work of decolonisation within the museum space. The term 'decolonisation', drawn from long-established academic study, is widely used (and widely abused) inside and outside the museum world; as a term, it has become unfortunately reflective of what any given institution or writer needs it to mean. It is used with some nonchalance in academic circles, and lobbed about like a grenade in certain factions of our media. Ultimately, though, it leaves large swathes of the general public – the people we serve – none the wiser. What I believe decolonisation to mean, as far as museums

Gathering of Strangers

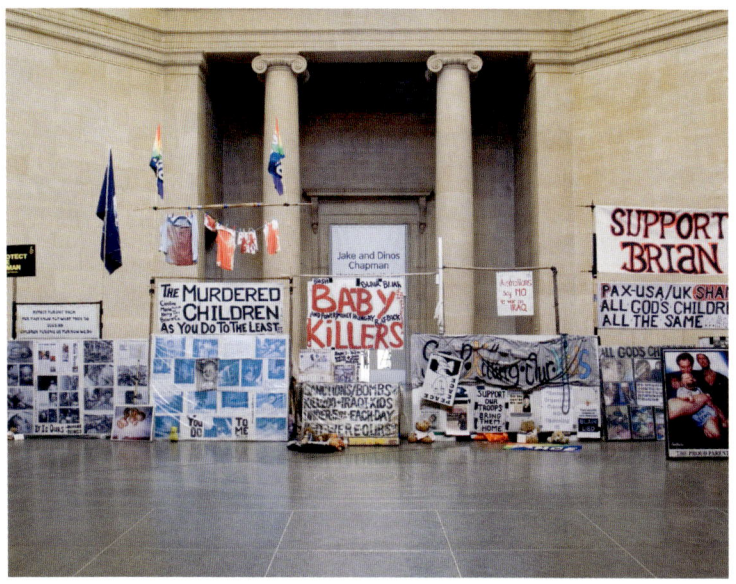

Mark Wallinger *State Britain* 2007 p.86

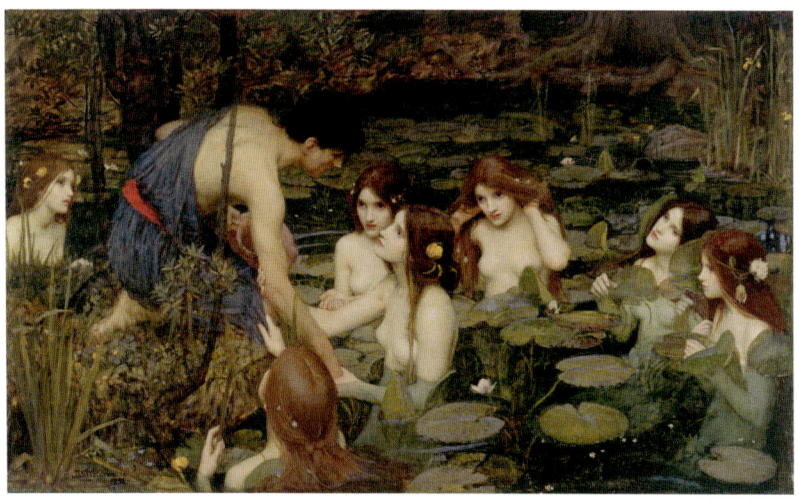

John William Waterhouse *Hylas and the Nymphs* 1896 p.117

Gathering of Strangers

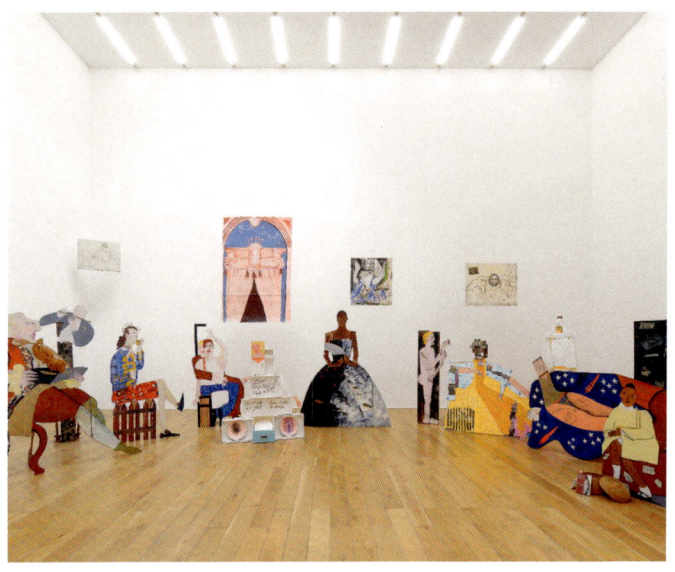

Lubaina Himid *A Fashionable Marriage* 1986 p.120

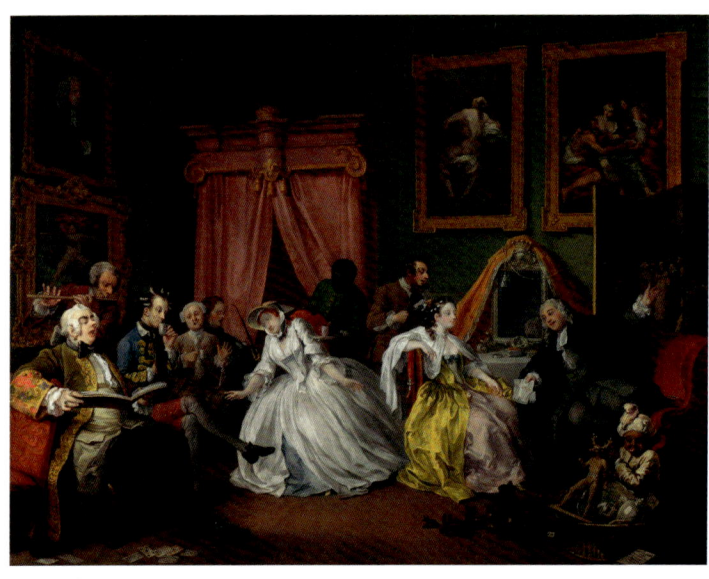

William Hogarth *Marriage A La Mode: 4, The Toilette* 1743 p.120

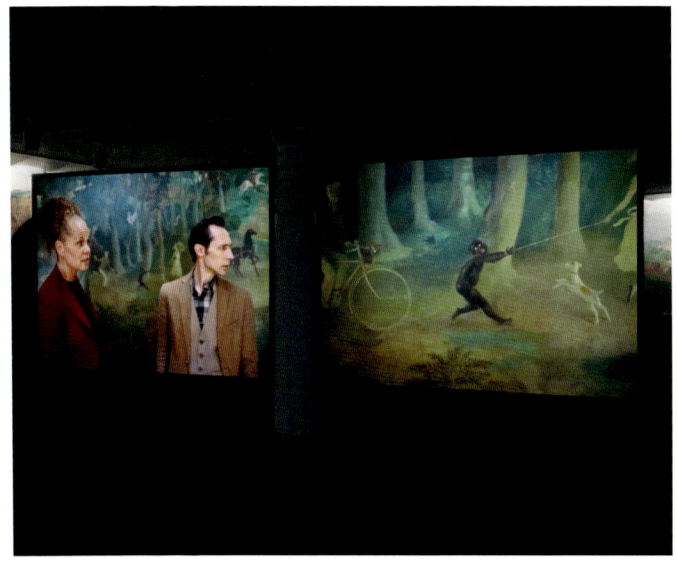

Keith Piper *Viva Voce* 2024 p.134

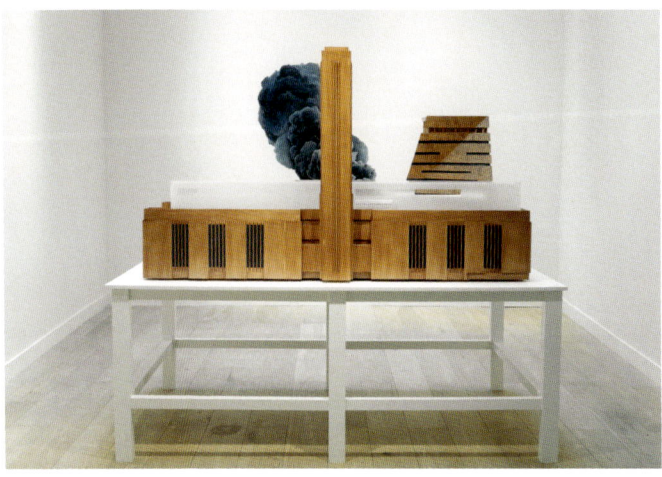

Nathan Coley *Tate Modern on Fire* 2017 p.138

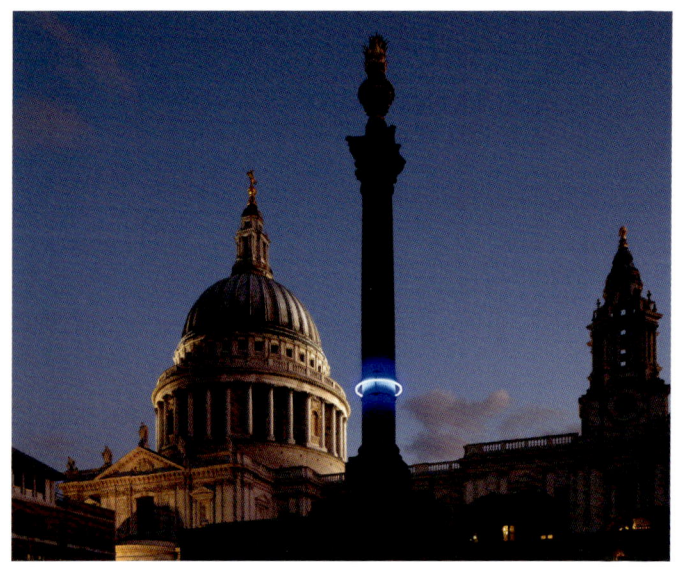

Michael Pinsky *Plunge* 2020 p.170

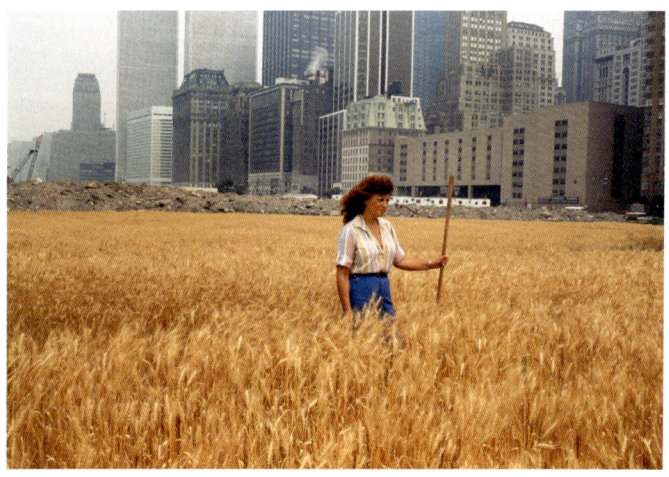

Agnes Denes *Wheatfield – A Confrontation* 1982 p.178

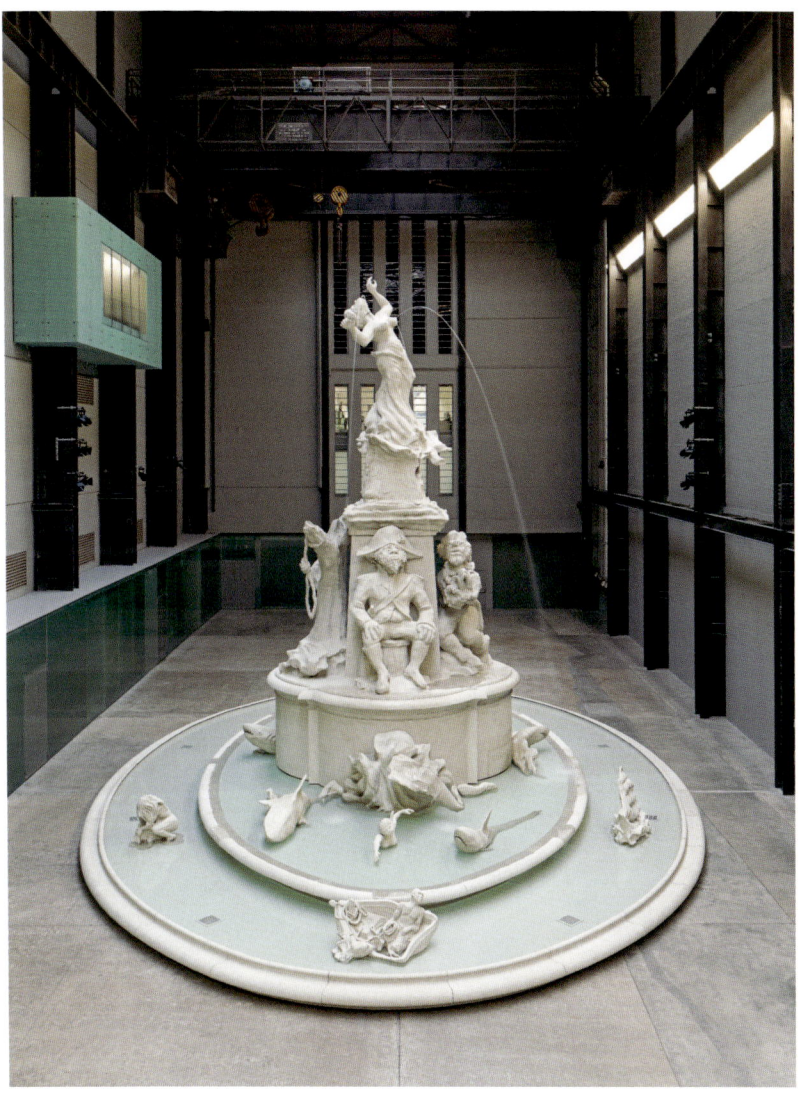

Kara Walker *Fons Americanus* 2019 p.186

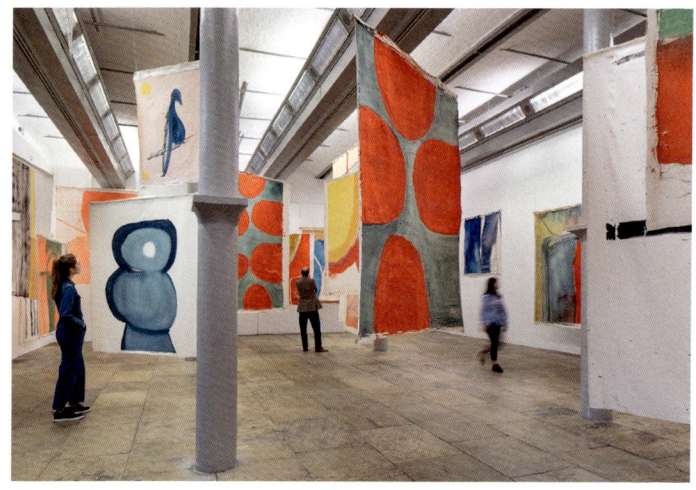

Vivian Suter *Nisyros (Vivian's Bed)* 2016 p.180

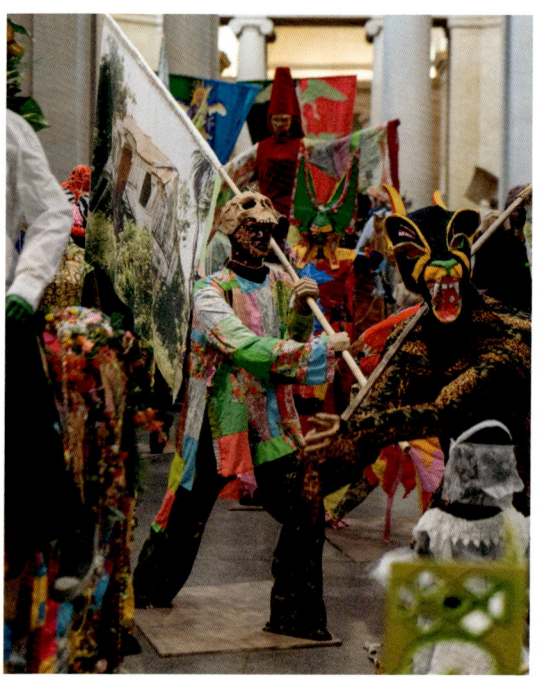

Hew Locke *The Procession* 2022 p.197

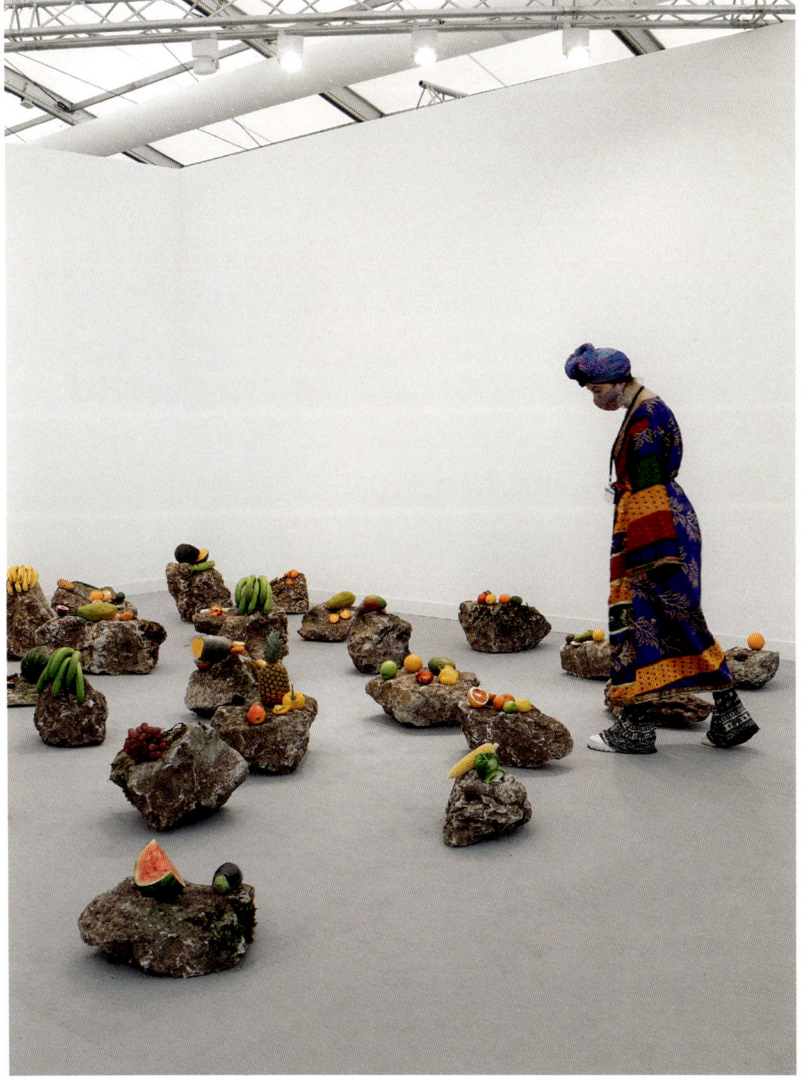

Edgar Calel *The Echo of an Ancient Form of Knowledge* 2021 p.208

Gathering of Strangers

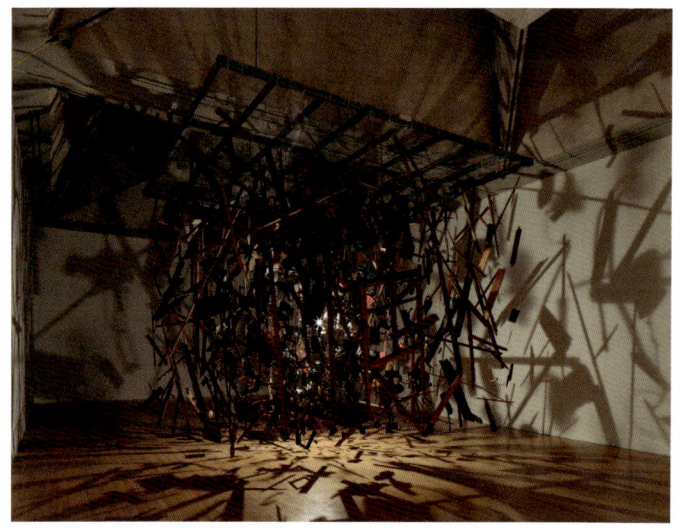

Cornelia Parker *Cold Dark Matter* 1991 p.211

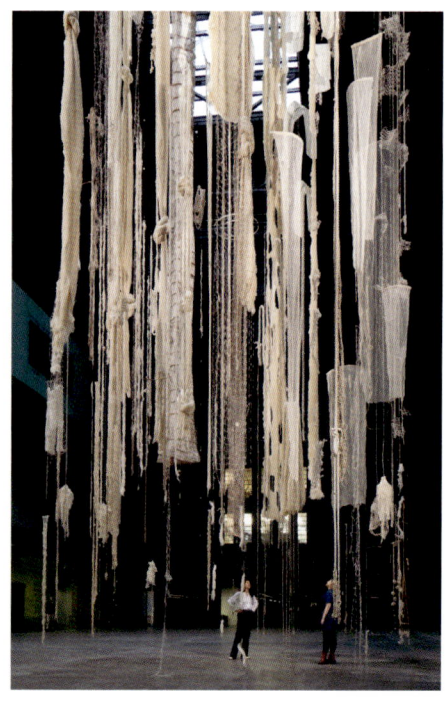

Cecilia Vicuna *Brain Forest Quipu* 2022 p.231

are concerned, is this: a careful, systematic process that examines the ongoing impact of imperial narratives, resulting in sensitive and meaningful action to tackle the framework of inherited inequalities, shift long-established biases and emphases, and make our museums more inclusive spaces. All the examples I cited above manage to do this: shift thinking, surface multiple world views, and foster and share new ideas and knowledge generously.

Decolonising work at Tate takes many forms, and has been fostered by many colleagues, especially colleagues of colour, over the long term. I want to acknowledge here the importance of their work, and its ongoing nature. If we look back, we can sometimes see it unfurl in slow motion – such as with a rather striking painting by John Simpson. When this painting was first exhibited in 1827 in the British Institution, it was called *Head of a Black*. When it was first engraved in the *Art Journal* in 1853, it was simply titled *The Negro*. Years later, in 1919, it was taken to Tate and given the name *Head of a Negro*, carrying that name until possibly as late as 2013, when it went on permanent display in Tate Britain. Today, it is known as *Head of a Man (?Ira Frederick Aldridge)*. Ira Aldridge was a famous actor and, although we cannot be certain, it is thought that he was Simpson's sitter. Yet this is not necessarily all neatly sewn up. Was Tate right to give the painting this title? Perhaps simply *Head of a Man* is appropriate because it qualifies the sitter as a man, rather than as a Black man, reducing the risk of the subject being seen as a figurehead for his race. But to use that shorter title might be to rob the sitter of his identity. Yet does *(?Ira Frederick Aldridge)* in the title do enough to hint at the possible identity of the sitter? And does the title *Head of a Man* do enough to recognise the sitter's race?

Another example of this sort of evolution of presentation is that of John James Baker's *The Whig Junto* 1710. The painting is the only known portrait of the Junto, an ideologically close-knit group of political peers who formed the leadership of the Whig party in the late seventeenth and early eighteenth centuries, and was acquired by Tate relatively recently, in 2017. Even then, the accompanying caption omitted to mention the presence in the work of a Black servant. This work is one that was allocated to Tate through the Acceptance in Lieu scheme, which allows that works of national importance can be given to public institutions as part of inheritance tax settlement; Baker's painting, therefore, already comes to us with the freight of high cultural importance and with a long history of being described and esteemed as a notable historic painting – it does, after all, portray those who led the country in this period. Perhaps this contributed to the absence of critique in the way the painting was described. Perhaps it contributed to our failure to correct the mistake. We inherit attitudes and words about the work as well as the painting itself. The omission of the figure of the servant was revised only after a visitor pointed it out.

The action of changing how we described this work then brought about a much larger programme of research and rethinking within the historic fine art team, and this work now sits in a room in the recently rehung Tate Britain named 'Court versus Parliament' that much more thoroughly explores the prolific dissent against majority culture in print culture of the time, through the inclusion of wallpaper, furniture and a sound piece by contemporary artist Nils Norman. This gives the visitor a sense of the context of Empire, of working class dissent and the evident resistance to the ostensibly stable leadership of the nation and the world that underpins the portrayal in the painting. This polyvocal approach characterises our current overall way of telling histories (plural) through the collection at Tate Britain.

The most difficult challenge for Tate in recent years in this arena has been an example I mentioned in the last chapter: the case of *The Expedition in Pursuit of Rare Meats*, the mural by Rex Whistler which runs around the walls of Tate Britain's former basement restaurant. Commissioned by Tate's inaugural director Charles Aitken in 1926 and completed in 1927, the mural depicts an imagined hunting expedition involving the Duke of Epicurania. It contains highly offensive racist imagery, including a depiction of an enslaved Black child chained to the back of a cart and the child's mother being chased up a tree. Elsewhere on its tour of the world, the mural visits China and includes derogatory caricatures of Chinese figures. In its general sweep around the globe for rare meats for the delectation of the elite, it reifies and amplifies an empire in the last stages of its collapse.

The uncomfortable images contained in the work have been raised at various points during the nearly 100 years of its existence, but its presence in the museum since its very early decades (and the fact it is painted directly on the wall) has made it very difficult to decide what to do with it. Art historian David Dibosa calls it a peculiarly 'embarrassing' and shameful object: he means the term 'embarrassing' to be unsettling to us, and his description of shame relates not just to the work itself but to his and others' feelings about having lived 'alongside' it, without making overt commentary, for such a long time.[19] Certainly, I share David's ambivalence and shame here.[20] This work has become totemic because we did not find a way to do what museums usually do with such objects, which is to take them off display and consign them safely, if still with a certain degree of shame, into the store where they can no longer offend the visiting public. The mural's racist tropes are sadly not unusual across fine art, nor in popular representations in this period. Nonetheless, there is an enormous difference between an offensive piece of art hanging on a gallery wall with accompanying interpretation explaining its context, and it decorating the walls of a restaurant where people sit down to lunch.

Colleagues at Tate had been raising for a long time how unhappy they were about the mural being on display, and we had numerous examples of visitors expressing deep concern about it. Several ethics committee discussions had taken us to a point where a long and somewhat awkward interpretation panel was placed at the entrance to the room, in which we attempted to give the mural some critical context. But the panel was rarely noticed, while the mural continued to make many feel uncomfortable, or indeed hurt and angry, as it remained present but unresolved.

It was exactly this point that exploded for us, in the wake of global Black Lives Matter protests, at a time of deepening concern about the racial issues that museums were not talking about. Protestors used a quote from a restaurant review from 1927 which the museum had happily used in the 2000s – 'the most amusing dining room in Europe' – to point out our ongoing toleration of the racism of the work. Unsurprisingly, we had an explosion on social media that was as loud, and as understandable, as the tipping of the Colston statue into the water in Bristol. I would say now that, as painful this experience was, it raised necessary issues that we had been too slow and too uncertain to go near, and the challenge from a wide and angry public was entirely legitimate.

Since then, things have shifted considerably, not merely at speed but with the depth and seriousness that I think these matters actually need. The restaurant had been closed anyway because of the impact of Covid restrictions and we decided it would remain shut until we had formulated a plan to properly address this most uncomfortable of objects. We invited voices from outside Tate – including artists, art historians, cultural advisors, civic representatives and young creative practitioners – to explore possible options for the work and for the room it was in. The ensuing discussions built on many previous conversations and incorporated feedback received directly from visitors and colleagues. This was a painful, generative, profound and necessarily time-intensive learning experience. It was also an action in bringing to the surface some deep and unresolvable disagreement, as well as an attempt to move toward a position which does not seek to 'solve the problem' or make this uncomfortable object 'safe'. As Amia Srinivasan, Professor of Social and Political Theory at the University of Oxford, one of the participants in these discussions and a member of Tate's ethics committee, said:

> Conversations about the mural were open, rigorous, and filled with good-natured but deep disagreement: would keeping the mural open to the public accentuate its power? Would shutting it off risk doing the same? Could the space be used by artists of colour as a creative site of reappropriation? Or would this unfairly burden them with a problem produced by a historically white institution? One of the few points of consensus was that Tate had to take ownership of its history, and that whatever decision was made had to be an invitation to a broader conversation, not the end of one.[21]

As I noted above, the decision of Tate's trustees, informed by these difficult conversations, was to ask the executive to invite a contemporary artist, should they be willing, to make a new site-specific installation in the room, which would then be opened to visitors as a display space. This new work by Keith Piper, now in situ, is exhibited alongside and in dialogue with Whistler's mural, reframing the way the space is experienced. Alongside it, new interpretative material engages critically with the mural's history and content, including its racist imagery and the very significant disagreements that the various constituencies we consulted with shared with us. To invoke David Dibosa's terms once more, the mural prompts shame and discomfort – but we have found it more useful to surface this through discussion and to share these feelings with the public, since this is the past we still have to live with, however much we may disagree with it. *Viva Voce* 2024, carefully researched and brilliantly presented by Piper, stages this argument for us, so that the public can develop their own, better informed, views.

Through these debates, it became clear that it was important we did not remove the artwork – or 'cancel' it, to use the modish term. As museum directors and trustees, we are custodians of the museum's assets, be they beloved or reviled, and we pass on their power, for good and for bad. The Whistler mural, sitting in plain sight for many decades in our restaurant, is only one of the more visible examples of things we don't agree with or believe any more. Museums are full of them.

Meaningful Change

There is vital, ongoing work for museums that drills down into everyday practices essential in developing ethical, equitable and transparent readings of the objects in our collections. Stories such as the experience the Dresden State Art Collection faced do sometimes make me wonder if we have the stamina to do this work, in the face of critique that can go all the way up to governmental debate. It is tempting perhaps to think that this sort of quiet, unshowy decolonisation work should be kept safely in the corridors of institutions, for now anyway, until the fervour has subsided. But then I look at the sensitive and courageous discussions that have taken place in Bristol, or the intellectual and emotional labour of Black colleagues over decades in challenging and changing how we think about our past, and how this has made so much difference to the way we think about cultures in their plural realities – the ongoing influence of Stuart Hall or Paul Gilroy, for instance, just two of the very many thinkers I could mention.[22] Then it feels to me non-negotiable that museums should be doing this work, no matter how inclement the political weather.

When you look dispassionately at what museums are attempting now, it amounts to little more than common sense: why wouldn't a public body be as expansive and inclusive as possible? But sometimes, thanks to the wilful misinformation in circulation about decolonisation's purpose and intent, even the faintest scent of it can be alienating. And alienating audiences is the very antithesis of what we exist to do. It is then, again, part of our mission and purpose of 'expanding understanding' to carefully explain to audiences the reasoning and aims behind this intellectual work, and in language that allows respectful and informed conversation.

In some parts of museum culture, we see a gung-ho approach: to declare those wary of decolonisation work as bigots whose support we simply don't need. The idea that I wish to keep returning to in this book is that a public body is just that – a body of the public – and therefore, ideally, a museum such as Tate should reflect, as much as it possibly can, the divergent set of views making up the whole spectrum of the public mood. This is a near-on impossible task, but it is important to resist absolutism and to repeat that this is slow, sensitive, transformative work, and that we will not always get it right. Museums are sometimes considered unimpeachable, the last word in authoritative objectivity, but this, as I hope my discussions across these chapters demonstrate, is an illusion we can and should allow ourselves to relinquish. As I said in my Introduction, museums run on emotion, and are staffed by a body of people who are deeply passionate about what they do. Likewise, our public care a surprising amount about what happens in their museums. However bumpy the road, we should not be frightened when challenging historic power relations and reformulating our thoughts about our place in the world causes passionate reaction. The example of the Whistler mural lies at the more extreme end of the tensions that museums are attempting to navigate, but the need to accommodate dissent and different views on the situation are common to much of the work of museums today. That this takes place in an often challenging and very public spotlight is part of our increased importance, I would argue, even if it is often difficult to manage.

Museums are institutions for the long term, and usually not good at moving fast. This doesn't always serve them well in what is now a really fast-moving environment. Indeed, the collections and the buildings sometimes seem immovable, while staff and public passion swirl around them. Perhaps the real challenge, then, is how to shift from the conservative tendency to do nothing ('It will all blow over') to a recognition that long-term structural change is needed to address key tensions that have been stretching museums not just for years, but for centuries.

5

New Models for Museums

As we've seen, contradictions haunt the public museum. There are oppositions everywhere: between the challenges of the past and the ambitions of the present; between creating a welcoming space and inviting debate; between acquiring and caring for collections of the very best artworks but also challenging the idea of the 'very best'; by trying to tell stories of everyone but not claiming to speak for everyone.[1] It is time, I think, that museums allow ourselves to be a bit more at ease in our conflicted location, even if it sometimes feels like we exist between a rock and a hard place.

I want to hold on to the notion that a successful museum is or should be in a state of productive tension, in which objects, ideas and people are brought into constructive and not always resolved dialogue, and disagreement is allowed. This means the museum should strive to be an expanded space for deliberative conversation and reflection, as artist Monica Narula has proposed.[2] However, I also believe that unless we task ourselves to think and act differently, our institutions face significant challenges. I am not suggesting that we should burn the museum down, but I do, however, thank artist Nathan Coley for his image of Tate Modern on fire, as it encapsulates the idea that the museum has always been the subject of trenchant but also playful critique from the artists who make and show work within its walls, and the visitors who come to see it.

One big contradiction that I have yet to tackle in this book is one that, more than any other listed, could bring about the end of the museum as we know it. That is the clash between money, creativity and sustainability. In this chapter I want to propose some alternative operating modes for museums – ones that are potentially more socially, ethically, economically and environmentally stable than the current model. Now that museums have weathered and emerged from the extreme turmoil of the Covid-19 pandemic and the wider disruptions of equity and ethics I sketched out in earlier chapters, I think it is time to begin mapping out a more sustainable long view of the purpose and practice of museums, such that we – in the public museums at least – can argue with greater strength for the contribution they make to the creation of social and economic value. In using the terms 'positive' and 'sustainable social value' I am drawing on the critical thinking about the circular economy and so-called 'doughnut economics' set out by economic thinkers such as Kate Raworth and Mariana Mazzucato, which seeks to redefine value, in the case of museums' cultural and heritage value, outside standard capitalist (and especially neo-liberal) financial value frameworks.[3]

Degrowth

It is not surprising that discussions in museums about degrowth have become increasingly common in recent years. The concept of 'degrowth' has been borrowed from economic theory, in which context it is associated with an anti-consumerist and anti-capitalist approach to sustainable development. It is being explored more broadly now as part of debates about green-growth strategies and a mode of economic activity that is less intensive and less exploitative. Within museums and the arts, the degrowth debate has unfolded as a useful way of framing ideas of deepening social impact or extending museums' social learning capacity, as opposed to thinking that the museum must continually increase its size or its quantitative reach. Rather than an 'anti-growth' position, the concept of degrowth then becomes one focused on a sustainable long future. A plan for degrowth would mean understanding and making strategic decisions about the future for the museum institution and the sector more broadly – decisions that would focus on deepening our impact on and our connection to people, and would be anchored in an idea of social learning and dialogue about the shape of the past and the present, as well as a front-foot argument that the cultivation of enjoyment is also a social good.

It means taking a moment to sketch out the economics of the current museum model. It is an obvious but pertinent point that public museums are premised on market failure. The museum, as a collection of objects and activities, is too expensive to either assemble or maintain without the twin engines of state subsidy and private philanthropy – with, in the modern era, the ability to monetise some if not all of its activities acting as an ongoing underpinning. This does not mean that museums are bad businesses but that, in common with many charitable or public good activities, they provide a value that is more than the sum of their commercial output. Different museum ecologies have a different balance of these three core elements: in the USA, for instance, the government or state subsidy is relatively low and private philanthropy a much bigger proportion of any individual museum's annual turnover. In Europe, public subsidy generally accounts for 60–70% of museum income. In the UK, museums exist – usually – in a 30–30–40% balance; public subsidy represents the 40% in most institutions, with it standing at 30% in some of the largest museums (including Tate).[4]

Each model brings its own positives and negatives, but where public subsidy is significant there will always be an important obligation to provide public benefit in the form of knowledge shared, access to cultural capital, and learning as part of the experience. The museum visit, in short, must offer something more than simple entertainment. At the same time, all museums are, and have been, under great pressure to generate their own income. But what museums have faced up to in the modern era, adhering to the idea that to grow income has essentially meant growing visitor numbers, is not just the discovery that maximising the number of overall visitors has not made museums more diverse in terms of their reach (as we saw earlier), but that it has also risked diminishing the wider social learning benefits that can come from museum-visiting.

The experience of living with and through the Covid situation, and the period of socially distanced cultural life that followed it, has taught us some potentially valuable lessons, in ways we perhaps didn't understand at first. After the initial lockdowns of 2020 and 2021 we welcomed only a few tourists and a cautious local public back to our galleries. We had a responsibility to keep visitors safe, and so introduced distancing measures and mask-wearing, and capped capacity to reduce crowding. Even if we had been more relaxed, I doubt there were many members of the public eager at that time to be crowded into a confined, internal space, even to see something novel or exciting. Alongside this caution, however, was a newly awoken sense of enjoyment in an encounter with 'real things'. Seeing paintings, sculptures and textiles up close offered heightened delight as people appreciated the material quality and the haptic power that is sorely absent from onscreen artistic viewing. In Tate's case, our reduced capacity and limited space meant that our usually busy programme was temporarily paused, or at least slowed down somewhat. More broadly, museums started to leave shows up for longer, partly because of the difficulties in transporting artworks between institutions, partly to save money in a very challenging financial situation, and partly because the throughput of visitors was necessarily slower. Initial visitor feedback was positive, with many praising the less crowded environment. A symptom of the post-lockdown period, perhaps? Even if visitor numbers do return to the levels we saw in 2019 (and as of 2023 they have not), then I am fairly certain that the public appetite to put up with very crowded exhibitions has gone for good. This makes it all the more important to ask the question: if our growth failed to expand our reach, is this quantitative approach to judging the success of a museum even the right one?

We might also want to apply this thinking to the overarching model of growth on which museums have tended to draw. In this model, if a museum is successful, the next step would be to expand, and establish another space, then another, and another. This ideal is questionable. The ever-expanding 'multinational' museum model with branches sharing their 'riches' with other parts of the world often serves to reinforce the intrinsic inequalities of global cultural wealth distribution, and perpetuates what many recognise and critique as a colonial model. This is only exacerbated when the museums in question retain the best of the cultural wealth for themselves, defending the 'encyclopaedic' model and resisting the redistribution of assets that would recognise and help construct a greater cultural parity across nations, and especially between the Global North and South.[5]

The ethical and reputational challenges for established museums also bring greater pressure to be more self-sufficient. The need for cash to support the ongoing generation of income and keep the machine running is what drives museums towards ever more reputationally challenging modes of sponsorship and support. The business maxim 'speculate to accumulate' does not hold true here, either. We need to be careful that in our drive to diversify collections we are not asset-stripping new regions in a way that undermines local ecologies' capacity for and efficacy in growing – and growing differently.

This is before we even start to contemplate the operational habits of most museums, which are both ecologically and economically unsustainable. Thinking about the social impact of the museum and our engagement with the public we represent should have an impact on the varying streams of support we accept in order to sustain our spaces. As public bodies, we should not seek funds from sources that exacerbate the environmental devastation continuing across the globe, or perpetuate inequitable living conditions, or support war or conflicts. This really goes without saying, but it still happens far too often today.

Grow or Die

'Grow or die', another business maxim, derived from George Land's 1973 book of that name, is now largely discredited – yet we still find this principle embedded in the deep thinking of most organisations, and indeed most museums. As I set out in earlier chapters, the drive to expand museum infrastructure was the overriding feature of museum improvement from the 1990s to now. Museums simply weren't business-oriented until at least the 1980s, when dwindling support of the arts and of the public sector in the UK and the US forced those running museums to look to more commercial approaches to fulfil their role. There were certainly benefits of this turn to thinking about the visitor as an 'asset', among them a greatly improved visitor experience and more accessible museum buildings. At the same time, as I traced earlier in this book, we saw an expanded sense of museum-going combine with a desire to expand art and culture beyond the elite spaces of the capital city. There was a welcome and very successful creation of contemporary art and culture spaces in the smaller UK cities and towns, often – as with Tate Liverpool or, later, Turner Contemporary in Margate, Hepworth Wakefield, Baltic in Gateshead, Towner in Eastbourne or Mostyn, Llandudno – as anchors and engines of economic as well as cultural and social regeneration.

These galleries are all brilliant examples of art spaces that show international artists, of the past as well as the present, showcase some of the very best of national and international collection works, and also have a strongly articulated local social purpose. For example, Turner Contemporary's learning programme now engages with environmental challenges associated with ocean pollution that feel particularly acute given that the gallery looks out onto the beach at Margate. At Mostyn, digital creativity and digital literacy have become key focuses for a gallery that has a very dispersed rural and coastal community around it, as well as many summer tourists, with all the attendant challenges this poses for those most local to them. These institutions have, without question, extended the reach of the visual arts in the UK, and they represent an expansion of the ecology and diversity of the visual arts in this country that is unequivocally positive. Across the rest of the world, this period also saw the increasing globalisation of the art world and much greater distribution of museum and art spaces beyond the Western Euro-American axis of the nineteenth and twentieth centuries – again, with many positive benefits.

We are now twenty years beyond this big expansion of the gallery and museum landscape – but unfortunately we are still at a point where our thinking needs to get past the idea that bigger is better.[6] This has, almost inadvertently, lodged rather too firmly in the psyche of institutions today: in the thinking of boards of trustees, the funders and donors that support museums, and also the leadership and staff body of museums. In researching this chapter I could not think of a single museum that had redeveloped or improved in order to get *smaller*.

The power and influence of a museum is not dictated by size. I appreciate that this may ring hollow when you consider the ways in which Tate has expanded over recent years. I should say too that I am not ruling out growth altogether: what I want to do, however, is challenge the assumption that the measure of a museum's success is when it doubles its size or opens a new outpost.

The growth maxim is understandable if the fundamental purpose of museums is to share their collections, exhibitions and research with ever more people. Following this logic, surely bigger buildings, more collections and more public programmes can only be for the good? Larger collections are *surely* better than smaller ones? Many satellite branches, all over the world, are surely better than one or two? Here, visitor numbers become the shorthand measure of success. Never mind how much visitors enjoyed themselves, or how much they learned; we are still nearly always using proxy measures – and always quantitative ones – to measure museum performance. All of this output-based thinking weighs heavy on the sector, acting as a disincentive for the kind of change that would move us toward a more sustainable mode of operating and a richer relationship with a more diverse public.

In the words of economist Edward Hess, growth itself can 'destroy value as it outstrips a company's managerial capacity, processes, quality, and financial controls, or substantially dilutes customer value propositions'.[7] Many museums are seeing exactly these effects, yet they do not always act and think forward with this in mind. Instead, a kind of circular conspiracy arises from quantitative metrics and reward systems, encouraging 'more' and pulling us away from, rather than toward, our mission.

In terms of conventional museum metrics, there is no bigger boost than the blockbuster show. The so-called blockbuster emerged as a form in the 1960s (with Tate's Picasso exhibition of 1960 an oft-cited early example) and grew more numerous in subsequent decades as the museum sector shifted away from displays of private collections towards public exhibitions drawn from collections dispersed across the world and reassembled in public museums. At Tate, we enjoyed a run of blockbuster shows in the years preceding the pandemic – *David Hockney, Van Gogh and Britain, Picasso 1932 – Love, Fame, Tragedy.* All received a tremendous amount of attention, all drew in huge crowds, and all brought a large and diverse audience through our doors. But is quantity our best measure for good?

The debate about the pros and cons of the blockbuster exhibition model has been a long-running one. In a conversation at Art Basel in 2017, museum directors Frances Morris (Tate Modern) and Beatrix Ruf (Stedelijk) usefully explored the limitations of the large-scale exhibition driving the art museum's activities, suggesting instead a need to move away from familiar names and instead deepen the learning and social potential of a museum space connected to its locality.[8] This more locally rooted model of the museum – a common practice in regional towns and cities – offers new possibilities for national museums within an energised civic sphere. As I have been tracing, museums need to, and do, evolve; we should not be alarmed, therefore, that there is again a will to rethink how we share our ideas with the public. It may be instructive to note that in the movie business, following the seismic shifts in film viewing habits brought about by streaming platforms and the consequent renegotiation of the relationship with the viewing public, the term 'blockbuster' has been quietly retired. Cultivating online loyalty to subscription packages where content is selected by the viewer is at least as important. Perhaps it is time for museums, too, to cease using this loaded term. Certainly, the metrics of the past – as the 'big ticket' shows have tended to be of very familiar, usually dead, white and male, artists – will not serve a more multi-dimensional, intergenerational audience seeking new ideas or surprises as well as the culturally familiar. By 2024 at Tate, the steady building of a large and curious group of Members (approximately 150,000 in total) and the creation of exhibitions with a strong cultural story, has seen exhibitions like *Women in Revolt!* perform as the big public draw for a progressive Tate Britain. At the same time, the mass reach of really big art names will mean such shows are never truly retired – not least because, when the exhibited artists are completely famous, these exhibitions do attract a large and diverse audience that reaches beyond the usual arts attenders.

And what of the question of time and its effect on the visitor experience? Habits evolved across the global museum network have seen the 'normal' museum run of a big exhibition become, on average, no more than four months. As we have seen, this convention was overturned during the pandemic, with some museums extending their exhibitions simply because the works temporarily couldn't travel, and others stretching their shows in order to cope with diminished resources. Rather than a pandemic moment, this deliberately slower mode, with exhibitions staying for six, nine or even twelve months, might be here to stay – and will occasion little complaint from our public. The decision by the team at Tate Modern to retain the Yayoi Kusama exhibition (drawn largely from our collection, so within our control) for more than two years generated only relief and delight from our visitors, as it had consistently sold out each time tickets were issued. We also made the decision to limit capacity, ensuring that each visitor could have the space and time to properly experience the visual and emotional impact of the work. This had the effect of making the exhibition a permanently 'limited' experience, which only enhanced its appeal.

To move to a slower mode across the wider museum does, however, need concerted collective conversations and joined-up action. It would also entail significant changes to conservation, loan agreements and touring arrangements. The good news is that all of these are entirely within our control and could be implemented with next to no diminishment of our public benefit. In fact, visitor research tells us that there are typically *too many* exhibitions coming and going, and that we need to spend more time promoting and showing our programme, with particular emphasis on lesser-known artists whose work benefits from a slow burn, word-of-mouth build up in audience.

If we think of the 'blockbuster' as a large-scale, high-input experience (in operational, financial and material terms), we really do need to ensure that it stays with the museum that has undertaken the intellectual and logistical labour – to say nothing of the financial heavy lifting – long enough to create genuine value return, both in terms of visitor enjoyment and income generation. This income can then give the museum the opportunity to do more. In this sense, I think we need to consider our displays, exhibitions, activities and public offer as operating with multiple cadences, or usefully different speeds and scale. Some exhibitions can be deliberately designed to promote deep engagement, or to showcase new thinking and research, for a smaller audience. Others can be easier to navigate, encouraging wider participation at greater speed. These different modes might thrive better in an overall ecology of a museum that knows when it is good to go large and long, when it is right to be nimble and fast, and when it is best to offer a chance to rest and reflect. A different attitude and approach to those large, income-generating shows might allow for a broader range of engagement and a richer experience for our visitors. But what *about* the money, I hear you say. Don't blockbuster exhibitions, running for a limited period at a number of institutions, fund the larger work of the museum sector as a whole? There is an underlying assumption that successful exhibitions produce surplus income to invest in museum projects of 'greater' social value, but in practice, this is not always what happens. The drive to participate in a global circuit of 'landmark' exhibitions is rather like the income-generating parallel to continued capital expansion. Both speak of status and competition between peer organisations in different places. So across Paris, London, New York or Madrid, we still see a drive to create the 'definitive' exhibition of a small number of major artists (again, often white and male), or, in other museum fields, of a period of high-status antiquity (for example, Egyptian or Roman material). Such exhibitions require the investment of a huge amount of resources and tend to only happen across a self-selecting 'premier league' of museums who can afford the loan and transport fees. Were this to become the primary mode of the major international museums, it would be unsustainable in all senses of this word, reinforcing inequalities across and within museum ecologies – but also within countries, between capital and regional cities. It would additionally do little to help museums trying to adopt more ecologically sound practices or shift into a net zero operational mode.

Alongside this, I also think the blockbuster impulse – based as it is on a generally accepted set of star artists, artworks or objects – tends to drive museums towards making exhibitions that could really happen anywhere. Much more interesting, to my mind, is the 'star' show that also draws on the museum's own (often idiosyncratic) collection strengths, local patterns of connection and perspective, or specific research knowledge that has been developed by the museum in collaboration with its communities. We don't want to end up with a 'nationalism' of museum practice, missing out on the significant challenge to thinking that comes from international exchange and the encounter with objects from elsewhere, but the blockbuster tour has become over-valorised as the predominant mode, especially for the art museum. When you ask the directors of major museums, as organisers of a museum summit hosted by Louvre Abu Dhabi did, to describe a museum of the future, they describe a necessary turn toward a deeper, more locally focused mode of operation. To cite Max Hollein, director of the Metropolitan Museum of Art:

> The focus on the visitor as the main source of income is a very dangerous one. It's much more important to be connected to local audiences, but you [should] also amplify the role you play locally and also internationally as a provider of service, as a provider of experiences and education.[9]

It is clear, though, that our habits haven't quite caught up with our thinking. And I include myself here.

So what might these alternatives to the blockbuster exhibitions and tours look like? This question asks us to look afresh at the things that make each museum unique: the objects in our care. Described so often as the 'permanent collection', as if they are a fixed and unchanging asset, for most modern museums the collection displays are far from permanent, but rather in dynamic and regular circulation.

These collection works all too rarely take a starring role in the wider public messages about the museum. A more sustained focus on the changing displays, or on single objects that help tell a fresh story about the museum or the collection, is still quite a rare thing, but it can be very powerful. At Tate Modern in 2021, colleagues brought together acquisitions of Australian art made over a ten-year period in partnership with the Museum of Contemporary Art, Sydney, supported by Qantas, in a collection exhibition called *A Year in Art: Australia 1992*. The exhibition set out an important new perspective, exploring how the acquisition of works by indigenous artists has changed thinking about the very nature of our whole collection. Though not a ticketed exhibition, the show was recognised as a distinctive entity by critics and press, which helped to bring the works to greater public attention. That the works are all jointly owned with the MCA offers financial and spatial savings, as well as the potential for public exposure in two different hemispheres. Greater use of the collection in ways like this also addresses that criticism of museums as hoarders of 'stuff seen by no one'.

The public enthusiasm for learning more about contemporary indigenous art from Australia has spawned other strategic developments from Tate, changing our programme and our approach. So in 2025, Tate Modern will stage a major show of Emily Kam Kngwarray in partnership with the National Gallery of Australia, curated in collaboration with Hetti Perkins and Kelli Cole, Warumungu and Luritja, and Arrente and Kalkadoon women respectively, and with the engagement and support of the Alhalker and Anangker Country women, descendants of Emily and the community she was a part of. This partnership challenges us to build new methods of exchange. It will give us, we hope, a different model of the international 'star' show, this one premised on the centring of an indigenous world view as the main story in Tate Modern's exhibition spaces, and giving the Global North audience a once-in-a-generation opportunity to experience the deep wisdom and power of Kngwarray's work. This feels like a different kind of 'do not miss' show. The mode of exchange, practically and intellectually, is slower and more sustainable in every sense, as we strive to minimise the carbon impact of this cultural partnership and maximise knowledge exchange and cultural learning.

We also need to think about how we make greater use of our collection, in our displays and in terms of public engagement with our stored collection. There is great public enthusiasm for this. Collections Care divisions are too often the Cinderella of the museum; valuing the collection needs investment in those who care for it and make it accessible.

If it's not already clear from what I've said, then I should spell it out: museums rely on each other. But as we start thinking about models beyond the blockbuster, we also need to think about ways of forging connections and generating dialogue that do not come at an enormous financial or ecological cost, nor at the expense of smaller institutions. Our international partnerships need to be conceived not as the creation of new outposts, but as a set of evolving relationships based on knowledge-sharing within the complex and evolving global arts ecology.

There is a useful distinction to be made here between the commercial art world and the global museum system. However committed to the artists they represent they may be, the commercial art galleries are fundamentally 'for profit', and so for them global expansion is their best strategy – albeit some are beginning to question this, especially in terms of the environmental impact of their business.[10] For the 'not for profit' museum whose collections are effectively placed beyond the market and held in trust for public enjoyment present and future, value is generated also through non-monetary means. Most international exhibition tours, consultancy and advice bring a vital financial return for the institution; this is an important and growing part of the business of many museums, including Tate. If this is done without altruism, however, it is counterproductive. I would like to imagine international exchange that feels more like conversational exchange, in which local knowledge and ways of doing things meet open accounts of experience, all geared toward sharing our collections and our research more freely. Again, the restrictions imposed by the pandemic allowed us to test new modes of knowledge-sharing: indeed, the Hyundai Tate Research Centre: Transnational and many of Tate's international committees thrived during lockdown periods as discussions and debates took place on Zoom, providing a level playing field of access for all, rather than privileging only those organisations and people who could afford to travel. We all miss seeing a person or a crowd, but we need to hold on to the best of this online exchange, so that future participation can be more inclusive.

Furthermore, the relationships built through exhibition exchange can extend to professional development, including training colleagues to install and work with specific collections, bringing greater equity to these relationships, and expanding the pool of knowledge and experience beyond an originating institution.

Space

We've spoken of the limitations of capital expansion projects, but what of the broader question of space and the museum? Is there a way to create or develop new and different facilities that can really deepen or change a museum's impact, and remove the need for the growth mindset?

The storage of collections, to take one key example, is often a secretive, selective and back-of-house business. Typically, museums store large collections in their own facilities, which are inaccessible to all but the most dedicated of specialist researchers. In recent decades this has been challenged by institutions like the Schaulager in Basel, which was founded in 2003 with the aim of combining the research, display and storage of contemporary art. As their website explains: 'In the typical museum situation, "schauen" and "lagern" – "seeing" and "storing" – are mutually exclusive activities, which are brought together in the name "Schaulager" ... Storing works openly guarantees their accessibility for viewers, scholars and restorers.'[11] The Schaulager's example didn't foster many followers, however, since in practice the open display of stored objects tends to turn the store into another museum, requiring staffing and explanation if visitors are to make sense of the works they see. Even at the well-resourced Schaulager, open visits are actually monthly bookable tours, while the institution also mounts temporary exhibitions in the usual museum style.

More recently, some of the UK national collections have started to think about collections storage as part of community or scholarly engagement in ways that offer a more holistic sense of access to the knowledge as well as the objects held within collections. The V&A East Storehouse, located in East London's Queen Elizabeth Olympic Park, will 'take visitors on a journey across time [to] explore why objects are collected, how they are cared for, conserved and displayed and will reveal the latest research emerging from the collections'.[12] Alongside this, the museum is developing V&A East, a museum site focused on celebrating global creativity and the practices of making and designing. Rather than expanding simply to make more exhibition and display space, these sister sites have been conceived to engage more meaningfully with the globally diverse communities of East London, which remains – even after the sizeable Olympic Park investment leading up to the 2012 Olympic and Paralympic Games – an economically challenged part of the capital. Moving its stored collections away from a central London location gives the V&A the opportunity to connect meaningfully to communities that typically do not engage with the work of museums, offering a qualitative step change for the whole organisation and its global collection.

The Natural History Museum and the Science Museum are also part of major storage reorganisation projects (the three organisations previously shared storage at Blythe House in Hammersmith), with the Science Museum Group collections moving to a new National Collections Centre on the former RAF Wroughton airfield near Swindon. As well as providing research and schools learning access to the stored collections, the complex will be a science and innovation space for projects such as testing solar- and wind-powered future technologies. The Natural History Museum has taken a similar approach, and will move its collections in coming years to a science and digitisation centre based at Thames Valley Science Park developed in partnership with the University of Reading. The centre will allow museum scientists, researchers and academic collaborators to use the collections for natural science research and innovation.

All three of these institutions are moving from treating collections as material needing to be securely stored towards seeing them as knowledge assets that can add to public engagement and, most especially, the learning potential of museums. As such they actively resist an accumulative growth trajectory, instead seeing their collections as a potential source of deepening relationships with others.

It is also the case that most museums need to invest in their current or new storage facilities, especially if we are to find less carbon-intensive ways of caring for our collections. This is typically seen as the least sexy long-term commitment museums can make in the present moment, but it is probably the most important one. To me, this is not an 'operational' or 'back-of-house' issue: the drive to make our collections more accessible, and held and cared for sustainably, really is the best way to set ourselves up for success in the future.

I will examine this particular challenge in more detail in the next chapter, as it is a vital shift museums must make if they are to operate in more environmentally sustainable ways.

Five Million Incidents

In thinking about growth, we have to ask what else visitors might want from a museum today. The answer is far from simple. In a conversation about a different direction for the post-pandemic art ecosystem, Monica Narula of Raqs Media Collective described a project they initiated in India called *Five Million Incidents*. Born out of a series of collective conversations, the project ran for a year at the Goethe-Instituts in New Delhi and Kolkata, and involved a range of cultural practitioners – artists, dancers, actors, photographers, writers – engaging their audience around the idea of the 'process of making'. Beyond the scale and ambition of the project itself, it is Narula's description of the 'incident' that I find most interesting:

> An incident is a fold in time – a quickened heart-beat, an epiphany, a flash of insight, an outbreak of goosebumps … an incident is anything that transforms the way we live or think, a conversation that carries a surge in its wake, an event that makes us rethink everything.[13]

This is a more poetic and profound description than any I could have summoned for what happens when a visitor really engages with what we put on our walls or share in our spaces. As Narula goes on to say, an incident is 'a mode of conscious engagement with time', a description which hints at a different way of conceiving of the work of the museum. This is a different kind of growth model – one that asks us to think about time, rather than space, as the vector of progress.

Although we are now very good at talking about the deeper health and cultural benefits of museum visiting, we have still not come up with good overall measures of the qualitative impact of museums beyond specialist studies or falling back into quantitative measures of these qualitative things. We argue for *more* schools engagement or *more* young people engaging with us, rather than focusing on the quality of the engagement or the transformation it might bring about.

Still less have we understood how we could see deepening qualitative impact as a necessary driver for the future shape of our museums, and a sustainable basis for a business model. Is there a way to measure a museum's social and cultural impact or the diversity of its public reach in social, cultural and economic terms, rather than merely looking at the number of people who cross the threshold? If we look to the evolving business environment around us, we are in an era in which companies have come to realise that their 'happiness index' is a significant factor in employee productivity, talent retention and business impact. Museums should be leading public debate and driving understanding of the wider social wellbeing that comes from active participation in culture – especially in museum cultures, whether that participation means schoolchildren learning, or an adult wandering our gallery spaces on a Sunday afternoon.

In the meantime, developments in the Global South are usefully different from what has happened in the past in the UK, across much of Europe and in the US, and may indicate the direction Western countries' museums should take in the future. The creation of institutions such as the Museum of West African Art (MOWAA), located in the heart of Benin City, or art venues such as Yinka Shonibare's Lagos complex Guest Artists Space (GAS) speaks of the need and wish for spaces to hold the art and the narratives of these nations in the twenty-first century.[14] These projects already suggest to us a different way of conceiving of the future museum, one that does not follow the modes of growth or the ideas about purpose that have traditionally structured the Western museum model. In the case of GAS, Shonibare's space gives time as well as space to the beneficiaries who visit, and leaves the desired (creative) outcome to be defined by those visitors, whether they are writers, artists, makers or scholars. Other generative elements of his space are focused on ensuring it is of sustainable benefit to the local community: a productive farm, local employment and resource from international visitors benefiting those who live there.

At MOWAA, renegotiation of the colonial legacies that have removed so much of the cultural materials of Benin and the Edo region is happening as part of the creation of the museum space likely to reshape that history itself. It is through the creation of a museum space that can actively shape decolonial practice that we will see new museum models emerge. As the recently published vision document for this future museum states:

At the core of MOWAA's vision is a commitment to inspiring the next generation of creatives in West Africa. By re-evaluating the concept of the museum in a twenty-first century African context, MOWAA seeks to ensure relevancy to contemporary artists, artisans and cultural professionals.[15]

They go on to talk of being a catalyst for deepening connections between contemporary arts and the rich cultural heritage of West Africa. Whilst we are yet to see how the museum will operate, its foundations speak of an expansive building of knowledge, rather than just focusing on the objects they may eventually hold. This is hopeful since it may address from the outset some of the problems that have accrued to the Western museum model.

In this light, we need to appreciate and attempt to cultivate the museum visit as part of a wider social experience: one that is more porous to, and more inclusive of, the world around it. This means offering people something new but also something familiar – if one thing can beat the excitement of new discovery, that is the nourishment gained from a long-held and regularly sustained relationship with particular spaces and particular works of art. Tate's *Australia 1992* exemplifies, I think, the value of new narratives for visitors and the scope for curatorial innovation; yet we also need to remember to leave some things be. The Horniman's overstuffed walrus is one example of this, as is Millais's *Ophelia* 1851–2 at Tate Britain. When that particular painting goes on loan, as it very occasionally does, we have to carefully brief our front-of-house teams and provide an explanation for visitors. Even then we get many grumpy complaints. We need to understand better the balance between reassurance – the visitor coming to find something they love and want to see – and revitalisation, in which the visitor is taken on a journey toward enjoying something new.

Human bodies also need places to pause and rest, take time to read, or to have a cup of tea in the café, a mid- or endpoint in itself, not just a convenient facility. Extending our offer to visitors builds loyalty (it also, pleasingly, increases spend per head). It is also the very antithesis of that early nineteenth-century museum experience I mentioned in my first chapter: of being 'hackneyed through the rooms with violence'. Sometimes, the very comprehensiveness of the larger exhibitions assembled for people's enjoyment leads to very tired eyes and feet. More is not always more. We should also share our exhibitions, narratives and stories by different means – the Spotify soundtrack, the LP and the product made by the artist all make the exhibition sing, both as it is seen and, later, in the memory.

None of these examples are that unusual. Done well, however, with the same ethics of care and artistic quality that we apply to the exhibition itself, they make a show live beyond its space and time on our walls. These points of connection deepen the relationship between the museum and its public alongside as well as around our exhibitions and displays.

Back to School

This cultivation of more time holds true for our educational teams as well as for our general visitors. The giant school group in their high-vis vests is a familiar sight in many museums, and there is enormous value in the group trip and the first encounter with art it offers to many children. However, most museum educators now emphasise the benefits of a visit for a smaller group, allowing children's ideas and responses to be placed centre stage and the different space of the museum and its objects to come into its own. As former Tate Director of Learning Anna Cutler has eloquently argued, it is only through a commitment of time and attention that we will learn from young people what the museum space can become.[16]

At the Horniman Museum, the post-pandemic recovery strategy has included halving the number of school sessions, but making each session twice as long. The museum is also prioritising schools whose pupils have the least opportunity for engagement with the arts. Without really meaning to, the learning teams had followed a familiar path of measuring the number of visiting pupils as their reporting criteria to their main funder. The 'hard stop' of the pandemic, when museum learning was suspended, has allowed them to refocus on the quality of the learning encounter. We must also make sure appropriate resources are directed toward the learning and community-building that museums can do. This work should not be at the margins of the museum space, nor should it be the smallest budget line.

We should also consider how our programme and collection might blossom across all of the platforms available to the museum. A long-overdue recognition of the power to engage visitors through digital means is one of the biggest lessons from the pandemic – and taught us, with some speed, what works and what does not. As in the physical space, we have learned that it is not about how many people come but how deeply they explore, or the extent to which they offer their own views in return. We are really only at the beginning of this journey, but the potential of social media as a site for conversation or the online space for learning is now being embraced much more effectively by many museums. For example, the National Gallery used its pandemic closure to cultivate a new adult learning programme, sharing its knowledge with a receptive community that was happy to pay for access. At Tate, the past few years have seen younger, digitally savvy colleagues deepen connections to particular communities as part of developing a more polyphonic voice for the museum. Our digital presence is not yet an integrated part of all we do, in the way it is for leading commercial digital content creators, but we know that this has to be our direction of travel.

What I think is important to note is that our digital projects, like those of many other museums around the world, draw fundamentally on the resources of the collection to inform content. This varies in pace and intensity, from immersive campaigns to the social media equivalent of light Sunday reading, creating in some respects the same cadences of engagement that are now so vital in the physical world.

Holding Collections

We cannot leave the question of growth without spending some time looking at the basic foundations of almost every museum in the world: their collections. As I said at the beginning of the chapter, here too the historic trend has been 'bigger and bigger', as institutions competed to acquire the 'best' works or, more recently, have wished to address historic omissions by expanding and diversifying their collections.

Rather than pursue an active acquisition strategy, we need to embrace the idea that it might be better for museums (and for our public) to collect fewer works, and to acquire more strategically. As more work enters the collection we also need to think differently about how we use what we hold. There has been much written about the 'distributed' museum model, and we have seen recent innovations in that regard at a national as well as an international level, with institutions like the National Gallery and the Uffizi Gallery touring key works to non-museum spaces. There is, however, much more that could be done here.

We also need to be alert to the ways in which acquisitions can reinforce inequality. As an institution of the Global North, Tate, like many other museums, has to be sensitive to the localities and cultures we wish to engage with, and imagine the future from their perspective, too. This requires some adjustment of our institutional habits and, once again, a slower approach, so that we can properly understand, reflect and respect the history, geography and politics that objects entering the collection will bring to the fore.

It also seems to me, as uncomfortable as this is for UK museums, that we need to return to the question of deaccessioning strategies as part of a degrowth plan for collections. All museums, especially long-established ones, will have a portion of their collection that is very rarely exhibited, explored, or even thought about. And if it is not, the question for the holding museum is: why not? Do these works belong? Can they be properly cared for, or is there a better home for them? Museums have to redistribute and dispose of some objects if they are to remain both sustainable and relevant in our current time. We ought to see this as good housekeeping practice on the part of every museum, and indeed an increasing number of museums are adopting deaccession strategies. Some foot-dragging still occurs, however: an incredibly thorough collections review conducted by Glasgow Museums toward devising a 'disposal methodology' was widely admired when published, yet barely used by anyone subsequently.

We also cannot ignore the question of equity. The essential rules that govern museums come to us from the colonial period, and we shouldn't be surprised that they are being stretched to breaking point right now. It is easy for me to say, of course, as I am not the director of a museum that finds itself in the eye of a restitution storm, but this is an issue that is not going to subside. Museums can return objects in ways that properly recognise and accommodate the practices of relevant cultures; indeed, many are doing so, despite the so-called contested terrain. Whatever current museum statutes say, this demand for equity, parity and return is here to stay – it is, after all, counter to our sense of the museum being a space of exchange, tolerance and learning to rule some objects too important to release and some places not safe enough to receive them. At the time of writing, a number of museums are engaged in discussions about the return of looted objects and almost every museum is involved in constructive discussions across nations about how to reckon with this colonial legacy.[17] I will just observe that the cultivation of these relationships, the sharing of knowledge and exchange – which is not limited to but may also include the return of some objects – is surely the most interesting form of future expansion of a set of relationships, even though it may mean letting go of some things. A distributed and connected knowl-edge-sharing network of global museums working toward access, education and enjoyment beyond national borders seems to me to protect museum collections for a more equitable, and more exciting, future. The 2024 Venice Biennale gave us a brilliant example of this. Nigeria had a pavilion for the first time, which showcased the new West African museum being developed that will explore the colonial history of looted objects, amongst other things. Artist Yinka Shonibare is not content to wait for a future when the British Museum returns Benin materials. His vast pyramid of clay replicas of Benin objects from the British Museum, *Monument to the Restitution of the Mind and Soul,* imagines that future museum display, framed through a Global South lens, now. Powerful, challenging and reparative.[18]

The Future Good?

By combining many of these ideas in their future planning and day-to-day activities, museums may find a viable solution to the growth model. What is still not clear, however, is how that solution can be measured. What are the future performance indicators for museums?

Picture a dashboard mapping the increase or decrease in happi-ness across the museum community.[19] This same dashboard might be mapping the geographies of knowledge shared across the globe, and the impact that knowledge is having on colleagues and audiences alike. This would lead naturally to a mapping of network connections, where a richer and more diverse and interconnected nodal map would be the desired 'good'. As our visitors leave our spaces, we might ask them not what their favourite artwork was, but what their favour-ite idea was, thereby generating an ever-changing digital map of the ideas exchanged which might live as the landing page of our website or our museum app. We could also chart the number of conversations or encounters within the museum space, with staff, but also with fellow visitors. Building on this, we might also ask visitors to share the strength and range of their feelings about an exhibition or a display, dislikes as much as likes. Many museums do this already, of course, but I know that most still feel that any discontent expressed represents a problem to be fixed, rather than seeing it as part of the useful measure of a passionate engagement. The only worrying response might then be indifference – a marker that the museum is not stimulating people at all!

If this all looks a bit soft, I would contend that it is much harder, in fact, to focus on increasing the sum of local or global happiness than it is to simply count the number of tickets sold. These qualitative measures should also be combined with some tough targets demonstrating greater equity – in terms of people, across the collection, and in terms of the programme – so that the strategic direction for the museum is calibrated toward deeper social benefit. We can and should, therefore, be looking at who comes to our museums in relation to the demographic profile of our location; we can and should be setting equity targets for our acquisitions; and we should be thinking about who gets to see our collections, globally as well as locally. All of this data would look rather different from the key performance indicators museums typically report to their governing bodies or funders, but they much more closely resemble the motivations of museum professionals driven by a wish to share knowledge, and they must surely, too, be closer to the wishes of a curious public who come to museums to enjoy themselves and discover something new, or anew.

The impact of the pandemic and the ongoing environmental crisis, as well as debates about social equity borne out of anti-racist movements, have only sharpened the need for different models for the museum of the future. Discussions around these issues have not yet given us, however, a clear enough sense of what this new thinking is, nor how the business model would actually work. That is not a cop-out: we in museums are in the middle of this work now. As I hope will be clear from what I've said so far, museums also inhabit multiple times, geographies and politics. Here I try to bear in mind Homi K. Bhabha's notion of simultaneous 'slow and fast times' as a way of understanding the uneven impact of globalisation and the necessity of thinking from more than one perspective in our postcolonial moment.[20] What we are likely to need in coming times is the flexibility to move both slow and fast – by which I mean maintaining some sense of continuity with the scholarly roots of museums and their long history, while also allowing that our spaces and our collections can and should be used, enjoyed and learned from in multiple different ways at once.

More significantly, we must be aware that the museum collection or exhibition configured for maximum visitor numbers can compromise those aspects of the museum encounter that are potentially most enriching: the chance to appreciate and take in new knowledge, to pause, reflect and agree or disagree with what you are seeing or being told. Such 'blockbusters' do not make space for the recuperative, the reparative, the spiritual, the revelatory, the aesthetic or the political– the very things most people working in museums or practising as artists want to introduce as part of their work, and the aspects of the museum experience most missed in the long period of closure during the pandemic.[21]

Let me say here that I am not yearning for a return to the days when serene and often solitary contemplation of the deep wonders in the museum was seen as the highest order of experience. However, I do think we need to plan for a future museum world that isn't simply striving to sell as many tickets as it can, as if we are a straightforward tourist attraction rather than a social learning experience. We should be thinking about how we can give people space to appreciate all that we do, as part of a deeper social engagement with the museum, its collections, its research and its ideas. Visitor numbers will continue to recover, but perhaps (whisper it) they don't need to hit those peak crowds again.

One precondition for a different future is that we need business models which really hold to the triple bottom line of sustainable development thinking. I shall say more about this in the next chapter; for now, I would underline that this means thinking about measuring the museum according to the strength of its social impact as well as the quantum of its visitor numbers, in ways that are environmentally as well as financially sustainable. I would advocate that we need to work within better limits, using our resources more carefully. We must think about our own practices in relation to the wider global social and economic situation, with a remit to not exacerbate the evident inequalities within our own countries and the world at large. Perhaps then, and only then, can we occupy a position as a trusted guide for audiences, and truly understand what success looks like.

I will leave you with one final analogy, which I think bears pondering in relation to a more viable model for the future. I love food, and have long been interested in 'slow food' – a now global movement, founded in northern Italy, that not only advocates a more relaxed, meditative appreciation of good food, but also places emphasis on the provenance, terroir and locale, heritage and organic practice of what we eat. Most critically, it also recognises the social value of food and the benefits of communal eating: the importance of conviviality and generosity of exchange between people as they share not only nourishment, but also traditions and long-rooted cultural histories. Time – to cook and eat and understand the approach and perspective embodied in the food – matters more than size of portion or financial value. This simple analogy offers, I believe, much food for thought for the museum, now and in the future.

6

The 100 Year Future: Museums and the Climate Crisis

'We have reached a defining moment in the history of our planet, and the cultural sector has a unique part to play in effecting change...'

So began Tate's climate emergency declaration, published in July 2019 to coincide with the opening of Olafur Eliasson's exhibition at Tate Modern. The document was the endpoint of a series of discussions, debates and initiatives that Tate had undertaken in the preceding years to understand and interrogate its collective carbon footprint, and it articulated an ambitious plan for Tate to lessen its ecological impact and inspire a shift in thinking about the connections between art and the environment within the sector, as well as among the museum's wider public. It was, however, just the beginning. In subsequent years, global awareness has grown such that in autumn 2023 Tate hosted a COP summit for UK museums, where members presented agreed resolutions that should move museum practice towards lower carbon operations for the long term.[1]

As institutions of the long term – and as institutions that are fundamentally concerned with the preservation and presentation of human creativity across time and from around the world – museums must act if we are to preserve conditions for the future. If we do not, the heritage we are responsible for will cease to have relevance or meaning, and may disappear altogether. At COP27 in Sharm El-Sheikh in November 2022, Professor Debra Roberts, co-chair of the Intergovernmental Panel on Climate Change (IPCC), summed up the situation facing humanity:

> Our report clearly indicates that places where people live and work may cease to exist, that ecosystems and species that we've all grown up with and that are central to our cultures and inform our languages may disappear. So this is really a key moment. This is the decade of action, if we are going to turn things around.[2]

The time for action, however, may already have run out. July 2023 was the hottest month on Earth since records began. António Guterres, Secretary-General of the United Nations, said:

> The era of global warming has ended; the era of global boiling has arrived ... Leaders must lead. No more hesitancy. No more excuses. No more waiting for others to move first. There is simply no more time for that.[3]

What is especially critical about the role of museums in this context is the platform they can provide – the loudspeaker or the clarion call. For decades, artists have been at the forefront of demands for action. Some offer compelling visions for what our world could resemble if action is taken; others show us the brutal reality of life without change. There are thousands of works I could include here by way of example, but I would like to point to a piece of public art called *Plunge*, created in 2012 by the artist Michael Pinsky.

The work encircled noteworthy buildings and monuments in London with an illuminated blue line, showing the predicted sea level in the year 3012. The public who encountered these lines on their journeys around the capital were invited to imagine just how much of London would lie below the water's surface. The lines were also intended to suggest a protective shell, indicating that we may still be able to change our situation. The overarching message of Pinsky's work, however, was that adaptation is essential if we want our low-lying capital city to remain habitable.

This isn't just a prediction of a time 1,000 years in the future. Within our collections at Tate are the tidemarks of a previous inundation in 1928 which affected paintings in store. Some of these marks were themselves turned into an artwork by Cornelia Parker, in her *Room For Margins*, which she used to draw attention to the climate and nature crisis. Tate was lucky. Colleagues at the Lismore Regional Gallery in New South Wales are still dealing with the aftermath of flood waters rising to the second-floor ceiling of the gallery when the Wilson River inundated low-lying areas in February 2022.[4] Collections were significantly damaged but, as director Ashleigh Ralph said, the gallery's losses pale in comparison with those of the community, many of whom have lost everything. This was the second 'once-in-a-century' flood in five years.

We know that artists often sound the alarm about the crises we are moving toward. But as museum sustainable development leader Henry McGhie has argued, we have known about this 'crisis' of nature and environment for almost a century, yet continue to live and act as if it will not happen.[5]

Until relatively recently there was a belief, both individual and collective, that we exist somehow separately from the natural world, or at least alongside it. This sense of separation has enabled humans to look at nature as a sort of unlimited repository of resources, leading us to pursue unbound productivity. But the cost of this mentality has, of course, been vast. Museums have absolutely been party to this notion of estrangement from nature, but the past decade has, thankfully, seen a major shift in awareness. We have long understood that we are at the mercy of nature, but we are finally coming to see that we *are* nature. We embody it – our edges are not distinct – and, as cultural institutions, we need to lead the way in demonstrating that saving nature is saving ourselves: our people, our collections, our buildings, our lives. As the director of an organisation with four museum buildings facing water, it would be irresponsible of me not to think that the disastrous submergence indicated by Pinsky's blue line is possible within my lifetime. Yet despite the very many people who champion this issue within the sector, museums are not shifting their practice fast enough to make a difference.

The Conceptual Shift

What has not yet occurred, in my view, is a fundamental shift in our thinking about how we operate our museums as organisations of and for the really long term. Ultimately the message we are still sending is that the conservation of our objects is more important than the conservation of the planet. When museums insist on maintaining the 'best' conditions for the preservation of the objects in their care, without thought to the energy consumption required to maintain this perfection, we fail to acknowledge something we know from both contemporary conservation science and from our often long history of holding objects in far from ideal conditions: that our objects are gradually decaying, whatever we do with them, and they do so all the faster if we put them on display for people to see. The benefit to people needs to be balanced against the protection of the objects in the short and the long term. The notion used to be that collections were preserved for a far-off and unchanging 'posterity', but it is unclear nowadays what that posterity will look like – and there is little point in keeping objects in perfect conditions if this contributes to the damage to the planet for its inhabitants. We know all this in theory, but this knowledge has not always been translated into planning and acting differently in the present.

Museums have now begun to share knowledge, support and advice as well as to explore how their programmes and spaces can be utilised to drive greater change. There is now excellent guidance available on decarbonising buildings and switching to lower carbon operating modes.[6]

Tate, along with a number of other major UK museums, is also part of the Bizot Group of international lending collections, whose green protocol has now been in place for a decade. The protocol, recently renewed and strengthened, draws on the collective conservation research of many international museums, including the Getty Conservation Institute, The Art Institute of Chicago, MoMA and Tate, and states that blanket environmental parameters should be replaced by a more flexible approach, and that, where appropriate, care of collections should be achieved in a way that does not assume air conditioning or other high energy cost solutions. This is sane and sage guidance. The issue is that many institutions do not follow it.[7]

Where we need to make a real change is in rethinking our approach to collection conditions, which in turn directly influences the conditions employed for storage, display, loans and touring. Despite warm words about relaxing parameters for collections, a recent survey of the Bizot Group showed that only 50% of member institutions were actually following the group's own recommendations. Consequently, we are still seeing an assumption that air conditioning or air handling will be used in galleries and stores. In addition, loan periods are still restricted to, typically, three months; this has a significant impact on the number of exhibitions that museums feel they have to mount each year, at a time when many are trying to do two six-month shows per year rather than four three-month shows, for financial, operational and environmental reasons. Our 'objects before people' thinking is actually undermining what museums are created to do, which is to share collections with the public.

Advocacy from some Bizot member museums (and anger and despair from some of the Global South members particularly) led to a renewed work programme across the group, with those institutions whose conservation research demonstrates alternative approaches to keeping collections stable working to collate and share best practice.[8] It remains to be seen whether those holding tight to keeping 'their' objects in the 'best conditions' – itself a deeply questionable presumption – will accept the evidence and shift their parameters and practice.

The potential to both evolve our business models and amplify our common mission to deepen people's engagement with our collections and exhibitions also depends on changes to these core 'conservation conditions'. Thinking in terms of sustainable development goals – where people, planet and prosperity are seen as the triple bottom line for understanding museum impact and strategy – requires real change in how we work and how we see ourselves. Current stipulations (or habits) around couriering and transport also make it harder to achieve sustainability targets. Although many objects moved around the world under 'virtual' supervision during the pandemic lockdowns, there is still a surprising degree of resistance from many institutions to keeping this very sensible mode of working as the 'default' norm for museum object exchange.

So how should museums proceed through this crucially important decade toward 2030? Most larger museums now have sustainability strategies, drafted in the past five years, that set out their goals. Tate now has a climate emergency working group to build on the good work already in place across our estates, conservation and collections care teams, which has accelerated progress since we declared a climate and ecological emergency in July 2019: having committed then to reducing our carbon emissions by 50% by 2023, we achieved this ahead of target, and continue to make tangible progress towards net zero emissions by 2030. The sense, amid the urgency around this target, that we are learning as we go along is reflected in the fact that there is now an emerging consensus that aiming for 'net zero' is actually unhelpful. Net zero means offsetting, which is not always a sound or reliable practice, and in fact gets in the way of thinking about the really radical behavioural changes that are required to get to absolute zero. Better, many feel, to aim for absolute zero and fail, than to set a lesser net zero goal that may bring about future problems of its own.

Awareness-raising and engaging the public as positive advocates for change has been particularly successful. In my own organisation, Frances Morris of Tate Modern has really focused minds on how our programme and our collection can amplify issues, through such projects as Ackroyd & Harvey and Ben Okri's *On The Shore* 2021.

Yet even an organisation like ours, where there is passion and a commitment of senior leadership time and resources, is not moving quickly enough. It is as if there is a kind of treacle in the machine, slowing down change for fear of what the future *might* hold. Current temperature rises are, in the view of many scientists, already too high and indeed potentially irreversible – so the present we are in is already pretty catastrophic. We cannot afford to be faltering out of fear of what might happen to objects in a future where our institutions as well as our ways of living might be profoundly altered. What is certain is that if we do not accelerate on these issues, the future looks very uncertain indeed.

Below, I sketch out a brief checklist of how I believe this acceleration may be achieved, addressing practical concerns but also pointing to notions of equity and integrity that should not be neglected. It amounts to a ten-point plan for the museum sector future, one that has evolved out of ongoing conversations within and outside my organisation, and builds on the work of colleagues all over the world, especially as we draw on the knowledge and resources of those museums already living and operating in the face of significant climate challenge. While acting as a good advocate for the planet is vital for organisations that wish to still exist in future centuries, this plan goes beyond raising the alarm about current practices and future consequences, focusing rather on practical costed actions that can be carried out now, to help us steer the most positive course we can and, by doing so, act as good custodians of our collective history and our future.

1. Decarbonise

The decarbonisation of our buildings, our operations and our working practices is a non-negotiable matter. Museums have a particular obligation to decarbonise because we have to plan to exist as institutions and collections in a hundred years' time. We therefore offer a very long-value payback for making this investment, as well as urgently needing it in order to survive for another century.

Carbon literacy should be a mandatory part of museum training to ensure all staff are aware of the issues and of their own role in mitigating them. In the UK, the National Museum Directors' Council is lobbying for the next phase of government maintenance support to be directly tied to decarbonisation. Some museum directors are anxious about this, because old buildings are difficult to modify and they have many other pressing needs. Green 'invest to save' models must be central to the future development of the museum landscape; this would mean making the case that government infrastructure funds should be tied to stringent carbon reduction targets. This is not an easy task to undertake – but its being hard to do should be an even bigger motivation. The international museum community should also be collectively advocating for a green museums investment revolution to protect our long-term future, which would help these institutions (and buildings) of the past to adopt technologies for future sustainability. This is not simply a matter of financial investment: it will also require changes in planning and listing of buildings, and an understanding that museum infrastructure needs help in adapting to a different planetary future.

2. Listen to the Artists

Artists are the people who are imagining, and in many cases realising, our future. They are philosophers, forerunners, agitators, prophets. They inspire us, move us, and educate us – cultivating empathy and understanding, and driving behavioural change. Art can act as an early warning system, as we saw with Michael Pinsky's work. As critic Jerry Saltz puts it: 'Artists often channel the future, seeing patterns before they form and putting them in their work, so that later, in hindsight, the work explodes like a time bomb.'[9]

We see this very clearly if we look back over the past fifty years of art practice. The tradition of artistic statements about climate and nature, made for and with a wide public, goes back many decades. Over five decades ago, artistic movements (such as land art, developed by Robert Smithson) as well as individual practitioners such as Gustav

Metzger and Joan Jonas were questioning our collective impact on the land and the destructive impact of overproduction and overconsumption, and looking to older orders of knowledge drawn from indigenous land stewardship practices to understand how and why we should change. In 1982, with the help of the Public Art Fund, Hungarian-born artist Agnes Denes created the landmark *Wheatfield – A Confrontation*, planting two acres of wheat in downtown Manhattan. Over the course of a few weeks, the barren Battery Park landfill site was filled with over 200 truckloads of soil, into which volunteers dug 285 furrows, by hand. Then seeds were planted, an irrigation system was created, and the emerging shoots were nurtured and protected. For months, Denes and her team of assistants rolled up their sleeves and became agriculturists. Just two blocks from Wall Street, on land that was valued at $4.5 billion, the fruits of Denes's labour slowly grew, and by that August 1,000 pounds of healthy golden wheat sat serenely, surrounded by concrete. The work spoke of mismanagement, waste and world hunger, with Denes telling the *New York Times* that the idea was 'an intrusion of the country into the metropolis, the world's richest real estate' – as much a critique of an economy that was damaging the planet as a protest for environmental awareness.[10] The harvested grain eventually formed part of an exhibition entitled *The International Art Show for the End of World Hunger* and travelled to twenty-eight cities worldwide. The seeds were taken home by visitors and planted. Decades later in the UK, Extinction Rebellion infiltrates our cities with a very similar practice and message.

The notion of using the natural or built environment to impart an urgent message has, of course, continued across the decades. In 2014 Olafur Eliasson created *Ice Watch*, for which he shipped blocks of ice to a Copenhagen public square, then a year later to Paris, declaring that he wanted people to have a 'direct and tangible experience of the realities of melting Arctic ice'.[11] Like Agnes Denes, Eliasson was juxtaposing a fragment of raw nature with the artificial organisation of urban life, striving for symbols potent enough to break through into public consciousness. Eliasson repeated this project outside Tate Modern in 2018 as a prelude to his exhibition *In Real Life*, which was itself, as part of its public education mission, conceived to be a model of how to make a show in a way that had the lowest possible environmental impact .

In Real Life included a display of Eliasson's photographs of glaciers which articulated the profound loss of glacier ice over a twenty-year period. The show also featured its own carbon calculator, shared with the public as a way of highlighting its own mode of creation and consumption. This included investment in creating circular-economy products for the shop, and a locally grown or sourced lunch menu in the café. Eliasson's exhibition powerfully demonstrates how museums, working collaboratively with artists, can provide space to address a range of related issues. It also provided an example of an artist walking the walk as well as talking the talk.

It is easy to feel disheartened when looking back at how long artists have been raising these issues, to little perceptible change in the sector. But if at Tate we embrace the idea of our galleries as megaphones and the museum as a potential cultural convenor, we can hold on to our purpose as institutions of idea and memory, in ways that can help pave the way for changes needed by all. The writer and artist Ben Okri gives us useful words in this respect:

We have to find a new art and a new psychology to penetrate the apathy and the denial that are preventing us making the changes that are inevitable if our world is to survive. We need a new art to waken people both to the enormity of what is looming and the fact that we can still do something about it ...

This is the best and most natural home we are ever going to have. And we need to become a new people to deserve it. We are going to have to be new artists to redream it.[12]

Some artists are not so much making a campaigning point but rather modelling for us how adaptation can and should be a part of our tools for a different future. Vivian Suter's work is a good example. The Guatemala-based artist responded to her own experience of climatic disaster by allowing her local environment to, in a sense, 'co-create' her work. In 2005, a severe tropical storm flooded Suter's studio, leaving her paintings swimming in mud. She was, at first, devastated at the scale of the damage. But, she says:

[A]s the paintings started to dry, I saw that the natural residue had left a sharp line across the canvases, and that the paintings underneath were still visible above this line. So I saw a new potential to incorporate this, and it unified the whole work. Since then, I have also started thinking and feeling differently about painting and the conception of my work. The experience has allowed me to see my paintings as living materials that are testament to the destruction, decay and regeneration of nature.[13]

The interchange between art, artists, and scientific work and thinking is also illuminating. In 2009, curator Alice Sharp founded the charity Invisible Dust, with the aim of raising awareness of environmental issues by bringing artists and scientists together to create impactful works of art. She initially met some resistance among scientists sceptical about what the art world could do for them. Thankfully, many quickly grasped the potential of art to highlight the impact of climate change and agreed to participate. Air pollution was an early focus of the charity's mission: in 2012, artist Dryden Goodwin turned more than 1,000 drawings of his five-year-old son inhaling and exhaling into an animation that was projected on the roof of St Thomas' Hospital, opposite the Houses of Parliament. The piece confronted commuters and tourists with a moving image showing the 'universal act of drawing breath' which became, as the artist hoped, 'intertwined with the rhythms of the city'. The work was designed to draw attention to the research of King's College professor Frank Kelly, an expert on lung health and an advisor to the government on air pollutants. Kelly's research, the EXHALE programme, looks at the effect that measures such as the Congestion Charge and the Low Emission Zone have had on the lung health of children in East London. This marriage of art and science – a strong example of making the invisible visible – packed an incredible punch. As the debate around the Ultra Low Emission Zone in London has shown, it is clear that advocacy of this kind is urgently needed if we are to motivate individuals to act against their own perceived interest for a larger common good.

3. Change the Conditions

Museums sometimes think that they can stop the depredations of time, which is never the case, no matter how conscientiously we care for our objects. As one very wise conservator said to me when I moved to be director of the Whitworth in Manchester in 2006, we can only ever slightly slow the inevitable rate of decay of any object, be it painting, sculpture, textile or moving image. The perfect conditions for any object would mean keeping them in their stable storage, and never showing them. Keeping museum collections is already an always ongoing compromise between providing access to today's public and preservation for tomorrow's. However, I think our risk levels are currently awry. By using energy, technology and science to achieve near-perfect conservation conditions, we have become exceptionally carbon consumptive. What I say next may be seen as sacrilege in some institutions, but I would be interested to know what pragmatic choices we might make that would still protect the collections in our care but not so 'perfectly', prioritising instead the planetary impact and the benefit to people from learning about and enjoying the art – remembering that this is our mission.

Truthfully, this is the area where I feel most strongly about the need for change within the museum profession. Indeed, I am angry that there has not, to date, been widespread positive leadership and advocacy from directors of institutions such as mine. Museum directors today would do well to remember the conditions of the past. I recently revisited the Whitworth, which has a particularly fine (and fragile) collection of works on paper, including many works by Turner, mostly gifted more than 125 years ago. The wonderful archive of committee papers there tells us that in the 1930s many of these works used to travel to exhibitions at the National Gallery and Tate wrapped in anonymous brown paper, taken by hansom cab to the station and then popped on the train, to be collected at the other end by another cab. In Manchester, as at those London galleries, they were also displayed in unconditioned spaces – spaces which were still being used until the Whitworth's 2015 renovation, deliberately kept in use by architects and engineers committed to lowering the carbon footprint of the gallery. This was supplemented by essential Victorian passive heating and cooling in the main exhibition galleries, reusing the roof ventilation systems that had been there since the museum's foundation.

I'm not proposing a return to sending paintings across the country wrapped in brown paper – but the fact remains that these fragile works have been passed down to us largely unscathed. And there was science behind the practices then, too: keeping conditions consistent, not allowing too much light exposure, and, as an extreme example, moving collections to the extremely stable, very secure Cheshire salt mines during the Second World War. To a large extent, conservation is about 'pragmatic risk management', as research by the Getty Conservation Institute has shown.[14] And most conservators will tell you that the greatest danger to an object today is from the abrupt failure of conditioned environments – something that will become an ever more common occurrence in a world of isolated institutions, energy scarcity and more extreme weather events.

Nonetheless, I believe we need to relax. We need to relax the parameters for the conservation of objects, focusing instead on slowing the rate of change. More than that, we need to relax our mindset about our collections. I am heartened by the actions of conservation colleagues across the aforementioned Bizot Group who are supporting each other in researching and promoting a new, sustainable and evidence-based long-term care approach for the other 50% of Bizot leaders and the museum community worldwide to follow. Working together is the best way to really care for our collections in the long term.

Finally, to loop back to the related question of equity and access I explored above, the 'perfect conditions' we set for our objects effectively act to exclude many countries and cultures from the Global South from equity and exchange across the global museum ecology. Perhaps the worst argument I have ever had as a museum professional was with a museum director, then much more senior than me, who maintained that a Ghanaian kente cloth could not be lent to Ghana because they could not recreate the perfectly stable conditions he believed were needed. The 'need' was his, and not a step required to keep the cloth from damage. I hope that the debate has since shifted, but I fear that old habits and presumptions still linger, and we need to challenge ourselves to be bolder and braver if we are to reduce our considerable environmental impact in this area.

4. Move Art Differently

Perhaps the most challenging issue facing the art world is transport: how to move work around the globe in a sustainable fashion. The industry as a whole is carbon intensive, with work (and its couriers) shipped from country to country and audiences following in pursuit. At Tate, we knew we had to reconsider this approach. It turned out here that Covid, as it did in myriad other ways, provided an opportunity for such change. Faced with international travel restrictions, we had to trial a virtual-only courier approach, to ensure that we could deliver on international contractual engagements, sometimes in parts of the world that were not locked down, as well as continuing to share our collections and deliver our exhibition programme across the four Tate galleries.

This was entirely new territory for us. We were used to having a courier, often a conservator, accompanying our artworks from the moment they left our stores to the moment they were hung, many thousands of miles away. And it was, I admit, a little nerve-wracking to begin with. But in fact, this temporary arrangement allowed us to gain significant experience in lending and borrowing securely, without the presence of a physical courier. Tate Modern's 2020 Warhol exhibition, full of high-value loan objects, was successfully de-installed and transported to Museum Ludwig, Cologne, solely using digital communication and trackers attached to object crates: this, to my surprise, proved to be a more secure arrangement than we had been used to. Similarly, *Constable: A History of His Affections in England* was installed at Mitsubishi Ichigokan in 2021, with Tate colleagues joining their counterparts in Tokyo by Zoom to oversee the handling and installation of sixty works from Tate's collection. This way of working, not simply with digital couriering but also digital supervision through the whole installation of an exhibition, has been sustained across two very complex exhibitions developed by Tate for the Museum of Art Pudong, Shanghai. Across a nearly three-year lockdown period with limited travel available, two significant exhibitions of Tate works were opened to a Shanghai public that numbered more than 500,000 people.

In January 2021, having gained confidence from working in this way, Tate confirmed that it would move to a virtual-first courier policy. The policy has already brought about a significant reduction in courier travel and the associated carbon emissions. We have also since signed a memorandum of understanding with the Museum of Modern Art in New York to reciprocally agree that a virtual-first approach to couriers will be adopted for loans between our two institutions. We are hoping that similar arrangements will soon be in place with other partner institutions.

5. Curate Sustainably

There are numerous considerations for curators and registrars when planning more sustainable exhibitions: from thinking locally and ensuring that works from distant lenders are entirely justified, to curating exhibitions from just one lender rather than a multitude, to exploring options of transportation by land and sea rather than air and accepting the ensuing delay. These approaches need to be embedded as part of exhibition planning from the outset. At Tate there has been some pioneering work in this regard, and the presumption that we should strive to minimise carbon consumption has led to new ways of making and sharing exhibitions. The Zanele Muholi exhibition, which opened when many pandemic travel restrictions were still in place, saw the photographic works being printed and framed in the UK, then travelling in compact transport to the European venues. We were pushed to test this strategy by the fact that the artworks held in South Africa (and the artist themself) could not travel. It led to no diminution of the experience for the visitor, and was, in spite of lockdown restrictions, financially as well as environmentally sustainable.

Materials associated with exhibitions are also up for challenge and change, from moving to fixed exhibition layouts so that we do less 'build', to recycling materials: the scaffold boards that helped to create the raised 'studio-like' plinth in our recent Rodin exhibition, for instance, came from and then went back to the building trade.

Perhaps the most beautiful example is Kara Walker's Turbine Hall commission, *Fons Americanus* 2019. The monumental sculpture – a critical take on imperial public statuary – was fabricated with assistance from Millimetre, an innovative eco design and fabrication company based in Brighton. It was made from sustainable cork, then coated in Jesmonite to make it waterproof. The sculpture was designed to be zero-waste, as all the material was recycled into the manufacturing process. It not only gave us a zero-waste sculpture, but one that was in practical terms much easier to transport and install, and meant we did not need to reinforce the floor!

6. Collaborate

Collaborations between museums to allow more sustainable working modes must become normal practice, from the start to the end of the process. Tate Modern's *Surrealism Beyond Borders* (2022) was conceived in collaboration with the Metropolitan Museum, New York where it opened in October 2021, even though the project was initiated by research from a Tate curator. Teams across both museums worked closely to review the selection. The central goal was to ensure that we could present a transnational exhibition demonstrating the global breadth of surrealism, while reducing the climate impact of delivering a show of this ambition. The initial 'wish-list' included 390 loans from approximately 90 locations but, through collaborative discourse, this was reduced to 222 loans from 22 locations, with an emphasis on artworks from the collections at the Metropolitan and Tate. Active collaborative thinking across institutions can allow us to still make extraordinary international exhibitions, but with a much smaller carbon footprint. The 2024 exhibition exchange with the Lenbachhaus in Munich, where Tate swapped Turner works for a stellar selection of works by the Blue Rider group, mostly never shown in the UK before, was based on similar carbon reduction principles: all to the great benefit of the public in London and in Munich.[15]

7. Do Not Enable

Museums' involvement with fossil fuel companies and other environmentally damaging organisations speaks volumes to members of the public. If civic bodies appear ambivalent towards the exploitation of the world's natural resources, accept sponsorship from companies whose fortunes are made through oil and gas, or are not seen to be reducing their own carbon consumption, we can expect and deserve criticism from our public. This seems to me to be entirely reasonable.

For many institutions with ties to such companies, the level of protest and complaint around green- or art-washing has now become debilitating, and overshadows the work they are doing. As with the example of Liberate Tate, discussed in Chapter 3, the issue is not so much the protests themselves, but that organisations find themselves challenged in terms of their own values and ethics as institutions presumed to be committed to equity, sustainability and the preservation of the planetary future. Internal pressures, protests, press and wider public opinion thus come together.

In 2023, after many years of seeing protests inside and outside its building, the British Museum quietly indicated that it would no longer accept BP sponsorship monies. Victory was claimed immediately by Just Stop Oil and Culture Unstained, who had long been involved in coordinating protests against the sponsorship. There was surprise and anger, then, when in 2024 BP sponsorship was once again announced at the British Museum, this time for ten years, at a level that the institution appears to believe it could not decline. I feel dismay that the British Museum would make such a choice at a time when so many UK institutions have committed to not supporting companies whose green energy work can be said to be too little and too slow, in the hope that they will be motivated to move faster. I do not think the general public we welcome every day wish to see such ethical dissonance in museums they care about, and will likely continue to be active in letting the museum know so. That this will be one of the challenges in the newly appointed Director Nicholas Cullinan's inbox is certain.

8. Involve the Public

In July 2019, the Horniman Museum replaced the usual inhabitants of its aquarium display with the plastic pollution that blights those creatures' natural habitat, in a conscious effort to mobilise families and children as citizen advocates. The powerful letter from a five-year-old sent to his local MP asking him to take action to save the seas from plastic, and later shared with the museum and press, was only one of many resultant examples of museum visitors acting on behalf of the planet.[16]

The following year, local arts collective Plymouth Energy Community joined Art and Energy in inviting people from around the world to participate in *Moths to a Flame*, a huge collective project to address the impact of the climate crisis. They asked the general public to create moths out of recycled materials, and to send them in, along with recorded messages of hope and encouragement. The moths, which eventually numbered 20,000, sent from participants from Devon to Australia, formed an installation, along with the soundscape of whispered messages, at the Glasgow Botanic Gardens during COP26 in 2021. Art and Energy's Chloe Uden said:

> In a state of emergency, our thinking can become narrowed and limited. This is an opportunity for us to show that culture can not only be part of the *response* to the climate emergency, but also part of the potential *solution*. Creative thinking can help us to imagine things that haven't happened before, to create a new future.[17]

Clare Matterson, then Director of Learning and Public Engagement at the Natural History Museum (now Director General of the Royal Horticultural Society), worked with young people to develop a consultation and then a campaign for COP26 in Glasgow. The message from this younger generation was clear: 'Don't mince your words! Tell it like it is.'[18] Young visitors wanted museums to be honest, and to make use of their role as trusted experts to advocate on their behalf for our collective future. This 'activism' is not at odds with the museum's responsibility to share knowledge equitably and dispassionately. Rather, it goes to our core purpose – to expand and share learning for the public good.

9. Be Tough, but Real

It is important to note that none of this is straightforward. While all the points in this manifesto would ideally be adopted as museum practice, it would take a gargantuan effort to immediately implement even half of my suggestions across the sector. National museums are simultaneously local and global organisations and, as a result, there has to be a certain amount of travel and movement for us to fulfil our remit. The alternative to this would move us towards introspection, parochialism, and lack of connection to those global partnerships and collaborations that can also build strength to make significant change.

Museums' sustainability strategies must be just that – sustainable – as well as realistic. This requires determined, granular work to measure and understand environmental impact and then to act accordingly. Museums are now developing costed and detailed net zero plans which will require investment as well as culture change to implement. But we must have such plans. Indeed, I anticipate that they will in future need to be part of our public reporting, so that our wider public can hold us to account. Where activities that are carbon intensive continue, these will need to be balanced with recuperative actions (and I do not mean simple carbon offsetting here), so that the public as well as the organisation can see and judge long-term impact against short-term gains.

The Tyndall Centre for Climate Change Research at the University of Manchester recently undertook a long-term action research programme in collaboration with the band Massive Attack, who wanted to address the climate cost of a music tour but still be able to play in many cities.[19] The equally detailed work many museums are now doing to ensure costed 'absolute zero' plans for buildings and operations is tough, lengthy and unglamorous, but necessary if we are to change for the long term.

10. Encourage Optimism and Care

As I have mentioned several times in this book, Tate's statutory mission is to promote the public's understanding and enjoyment of art. This phrasing might seem quite mild, perhaps even ineffectual in relation to the urgency of taking action to address the climate and nature emergency. However, I would argue that our desire to take a strong public stand on addressing this crisis gets to the heart of what museums should do. We must share useful knowledge and thinking, helping people learn and understand the positive actions they themselves can adopt – whether through the insight of an artist or by offering well argued and publicly accessible scientific knowledge – because it is in our mission to do so. We can also be institutions that inspire and move people, through the beauty and the power of artists' engagement with our planetary emergency, thereby encouraging people to hold on to the optimism that they can effect change: this is the enjoyment bit of our mission.

In 2019 we held an extremely memorable public debate at Tate Modern with speakers including Olafur Eliasson, former Irish president Mary Robinson (now a member of the Elders, the group of global independent leaders working to address matters of peace, justice and human rights) and one of the leaders of Extinction Rebellion (XR), Clare Farrell.[20] The debate got feisty when Robinson suggested that XR's mode of activism tended towards alarm and doom. This, she argued, was not going to help build the energy for the long journey of adaptation and culture change we all need to pursue as citizens of a planet we want to protect.[21] I sit between their two poles. Sometimes, as with Michael Pinsky's work, we need to look squarely at the catastrophe. But our museums and visitors need also to keep our collective courage going and enjoy the creative challenge of change, so that we shape a long-term future where all our objects can still do their work.

7

Where Now?
The Museum of the Future

The Art Ark

So here we are, gazing into the future, with perhaps some idea of the challenges and possibilities now facing the museum. But what does that future look like? I've focused on matters to do with our public, our reputational and ethical challenges, our relationship to our history and our business model as we adjust to the post-pandemic landscape, as well as questions of equity and diversity, the call we make on the planet's resources and the imperative to reduce our impact and thereby influence thinking about humanity's capacity to change. It has been fascinating for me, as a lover of museums – and after seven years as director of Tate – to take stock and consider what museums should do next.

It is easier, of course, to say what I *don't* wish to see. I want to thank environmental economist Laurie Laybourne for pointing me to a film that helped me understand the catastrophe I would like to prevent. Alfonso Cuarón's dystopian drama *Children of Men* (2006) is set in a London of 2027 when environmental disaster has destroyed much of the world, reducing human fertility as well as threatening human life as we know it. As in Margaret Atwood's novels of environmental catastrophe and fertility collapse, the *Oryx and Crake* trilogy, the rich in *Children of Men* are able to adapt to these hostile conditions more effectively by pulling limited resources unto themselves. One short scene shows a building close to my heart turned into a museum unrecognisable to me. Tate Modern has become an 'art Ark' in which the treasures of the globe have been collected and gathered to protect them for a posterity in which only those wealthy enough to survive the ongoing apocalypse will be able to visit them. It won't surprise you to know that this 'protected' elite space is the antithesis of all I have been arguing for.

There is another vision of the future that I am less sure of. The Museum of the Future, recently opened in Abu Dhabi, is, according to its website, 'the most beautiful building on earth'. Although the museum does hold a collection, its predominant interest is the immersive digital experience, and it stages ambitious, innovative and, according to recent reports, hugely popular digital exhibitions.[1] Digital technology is certainly a powerful tool for unlocking the stories and ideas that we are trying to promote through our exhibitions and our objects. It's true, too, that digital must become our immanent mode, rather than an add-on to our work, if we are to reach the widest possible audience. I think we delude ourselves, however, if we see it as the future in and of itself. Without the haptic experience that for me embodies the museum encounter, it is not my future museum at all. It takes my mind to another dystopian sci-fi movie, *Total Recall* (1990), where the lived experience takes place almost entirely within a headset.

I also worry about museums that are created just to showcase a personal collection, or corporate wealth. We see this happening increasingly in both the Global North and South, evident in the super league of institutions that can effectively afford to do whatever they wish, whatever the effect on the planet or equity of access. Though many of these private institutions are open to the public, they are almost never free and frequently have very high ticket prices. Nor do they usually challenge or offer any significant alternatives to the canon of received greatness passed down through art history.[2] I am also concerned about the increase in private influence that underpins the economics of museum practice in the USA. Many great institutions now rely on private money to a degree that can damage their public reputation. As the initial shockwaves of the pandemic rippled through the sector, it was somewhat disheartening to see financially well-endowed institutions in New York and elsewhere decide to make their museum educators redundant as an initial cost-saving step. I am not in any way saying that UK museum ecology is the best – rather that, in my view, the public good aspects of museum life, including the public purse helping to resource the museum, are vital if museums are to offer the maximum benefit to civic life.

Moving Forward

Enough of the grumbling. The first thing I love about museums is that we can and do change. This has been perhaps *the* defining characteristic of museums, and the reason for their persistence. In 2021 I was privileged to be part of the judging panel for the Art Fund Museum of the Year prize – in itself a wonderful and vitally important award that helps illustrate some of the arguments I have been outlining throughout the book. In previous decades, the prize tended to reward the best and most beautiful museum expansion. Over the past five years it has moved to reflect and celebrate the public benefits of museum practice, showcasing brilliant work by colleagues in museums small and large, and drawn from the four nations of the UK, across learning practice, social engagement and community engagement, as well as in the scholarly, historical and artistic innovations of museums.

As part of the 2021 judging experience I travelled to the far northeast of Scotland to visit Timespan, a museum that had recently and quite rapidly changed its relationship with both its local community and an international network of like-minded institutions. An utterly convincing contender in a close-run contest, Timespan has a glorious location in the tiny coastal village of Helmsdale. It attracts a certain kind of intrepid tourist, but also holds a global history that connects to its population today and belies its modest location. In recent years, Timespan has moved away from being a heritage museum straightforwardly depicting life during and after the Highland Clearances – the eviction of tenant farmers from the Highlands in the eighteenth and nineteenth centuries that created Helmsdale. Instead, it has put down deep local roots through its exploration of the global history of the Clearances and the way in which those events are connected with the exploitation of the Caribbean, particularly Guyana (then called British Guiana), through the plantation labour of an enslaved and then indentured workforce. Objects in the museum tell the history of the herring girls, who did perilously hard but lucrative work gutting and salting fish. The fish didn't feed the Scottish labouring classes, but were instead shipped to Guyana to be the concentrated protein for a labour force that was, in turn, cultivating cash crops such as sugar and cocoa for export rather than for local consumption. This embroiled history of working-class displacement connecting to colonial exploitation of enslaved people and land rights disputes around the world has been owned by the local community, and forms a counter-story to the heroic emigrant narrative so often associated with the working-class peoples of Scotland. Local people, working with academics and artists, have become storytellers of a different past and, subsequently, a reimagined future.

At Timespan, artists' practice, museum objects and educational programmes combine to generate a community-building spirit and an open hospitality, as well as a confident weirdness in the artists it brings into its ambit. The wonderful café offers food that reflects the colonial histories the museum explores, making it a shared part of revisiting relationships and histories through culinary exploration and the pop-up presence of different chefs. It is a relaxed space, but one with a finger on the pulse of global food debates in current times, and speaks to me of the concept of conviviality as the scholar Paul Gilroy outlined it in his remarkable book *After Empire*.[3] Conviviality, for Gilroy, means living with and through the experience of others: it is a way of acknowledging trauma and past wrongs, but also of constructing, through community practices in the present, a larger space for joy, connection and learning. Timespan's conviviality can be seen in the interventions they have staged in the social and economic conditions of the local population – leading campaigns to adopt green energy solutions in the village, for example, and actively promoting the development of local skills to address employment challenges. As a small museum it has recognised it can make a big impact in its local place, and can also connect, with integrity and meaning, to larger conversations happening worldwide, with the museum's digital conversations involving a small but growing global audience.

This movement from past to future makes me think, once again, of Hew Locke's *The Procession*, one of the most popular commissions to have been shown in Tate Britain's Duveen Galleries. Locke, who grew up in then British Guiana, is an artist whose navigation of British colonial history is both subtle and powerful, as it looks back to move forwards with a new and inclusive sense of what it means to be British.

Other dimensions of a future museum can be helpfully identified in some of the other nominees for the 2021 Art Fund Museum of the Year. The eventual winner, Firstsite in Colchester, is a space without its own collection, but one that has dedicated itself to the creation of art as the means to grow community, shaping the museum around that community need over the last several years. Firstsite's actions during the pandemic – which included becoming a hub for free school meals and an art space for children – spoke of a recognition that it could offer both exactly what the community needed and also what the museum was best placed to deliver: connections through making. Director Sally Shaw came to the rescue of desperate parents across the country when she launched Art is Where the Home Is, a series of 'make at home' activities from many well-known artists, to help encourage a sense of play and learning through artmaking at home. Among these was artist Michael Landy, originally from Essex, who devised a toilet-paper-stacking sculpture activity which proved enormously popular, even in the midst of what seemed to be a national toilet paper shortage. Shaw's project was so successful that it was expanded into a national 'at home' exhibition when the lockdowns came to an end.

What is notable and vital in this example is the way in which the thought processes of artists – and key artworks of our nation's collections – formed the bedrock of the project. Firstsite was able to provide a platform for a wide variety of artists and their ideas, and also showed – with minimal effort and maximum impact – that art could and should be for everyone, at home and within reach. In the end, Firstsite won Museum of the Year because I and the other judges felt it had generated the most joy in a year when there were very few reasons indeed to be joyful. Better yet, it did so without in any way compromising the excellence and innovation of the art it promoted and helped foster. In offering space to other local community organisations that were engaged in meeting social and civic need, such as a charity supporting newly arrived refugees, it also created a conviviality – that word again – of connection and purpose that brought together artmaking, placemaking and a sense of welcome in ways that felt politically powerful but full of kindness, too.

In the years since, exhibitions such as 2023's *Big Women*, curated by Sarah Lucas and drawing on a number of large (female) artistic personalities from Lucas's own friendship circle – and defying conventions of generational association or canonical appraisal – have continued an approach at Firstsite that places public engagement and public joy, including some very big female belly laughs, at the centre of the museum's practice.

A State of Tension

We've taken a look at the museums that might, and might not, sustain us in the future. But what unites the more successful examples? How to describe the ideal model?

The first idea I would point to here is disagreement. There are almost no spaces in contemporary culture where remaining in disagreement, constructively, is evident or encouraged. The collections we hold and the institutions shaped around them are subject to all the forces that influence society, history, identity, and our collective and individual sense of belonging, and so we will only very rarely come to a common point of view about our work. I was struck by the words of Souleymane Bachir Diagne, director of the Institute of African Studies at Columbia University:

It recently occurred to me that art objects should be called 'mutant' … they are at once many different things. This is

why I like the word *mutant*, because in French *mutant* is
... a present participle. In other words, the metamorphosis is
continuously happening to those objects.[4]

Diagne reminds us that instability is not only the essence of the
art object, but of the collection in its entirety: museums are part of a
much greater flow and a more complicated set of narratives, some of
which we are able to grasp and others of which we do not even know
about yet. The museum, Diagne suggests, needs to be 'a place where
many different objects would be talking to each other'. This notion
of the future museum as a space for dialogue without the desire for
resolution is one of the most inspiring thoughts I have come across
as a museum director.

It's tempting – certainly for museum directors and boards who
have felt rather beleaguered these past few years – to imagine that
the present turmoil will pass (one peer of mine is very fond of the
'This too shall pass' incantation). I do not think, however, we will
or even should be moving beyond these tensions. Consciously or
unconsciously, museums have always sought to manage a series of
incompatible demands. Serenity of status is really only ever achieved
through the covering up or ignoring of the workings of power that the
museum helps to produce and reify. We should really be embracing
the arguments. If we don't, who will?

Nevertheless, museums must tread with care here – not only to
protect themselves from unnecessary attack in the press and online,
but because society at the moment needs us to be a less judgemental
and didactic voice. We should not go back to the turn of the twentieth century and the Victorian civilising mission that motivated
many museums to welcome 'people of all social orders' in order to
pacify a potentially revolutionary working class. In our desire to share

knowledge and expand understanding we inevitably stray into a didactic mode, but I want to think that in my imagined museum of the future we can take pride in our knowledge and our position as trusted expert, but resist suggesting that we have all the answers. Nor should we ever present a belief system that visitors must subscribe to. Our spaces must be ones where different ideas can be held and explored, and where we underline that disagreement is useful.

Each time I have sat down to write a chapter of this book, Tate has faced a different 'live issue' to grapple with. Early in 2022, to offer one example, I found myself at meetings discussing the complex geopolitical implications of Russia's war in Ukraine, and others considering gender-critical feminism and trans rights occasioned by the screening of Marin Håskjold's film *What Is A Woman?* At the same moment, the Horniman Museum was officially handing over its seventy-two Benin Bronzes to the Nigerian government in a ceremony at the gallery; Hew Locke's magnificent *The Procession* continued to generate debate about British colonial history, including that most totemic of figures, Winston Churchill, as well as drive visitors to Tate Britain in droves; and a partner organisation was caught up in a complex cultural argument about free speech, Israel and Palestine. On all these matters we can expect that there will be strong government views to navigate, strong public views to navigate, and strong internal views to navigate. And in each such situation, it is vital that we remain engaged and compassionate, and strive to hear all sides. I want to say firmly that these issues are not *problems* for the museum, but the natural outcome of a healthy, disputatious ecology. Rather than wishing them away, therefore, we need to find ways to continue to engage productively – to remain in a 'mutant' or dissenting state.

The Question of Care

Some readers, and indeed some colleagues, may read this and worry what a site of perpetual disagreement might resemble. To navigate this, we need to maintain a culture of care at all levels, from the base to the top of organisations. It is hard work to keep an open mind and generous spirit when critique can be personal and very hostile. This ethics of care would be another summary point, where museums switch into a 'slower mode' that seeks to amplify the knowledge it shares with people and to steward resources for an uncertain future. Under this banner of 'care' comes, of course, how we treat our people – our audiences, our collaborators and our workforces. And it also speaks to the question of how we reduce our negative impact on the planet. Growing this sense of care and connectedness is key to deepening the relevance and significance museums have for people, for their communities and for the localities they help shape.

The past few years have presented a number of sobering global crises – health, environment, the question of racial equity, and now war – that demand the utmost care in how we proceed. Our position, both individually and collectively, has been revealed to be precarious – something we always knew but could so easily overlook. As the director of MCA Chicago Madeleine Grynsztejn has argued, the 'reckoning' that occurred in the wake of Black Lives Matter protests in the summer of 2020, which continues to make itself felt in museums across the world, asks us to turn the museum toward engaging with and serving not just the largest and largely undifferentiated public, but rather the close communities that find themselves most vulnerable today. I find this a compelling idea, since it presumes that the difference a museum can make will necessarily be calibrated in relation to the community it is part of, and in relation to the objects and histories that it holds. It can use the special tools at its disposal, but it can also take action according to need. This framework helps us understand the particular power of the work of FirstSite, as an example.

Artist Tino Sehgal describes the museum as 'a place for secular ritual, where categories that constitute the basis of our society are enacted and exercised'.[5] So museums are places where we can test out variations of behaviours and beliefs. In the museum we can explore, we can mediate – but ultimately, we must be openhearted, inviting each visitor to investigate the dimensions of our shared humanity, no matter that individual's stance on the fracturing questions of our age. With this in mind, we must accept that museums are spaces riven, just like society, with contradiction.

When we got down off our plinths and pediments to connect to a wider public interest, we dismantled the church-and-state division between the museum that shows and informs and the public who come in to engage. For me, this means that the future of museums is no longer about quantitative growth, the new wing or the additional outpost – at least, not only about this. Growth can mean development toward ongoing transformation; a restlessness that leads to a commitment to the process of enquiry. It invites a polyphony of voices, both from within the gallery walls and from outside. It resists the temptation to batten down the hatches until calmer skies arrive.

What We Have

As we move toward the next productive iteration of the museum of our now, it is the objects that I want to place centre stage. Objects – these mysterious, banal, obscure or obvious things that we hold for the future on behalf of the public – are what make museums unique. Objects also place a useful indeterminacy – or mutant thinking, in Diagne's term – at the heart of the museum project. What they mean depends not just on their own material qualities but on the knowledge offered about them and on the person who looks at them. This is why they are contested, it is why they matter so much, and, in holding them, it is why museums are so useful to us now.

For me, the objects we hold, our care of them, and our ability to connect them to our public, form our foundation. These objects need to be at the heart of the story we tell: our collections, what they are and how we use them, the stories framed around them, and how they create and anchor our relationship with the public are all factors underpinning everything I have discussed in these chapters.

So much has been written academically and by art historians and museum professionals across the cultural sphere – and so much work has been done by colleagues at Tate – to challenge the canon, to regender it, to consciously and purposefully disrupt the Western, Eurocentric foundations of nearly all collections. We are, I would contend, not in a state of crisis in terms of thinking about the future of collections and what they can mean for people, but rather a state of brilliant diversity and expanded understandings. There is still much work to be done to ensure our collections represent and come into dialogue with the world as we understand it today: it is an active and continuing project. The changing focus of the British and international collections which underpins our work at Tate is typified for me by the movement away from a largely Western canon, towards a transnational understanding of the interconnected evolution of twentieth- and twenty-first-century art across all continents.

The latest phase of this project includes a strategic focus on work by indigenous artists, a subject only made visible within Tate's collecting strategy in the past four years, a renewed focus on Global South modernisms and queer and neurodiverse histories; all rather brilliantly explored in Adriano Pedroso's 2024 Venice Biennale, titled *Foreigners Everywhere*. Whilst there was a huge amount to learn from Pedroso's firmly Global South perspective, it was also a path into the future that colleagues at Tate are also exploring and that we can happily affirm and continue to amplify.

The shift of focus also means redefining what we think about British art. It cannot stand alone as a marooned 'island nation' story, and the 2023 rehang of Tate Britain's collection by Alex Farquharson and his team was a globally interconnected one. Likewise in the British Pavilion in Venice 2024, John Akomfrah's *Listening All Night to the Rain,* is a layered epic exploring multiple British histories and landscapes, with a fluidity and nuance embodied by the flow of water running through the extraordinary visual land- and soundscape. That it was created, like so much of Akomfrah's work, through collaboration with his fellow artists, who are also travellers in the work itself, is part of its subtle power.[6]

Collecting now, and in the now, entails being open to the provisionality of any attempt to write an art history. Furthermore, I believe we need to change the focus of our collecting not simply to be accumulative, but to grow our understanding of our collection, connecting it to a web of museums and their collections across the globe and to an expanding nodal understanding of the art ecology, such that, in Édouard Glissant's terms, we give up the fantasy of representing the 'tout-monde' in favour of a humbler sense of aimin for 'mondiality': operating with a sense of the world and especially 'other world views' in mind.[7]

A museum's collection, its locality and its origins are what make it unique. Our idiosyncrasies are everything. The global museum 'star show', as gratifying as it can be, can ride roughshod over this. Such shows have less relevance to the local, and can quite often pay little heed to the institution itself. Of course, we can continue to hold exhibitions of globally and historically renowned artists, but our starting point should always be what makes our collection unique, since this allows us to tell a story connected to and authentic to us.

Tate's own practices have been shaped not only through the actions of all those directors and curators who have helped build and develop the collection, but also because of the evolution of the visual arts world in London, including the other museums and the art market forces that have swirled around it. It has also been marked brilliantly by UK regional politics – whether this was the post-industrial cultural regeneration in Liverpool in the 1980s that led to Tate Liverpool, or the nostalgia for artist colonies of the past that took Tate to St Ives where it became part of a locally rooted cultural community in our own time. Tate responds continually to multiple contexts and, through our locations and our relationships, we are part of a network that is helping to shape new activity that is less hierarchical, less London-centric, and more reflective of the needs of our contemporary moment.

Thinking about our collections in terms of 'We have this. What does it connect with?' might give us a better route map for an interconnected, post-colonial mode. The result of such thinking might be more exhibitions that seek to capture a mood of social change, or speak to particular cultural moments. These kind of shows are often put together by drawing on existing collections or helping to shape them. 'Zeitgeist' shows are often put together largely from existing collections; this was the case with my earlier examples of *Queer British Art* and *Life Between Islands*, both of which worked to challenge preconceptions and open up new narratives, as well as build new stories into our collection. Both of these exhibition concepts were developed by individuals and groups within Tate, and were connected to complex local and global networks of interest and relevance. Their carbon footprint was much lower, their cultural impact significant.

Revelatory, personal, political – these exhibitions are examples of an alternative, qualitative kind of growth in thinking about art as well as building different connections to people.

Many, if not most, public institutions want to open up, share, extend, and be attentive and responsive to the changing social and cultural landscape around them. As a distributed national collection and a globally connected and locally relevant institution, Tate should be open, generous, connected and in motion. No matter how hard we try, however, we will get many things wrong – and we need to learn to be OK with that, even if it is sometimes excruciating and personally painful, because we are learning and trying to do something new, maybe even revolutionary: to be an art museum that reflects its locality and its citizens, and tries to shape a more open world.

At the end of her tough-minded call for museums to do better on questions of equity, Madeleine Grynsztejn concedes that the list of things we hate about museums is long but insists that we should 'take a beat and instead ask ourselves what do we love about museums? What do we want to save? Take that challenge seriously and act on it.'

I would answer these questions by saying what makes museums so special is that they are institutions built on 'stuff' – profound, ephemeral, dusty, not dusty, remarkable, prosaic stuff. Stuff: I use that word to entertain my most long-standing academic compatriot whose influence is threaded through this book. As young academics, on bad days when we were tasked with devising from scratch a first-year lecture course on topics we felt ill-equipped to opine on, we used to fantasise of a degree programme called 'Stuff Studies', where you would graduate with a degree in *things*. Thirty years on, I realise that I was only really channelling my interest in critical museology, and today I see the museum of the future as one which will continue to take the stuff we hold for future generations very seriously indeed.

Custodians

I have one final contemporary example to share, and I think it's important because it again sets us thinking about how museums have to change if we are to build relationships with new communities – particularly those previously excluded from the very canons and histories our museums help shape.

This work by Edgar Calel, a person connected to the Kaqchikel community from Guatemala, is entitled *The Echo of an Ancient Form of Knowledge* 2021. It was selected for Tate's collection through research carried out by Tate curators working with external curator Hammad Nasar and artist Grada Kilomba. Calel sourced the rocks that form the foundation of the work in Surrey, choosing them for their organic, natural appearance and their mossy surface. He didn't want anything too polished, and certainly nothing too complicated – just rocks. To enact the work, the rocks are positioned as altars – 'a sacred site for rituals'.[8] Locally sourced fruits and vegetables are placed on top of each rock. Thereafter, a member of the Kaqchikel community conducts a ritual without which the work cannot be considered complete. Calel himself intended to carry out this ritual but, in light of the pandemic travel restrictions in place at the time Tate selected the work, he found an artist in London to help – someone who, in a private moment, cut open some of the fruits and replaced them on top of the rocks.

Calel's work evokes a connection to his ancestors, and pays homage to his local indigenous communities in Guatemala. What he has produced is best understood as a visual chant, as an embodied poem, or as Naoj – there is no word for art in the Mayan language as it is spoken in the artist's hometown, and Naoj is often considered to be the closest term, encompassing the idea of 'knowledge-wisdom-understanding'. Calel's work reflects a Mayan cosmology which differs from Western perceptions of the world. Indeed, the work is not even an art installation as we might traditionally think of it: rather, as an offering to the artist's ancestors, it is designed to make us consider the complexities of indigenous cultures, and the ongoing effects of their destruction. What Calel is evoking here is the invisible, the untranslatable, and the ungraspable.

And this is where Tate was asked to approach the work differently. As part of the acquisition agreement, Tate cannot ever own the work. Instead, the artist has invited Tate to become a custodian for a period of thirteen years. As the artist said: 'I am thankful to our ancestors for giving us the license and allowing us to spread their knowledge and wisdom.' After thirteen years, a new agreement will be made with the artist and his community – either to renew our custodianship, to pass it on to another institution, or to return the elements of the work to the earth. Through the work, we've essentially entered into a knowledge-sharing arrangement with the Maya-Kaqchikel people, as a part of which Tate will not only acquire the custodianship for Calel's artwork but also make a donation to the Kaqchikel community, contributing to the ongoing creation of social good.

What Tate is being asked to take on here, we should note, is responsibility for knowledge-sharing, cultural learning and the building of social relationships in the now. It is this, not the rocks themselves, nor the fruit that rots, which makes us guardians or custodians. In addition, it is a relationship that has to be renegotiated each time the work is (re)made. When *The Echo of an Ancient Form of Knowledge* was shown in Tate Liverpool in 2023, the artist was able to attend in person to inaugurate the work again. This time the organic matter came from the central vegetable market in Liverpool. With Tate Liverpool's director Helen Legg in attendance, along with other community and museum colleagues, a burning ceremony took place that featured incense and other organic materials (in itself putting the event outside the usual parameters of collection care behaviours), and the work, carrying with it the wisdom of the Kaqchikel ancestors, was offered for consideration by the visitors in Liverpool.

With this acquisition – and the support of our trustees – Tate took a surprisingly easy step into an entirely new relationship with the world, which rather mirrors the changing relationship we are trying to build with our multiple, polyphonic histories. It marked a momentous shift, moving us from an institution founded on principles of exclusivity and cultural power to one that, while imperfect, is nonetheless open to new ideas, new ways of working and new relationships with the artists and public we serve. The events of history are what they are, but the way we understand, hold or own them is not. The perspectives we take on history are various and non-linear; they cannot be reduced to a set of objective facts. As such, we need to be able to hold many views and orders of knowledge within our spaces and allow there to be – even actively seek out – multiple voices. This in turn speaks to the ethics of care – for objects, for people, and for the history we carry and shape in our now – that is, for me, a vital part of the future for museums.

Perhaps my grandest suggestion is a rather modest one. It is simply the idea that the future museum *needs* to be imperfect, as it will be – to use that very old-fashioned museum phrase – 'in the course of rearrangement'. This could include an attitude of mind that states, to draw on a concept proposed by Josh Cohen, that we need to hold onto 'vigilant humility' as a way of navigating a complex past and a disputatious present.[9] This attitude of mind would allow that, while museums hold knowledge, expertise and also often the best examples of our collective cultural ingenuity and brilliance, they do not, and cannot, hold the whole truth. They will never be complete, nor should we want them to be: rather, we should want them to be an ongoing work in progress. That way, by resisting cultural absolutism and a desire for certainty, museums might become model civic institutions for engaging in the arguments we need to have as a society, in a tone and with manners that permit dissent, which in turn allows us to be more inclusive.[10]

The Journey Continues

This book began with my own cultural journey toward museums and we left that life history with me, aged eighteen, exploring Tate Liverpool. Much has happened since then to make museums central to my life, and to shape the cordially dissenting position I have tried to adopt throughout this book. Most if not all of that world view has been shaped through engagement with art practice and artists, and to close this book I want to return to art's place in my life history.

From around the age of twenty-one I started to travel, every few weeks or so, to look at art. And as my journeys were, more often than not, to public museums, I don't recall ever having to pay to see the art. These adventures started with a lengthy bus journey east across London to see an explosion frozen in time. Over the following years I saw a house cast in concrete, I saw a miners' strike restaged by an artist and an army of volunteers, I saw a man cut his arms and walk down metres of canvas dripping blood, I saw apples slowly rotting on the branches of bronze trees. I saw in the paintings of African American modernist artists a deeply politicised racial consciousness that prefigured the civil rights movement of the 1960s.[11] I saw On Kawara's date paintings and struggled to understand, or to explain to my son, what they meant.[12]

I was not always concentrating on these journeys. Sometimes I was there laughing and joking with friends or trying to impress boyfriends. At other times I was there in conscious solidarity, scribbling in my notebook, seeing in the artwork an idea or a challenge that I felt passionately about. Sometimes I understood the artworks; at other times I couldn't make sense of them at all. They have remained seared in my memory nevertheless.

I don't recall being told what to do or what to think. No one will tell you off in a museum these days for dawdling, dreaming or lazily spending a pleasant part of your day. As Josh Cohen has eloquently argued, there is power and a necessity in idle thoughts; perhaps the most under-recognised virtue of the museum is that no one is really checking whether you are paying attention.[13] This sense of simple, light-hearted pleasure should be appreciated as a significant part of the wellness benefits of museums. Museums aren't a medicine to be administered to the masses – indeed, we should remember that museum narratives have often been used to exclude the histories of many whose experience has not been part of elite or dominant social order. In our highly orchestrated and over-regulated world, simple pleasures should not be taken lightly. The capacity for divergent thought they engender is genuinely mind-expanding and life-enhancing. As someone who is always suspicious of being told what to think – about anything, even things I generally agree with – I have always liked working with visual art and with living artists. Here, meaning is rarely literal or easily read, and there is often a satisfying lack of clarity about what a thing does or could mean. So many of the objects in all sorts of museums pose a satisfying resistance to being explained – part of the reason, I believe, that museums are so fascinating. We should treasure the importance of this non-didactic space for imagination and discovery.

All of my early journeys to see art were important and, I would argue, interrelated. Each journey, each artwork, helped to shape my consciousness as a young adult, as a young academic and, eventually, as a young parent. Each also helped me see the world as an interconnected set of ideas and challenged my thinking about my own place in that world. Now that my children, Lily and Jake, have become fellow travellers, I can see how they benefitted in their youth from the playful opening up of sensorial experiences in museums, from *The weather project* at Tate Modern to Ikon's chocolate-coated walls. As adults, they inhabit a museum world that offers them a wide and dynamic reflection on their own life experiences. This was not always the case. On my first visit to the Venice Biennale I do not remember seeing a single woman artist, a single artist of colour, or a single artist from beyond the Western world. A couple of years ago, Lily walked around a Biennale made up of more than 90% women or non-binary artists, where the winner of the prestigious Golden Lion Award was the British-Caribbean artist Sonia Boyce. I type these words only a few months after we closed *What Freedom Is to Me*, Tate Britain's landmark retrospective of the renegade Black queer film maker (and Royal Academician) Sir Isaac Julien.[14]

Reflecting on an extremely turbulent few years for museums, I can still say I am optimistic for change. This is thanks to artists themselves, who create positive change both inside and outside the museum world, and also thanks to the curators, academics, researchers, directors and museum professionals who argue for the inclusion of a multiplicity of practices, identities and political views. It is also due to you – a public whose embrace of a broader story and a richer diversity of ideas far exceeds the posturing of those who wish to sow discord for an easy soundbite or political gain.

The mutable nature of museums, the ever-changing nature of their stories and their collections, is what makes them valuable. We may gather as strangers in museums but through them we can find common ground – and hopefully, dare I say it, new ways of thinking, and living. As Cohen says, 'this isn't much, which is why it might also be the most radical imaginable prescription'.[15]

Afterword:
Gathering of Strangers
and Friends

This book began life as a series of lectures delivered at Murray Edwards College, University of Cambridge in spring 2022, when I was Slade Professor of Fine Art. I was invited to take up the Slade Professorship by Professor Rosalind Polly Blakesley at Pembroke College. I was then made a Fellow of Murray Edwards by President Dorothy Byrne, a great advocate for the women's art collection at Murray Edwards College – and for women in general. Dorothy has enriched my life with her fabulous, feminist leadership and friendship. Week after week, I was looked after by the wonderful Dr Rachel Polonsky, then Vice-President of the college and Fellow in Slavonic Studies and by Professor Alyce Mahon, from History of Art. I owe all four of these remarkable women a great debt of thanks for their support.

Those lectures were written over a period of three months, during which I spent a day or two each week as resident in the academically adventurous shelter of Murray Edwards College. The college itself possessed a powerful feminist atmosphere and the ethics of care that made this writing possible even alongside my role as Director of

Tate. It also offers the same care for the students who make the space their home for the duration of their studies. As Homi K. Bhabha (who taught me when I was a student) reminds us, hospitality is the vital condition of our ability to think together about difficult things, and I certainly felt that during my time at Murray Edwards.

I approached my residency with some sense of awe, having been aware of the work of the college and its women's art collection since making an exhibition with renowned feminist artist Mary Kelly. She too had spent a formative period of her life in Cambridge, as artist in residence at Kettle's Yard and at what was then New Hall College, now Murray Edwards, in 1986. Mary's time at Cambridge and the work she made there laid the foundations for the college's collection of women's art, which was developed from 1996 onwards; today it is the largest collection of women's art in the UK and it lives on the walls of many of the communal spaces at Murray Edwards for the benefit of the college's students. It is a remarkable thing to sit and eat in the communal dining room alongside the powerful magic of Paula Rego's paintings, or to see Tracey Emin's work as you pick up your post at the reception. Although the college is not a museum, it acts as a rather good one – a space for inspiration, inquiry and dissent fostered by an adventurous programme of exhibitions such as a solo show of Scottish-Ghanaian artist Maud Sulter and a group show of international female textile artists, curated by Naomi Polonsky, that took place while I was delivering my lectures. The collection continues to evolve under the guidance of President Dorothy Byrne and deserves to be better known.

Alongside these new-found academic fellow travellers are others who have walked with me through much of my adult life. I cannot quantify just how much Professor Helen Laville has enriched my life and thinking; her curiosity about the past and the future, and her sense of pragmatic optimism, can be felt throughout this book. Lifelong friends Professor Josh Cohen, whose thoughts on the value of losing helped me find a suitable ending for the book, and Mark Ball, whose rebellious artistic spirit has always guided me, deserve huge thanks for their friendship and their wisdom. Deep gratitude to Duro Olowu, whose wisdom, laughter and creativity has sustained my thinking about the world as well as my sartorial instincts.

The wider formative hinterland of this book is populated by the museum professionals and artists whose ideas and passions have ignited and guided my own throughout my career. When I look across this extraordinary group of people I can see that we are collectively forging a different ecology of cultural value – one based not on established hierarchy or status but on art's capacity to enrich and challenge us. Readers of this book in draft form deserve special thanks first: Esme Ward, Director of Manchester Museum; Gus Casely-Hayford, Director of V&A East; Caro Howell, Director General, IWM; and Olivia Laing, writer and special connector to the energy of Derek Jarman. I also want to thank Bryony Bond, Mary Griffiths, Dominique Heyse-Moore, Samantha Lackey, Ed Watts, Amy George, Clare O'Mahoney, Helen Stalker, Fiona Corridon, Clare Gannaway and Natasha Howes for their visionary work at the Whitworth and at Manchester Art Gallery, as well as Dr Monica Pearl at the University of Manchester, and Peter Saville and Jon Savage, creative agitators both. Architects MUMA (Stuart McKnight, Gillian McInnes, Simon Usher, Simon Branson) must also be thanked for their visionary transformation of the Whitworth, allowing us to gather strangers, and special thanks are due to artist Nathan Coley for the work that became the signature of the new gallery and gives this book its title. In Manchester I was also given support and permission to be ambitious by Dame Nancy Rothwell, Vice-Chancellor of the University of Manchester, and by Sir Howard Bernstein at Manchester City Council and Sir Richard Leese – two unforgettable men who changed the culture of Manchester and the North for the better, and for whom I have the utmost gratitude and love.

The Clore leadership programme gave me my first experience of the rich diversity of leadership in the arts sector, and of how a new cohort of leaders could be differently powerful. Thanks to Kathleen Soriano, Moira Sinclair, Ciara Eastell and Axel Rüger for being the friends who hold me up and keep my feet on the ground; to Dame Vivien Duffield for setting us all off on a new course; and to Lord Chris Smith and Sue Hoyle for being guiding lights throughout this transformational period.

The Whitworth Art Gallery, Manchester Art Gallery and Tate have provided challenge and inspiration throughout my career, and these institutions help provide the rich flavour that brings my thoughts in this book to life. Colleagues at all three institutions have been inspirational, and I thank them for their work and their friendship. At Tate, I owe a special vote of thanks to Josephine Maxwell, the writer and researcher who helped me compile the original Slade lectures, as well as to Holly Matthews and Martha Greenhough, assistants beyond compare, who did such sterling work to source images and turn them into presentations that made sense. My colleagues Carmel Allen, Eleanor Appleby, Anne Barlow, Liam Darbon, Alex Farquharson, Samuel Jones, Helen Legg, Mark Miller, Gregor Muir, Polly Staple and Catherine Wood, alongside the many other curators and educators who bring such value to the public who engage with Tate, have all created the environment of curiosity, intelligence and kindness that makes for the best of museums: I have learned so much from them all. Special thanks go to Tom Avery, Director of Tate Publishing, who has been the instigator and best-ever editor of this volume. His enthusiasm, care and rigour have made this a much better book and transformed the difficult task of finishing it alongside my daily work into a pleasure.

I also want to thank Tate's Chair of Trustees, Roland Rudd, and his fellow Trustees, for all their support and for giving me lively encouragement towards getting this book written. Tate would not be what it is without their commitment and guidance. I owe much to the creative wisdom of the artist Trustees I have worked with: John Akomfrah, Stephen Witherford, Dexter Dalwood, Rosalind Nashashibi, Farooq Chaudhry and Kwame Kwei-Armah. There are a group of women leaders whose counsel and kindness down the years have helped shape and sustain my thinking: Sharon Ament, Hilary Carty, Janet Beer, Sally Luton, Koyo Kouoh, Sadie Coles.

Throughout the book I look to artists for the best examples of how to stay in dissent, with empathy and without judgement. Their work and working practices have consistently shaped how I perceive and understand the world. I want to thank Marina Abramović, John Akomfrah, Sonia Boyce, Nikhil Chopra, Nathan Coley, Tracey Emin, Lubaina Himid, Isaac Julien, Mary Kelly, Lynn Hershman Leeson, Sarah Lucas, Kira O'Reilly, Cornelia Parker, Keith Piper, Nico Vascellari, Joana Vasconcelos, Richard Wentworth, Lynette Yiadom Boakye and the inspiring spirit of Derek Jarman. Their collective disputatious and beautiful passions have helped define the ideal museum as a space for nonconformity, ever-evolving argument, and joy.

My experience as a museum professional has been profoundly shaped by my experience as a mother, a stepmother, and the partner of another museum professional. Museums were not a part of my early cultural experience in a working-class family, and discovering the pleasure of unstructured and self-directed wandering – for me, the keenest pleasure offered by the free-to-enter museum space – was a liberation as well as a joyous education. I shared this with my children without any conscious thought that this was 'good for them'; it was because museums offered spaces where we could please ourselves and do so together. Understanding my children's likes and their dislikes, and experiencing the museum through their eyes and actions, has been the most influential force on my professional attitudes. This needs saying, and matters a lot, because it is still by no means commonplace that the director of a space of great cultural capital like Tate should be a woman with children who still retains some working-class imposter syndrome about being allowed in through the hallowed doors. My deepest love and thanks go to Jake and Lily Kennedy, who have been to probably too many museums with me and yet still show up and smile, and to my stepsons Robert and Lucas Merriman, whose interests meant I kept up with science as well as art museums.

This book was conceived and written as we all emerged from the deep human shock of the pandemic period. During this time my father died after a long illness, followed by my mother dying after a very short one. I was fortunate to have her live her last months alongside me as I worked from home during the lockdown. My hourly Zoom calls meant she heard much more about museum management than any regular person should have to endure, but we came to know each other much better over these months and her presence kept me grounded during that difficult time. I understand now that my passion for a creative education and a culturally rich life was rooted in her experience as an early years teacher, one who believed in igniting a child's creative talents as part of their basic human rights. She heard the outline of what these chapters might be, and I am still very sorry that she did not get to hear or read some of them; I know that she was very proud of what I do and would have liked to have this book on her shelf, even if she wouldn't have been quite so bothered to read it all. As for my dad, he just loved an argument, and that spirit is in this book too. So too is the rebellious energy of my Aunt Sylvia, who featured in my lectures as a community artist in a feminist shocking pink tutu, and whose commitment to cultural democracy gave me a grounding philosophy for all my work. It is a further deep sadness to me that she passed away the year after my mum and so did not get to see herself in the hallowed halls of Cambridge. Her daughters Anna Higgs and Katy Jackson continue the creative adventure with me, as together we shape our next generation of museum lovers in the form of Anna's sons, Albie and Stanley, creative chaos merchants.

The last word has to be for my husband Nick Merriman, whose love and faith in me, not to mention his deep museological wisdom, have sustained my career in museums. He is the very model of a dedicated, dissenting museum director, whose reasonable demeanour disguises a deep radicalism about the potential of museums that engage the public actively as partners in shaping a better world. Our agreements and disagreements about what we do as daily professional practice have shaped this book, as they have shaped our lives together. I hope we keep the arguments and the spirit of joy going until the end of our days.

Notes

Introduction: Museums Now

1   'We see this reflected...' from Tate's Governance and mission statement, available online at www.tate.org.uk/about-us/governance.

2   'In recent years...' Between 1960 and 2023, a total of 3,235 museums opened; 882 museums closed during that same period. See 'Mapping Museums', Birkbeck, University of London 2023, https://museweb. dcs.bbk.ac.uk/browseproperties, accessed 27 Feb. 2024.

3   'We just cycled past it...' Adapted from 'Indie band's song adopted by NFL franchise', BBC News, West Midlands, accessed 25 Jan. 2024.

Chapter 1: Museum Origins

1   'This dispiriting phrase...' See Vanessa Trevalyan (ed.), *Dingy places with different kinds of bits: An Attitudes Survey of London Museums Amongst Non Visitors*, London Museums Service, 1991.

2   'There are many tomes...' See Donatien Grau, *Under Discussion: The Encyclopedic Museum*, Los Angeles 2021.

3   'The museum remains open...' For more information, please see 'The

viewpoints of the museum' section of the RMCA's website: https://www.africamuseum.be/en/about_us/viewpoints.

4   'Most so-called national collections...' In the case of the British Museum, it was the collection of Sir Hans Sloane; the National Gallery began with the picture collection of the banker John Julius Angerstein; and Tate's collection began with the gift of sugar industrialist Henry Tate's collection of British art and funds to build the gallery at Millbank.

5   'Objects may also...' See Dan Hicks, *The Brutish Museum: The Benin Bronzes, Colonial Violence and Cultural Restitution*, London 2020.

6   'Although governmental moves...' See the National Gallery website for details on the building's history and the choice of location: https://www.nationalgallery.org.uk/about-us/history/about-the-building?viewPage=2, accessed 19 Feb. 2024.

7   'The early model...' Pierre Bourdieu, 'The Forms of Capital', in Mark Granovetter (ed.), *The Sociology of Economic Life*, 3rd edn, New York and Oxon 2018, pp.78–92.

8   'It is useful to bear in mind...' See Grau 2021 for a thorough interrogation of 'encyclopaedic' in this context.

9   'Indeed, as many have observed,...' Tony Bennett, Mike Savage, Elizabeth Bortolaia Silva et al, *Culture, Class, Distinction*, London and New York 2009.

10 'Although we might not like to acknowledge...' Orian Brook, Dave O'Brien and Mark Taylor, *Culture is Bad for You: Inequality in the Cultural and Creative Industries*, Manchester 2020.

11 'The noted museum pioneer...' Lieutenant-General [Augustus Henry Lane Fox] Pitt-Rivers, 'Typological Museums, as exemplified by the Pitt Rivers Museum at Oxford, and his provincial museum at Farnham, Dorset', *Journal of the Society of Arts*, vol.40, Dec. 1891, pp.115–22.

12 'Modern innovations such...' Rachel Bowlby, *Back to the Shops: The High Street in History and the Future*, Oxford 2022, and Tony Bennett,

The Birth of the Museum: History, Theory, Politics, Abingdon 2013.

13 'The park - 'a green and social...' For more information, see *The Whitworth Art Gallery: The First Hundred Years*, Manchester 1988.

14 'As writers such as Dan Hicks...' Hicks 2020.

15 'This was argued...' Eric Williams, *Capitalism and Slavery*, New York 1944.

16 'Although the London Borough of Hackney...' For some history of this controversy, see Harriet Sherwood, 'Museum of the Home considering moving statue of slave ship owner', *Guardian*, 18 Nov. 2011, https://www.theguardian.com/uk-news/2021/nov/18/museum-of-the-home-considering-moving-statue-slave-ship-owner-robert-geffrye, accessed 28 Feb. 2024; 'Museum of the Home reconsiders stance on Geffrye statue', Museums Association, 18 Nov. 2018, https://www.museumsassociation.org/museums-journal/news/2021/11/museum-of-the-home-reconsiders-stance-on-geffrye-statue, accessed 28 Feb. 2024. See also the Museum of the Home's own statement, 'Geffrye, his statue and its future', https://www.museumofthehome.org.uk/what-we-do/our-story/the-statue-of-robert-geffrye, accessed 28 Feb. 2024.

17 'So, several years ago...' Centre for the Study of the Legacies of British Slavery, https://www.ucl.ac.uk/lbs, accessed 19 Feb. 2024.

18 'In recent times...' See, for example, the Whitworth's exhibition *Cotton: Global Threads* (11 Feb. – 13 May 2012) and 2006 symposium *Who are you? Where are you really from?*.

19 'Having had such holdings...' Among these exhibitions are *Althea McNish: Colour is Mine*, Whitworth Art Gallery, Manchester 2022–3 and *Material Power: Palestinian Embroidery*, Kettle's Yard, Cambridge 2023. The latter was an expanded version of an earlier exhibition, *At the Seams: A Political History of Palestinian Embroidery*, Dar el-Nimer, Beirut 2016.

20 'Within the labour movement...' See Sue Bruley, '"It didn't just come out of nowhere did it?": The origins of the women's liberation

movement in 1960s Britain', *Oral History*, vol.45, no.1, Spring 2017, pp.67–78; Jon Savage, *1966: The Year the Decade Exploded*, London 2015.

21 'Fostered in the last decade...' See Arte Útil, https://www.arte-util.org/studies/museum-of-arte-util, accessed 19 Feb. 2024. The movement takes its name from Argentine artist Eduardo Costa's *Manifesto de Arte Útil* 1969.

22 'Not long after the work opened...' This story serves as a useful reminder of how much things have changed in subsequent decades: Tate Britain's *Life Between Islands: Caribbean-British Art 1950s–Now* (2021–2) included audio installations that on occasion deliberately bled sound into other spaces in order to create the desired atmosphere, as well as Michael McMillan's 1970s Caribbean living room, which has its own soundtrack .

23 'As Robert Hewison...' Robert Hewison, *The Heritage Industry: Britain in a Climate of Decline*, London 2023.

24 'Anya Gallaccio's exhibition...' *Anya Gallaccio*, IKON Gallery, Birmingham 2003.

25 'The resulting confusion...' This 'sit/don't sit' paradox exists before we even get to the vexed question of museum seating! There is never enough, according to visitors, who find it tiring to walk the modern large museum, but curators and artists grumble that too much of it makes galleries look cluttered – and so the debate rolls on.

Chapter 2: Whose Museum?

1 'This was a momentous...' See the Arts Council website for more information on their history and current stategy, https://www.artscouncil.org.uk/lets-create/strategy-2020-2030, accessed 21 Feb. 2024.

2 'Lee's paper echoes...' Jennie Lee, *A Policy for the Arts: The First Steps* 1965, p.5.

3 'Often the impetus...' See Paulo Freire, *Pedagogy of the Oppressed*,

New York 1970; Antonio Gramsci, *Prison Notebooks*, ed. Joseph A. Buttigieg, New York 1992; Augusto Boal, *The Theatre of the Oppressed*, London 2019.

4   'Other examples from this period...' See, for example, the Black Arts Group, whose members included a host of Black British artists only now being recognised as the critical change makers that they were and still are: among, them Lubaina Himid – curator and artist participant of *The Thin Black Line* (ICA, London 1985) – which created a space for Black British women artists because the art world was not open to their practice, who has in recent years had a solo show at Tate Modern (2021–2); Sonia Boyce, who represented Britain in the 2024 Venice Biennale; and Marlene Smith and Veronica Ryan, both nominated for the Turner Prize in 2022, with Ryan winning.

5   'Devised and supported...' See the Jubilee Arts Archive 1974–1994, https://jubileeartsarchive.com, accessed 19 Feb. 2024.

6   'The legacy of this work...' See https://multistory.org.uk, accessed 19 Feb. 2024.

7   'Curators Linsey Young...' See Linsey Young (ed.), *Women in Revolt!*, exh. cat. Tate Britain, London 2023–4.

8   'It demonstrated my...' See, for example, Kabir Jhala, 'Germany has cancelled us', *The Art Newspaper*, 22 Sep. 2022. https://theartnewspaper. com/2022/09/22/documenta_15_closes_ruangrupa_exhibition_kassel, accessed 21 Feb. 2024.

9   'At the same time, the fight against...' The list of films that premiered on Channel 4 in the 1980s and early 1990s is like a counter-cultural visual lesson as well as a roll call of most of the important moving-image artists of our own time. It includes *Jubilee* (Derek Jarman, UK, 1978), *Young Soul Rebels* (Isaac Julien, BFI Production Board, UK, 1991), *Handsworth Songs* (John Akomfrah, Black Audio Film Collective, UK, 1986), *My Beautiful Laundrette* (Stephen Frears, Working Title

Films and Film4 Productions, UK, 1985), *Sebastiane* (Derek Jarman and Paul Humfress, UK, 1976), *Caravaggio* (Derek Jarman, UK, 1986) and *Edward II* (Derek Jarman, Working Title Films and Fine Line Features, UK, 1991).

10   'It was a sea-change...' John Holden's report *Future Options for Regional Agencies* 2001 was prepared for Resource, the Council for Museums and Libraries.

11   'In the first fifteen...' 'Universal free admission to the UK's national museums', Centre for Public Impact, 27 May 2016, https://www.centreforpublicimpact.org/case-study/free-entry-to-museums-in-the-uk, accessed 28 Feb. 2024.

12   'They included programmes...' Caroline Sharp, David Pye, Jenny Blackmore et al, *National Evaluation of Creative Partnerships: Final Report*, National Foundation for Educational Research, Oct. 2006.

13   'In retrospect, the cultural...' See Ben Cowell, 'Measuring the Impact of Free Admission', *Cultural Trends*, vol.16, no.3, 2017, pp.203–24; 'Evaluating the Evidence: The Impact of Charging or Not for Admissions on Museums', Association of Independent Museums, 2016, https://aim-museums.co.uk/case-studies/evaluating-evidence-impact-charging-not-admissions-museums, accessed 22 Feb. 2024.

14   'The core text...' Ken Robinson, 'All Our Futures: Creativity, Culture and Education', National Advisory Committee on Creative and Cultural Education/Department for Education and Employment, May 1999, https://www.sirkenrobinson.com/read/all-our-futures/allourfutures, accessed 28 Feb. 2024.

15   'Indeed, most museum and arts organisations...' See, for example, the Tate and RSC research project *Time to Listen: Evidence from the Tracking Arts Learning and Engagement Project*, Tracking Arts Learning and Engagement (TALE) and Arts Council England, Oct. 2018, https://researchtale.files.wordpress.com/2019/03/time-to-listen-

background-report.pdf, accessed 22 Feb. 2024.

16 'It's easy to understand why...' For analysis of this phenomenon, see Naomi Rea, 'As Museums Fall in Love with "Experiences," Their Core Missions Face Redefinition', *Artnet*, 14 March 2019, https://news.artnet. com/art-world/experience-economy-museums-1486807, accessed 22 Feb. 2024.

17 'But *The weather project*...' Kusama's *Infinity Rooms* at Tate Modern have been running at capacity, with fresh waves of tickets selling out in mere hours upon release. More than 750,000 people have now seen the work during its run.

18 'We might do well to remember...' Cedric Price, *Fun Palace for Joan Littlewood Project*, 1959–61.

19 'As I noted earlier...' For more on this, see Brook, O'Brien and Taylor 2020, *Culture is Bad for You: Inequality in the Cultural and Creative Industries*, Manchester 2020.

20 'Each work wears its radicalism...' Tate's Uniqlo Tate Play programme, of which *Mega Please Draw Freely* and *Zero to Infinity* are a part attract an audience that is 33% to 38% under sixteen, compared to 10% under sixteen at Tate Modern more generally, and 30% to 36% Black, Asian and Minority Ethnic compared to 16%.

21 'Furthermore, it is sometimes the case...' See, for example, the manifesto of Arte Útil, the Useful Museum movement (www.artutil.com). The movement has successfully harnessed the energy and thinking of socially engaged artists – and garnered much support within some sections of the museum world – but it is quite a didactic and intellectually demanding practice, and one in which objects themselves play a lesser role.

Chapter 3: Museum in the World

1   'The way that Jarman...' For the most eloquent first-person account of this period, see Derek Jarman, *Modern Nature: Journals, 1989–1990*, vol.1, London 2017.

2   'They went on...' For more information on 'A Minute's Violence', please see Greg Thorpe, https://www.gregthorpe.eu/minutesviolence, accessed 21 Feb. 2024.

3   With thanks to Samuel Jones, Head of Governance and Strategy, Tate.

4   'And it is worth noting...' The activism involves glazed artworks, so that the damage is spectacular but not capable of destroying the works. These incidents are also incredibly well researched in terms of choreographed social media and press impact. The activist groups themselves are aware there is a fine line between drawing attention to their cause and alienating the wider museum-going public.

5   'This kind of practice...' The nominated artist collectives were Array Collective, Black Obsidian Sound System, Cooking Sections, Gentle/ Radical and Project Art Works. See 'Turner Prize Shortlist Revealed', 7 May 2021, https://www.tate.org.uk/press/press-releases/turner-prize-shortlist-announced-0, accessed 22 Feb. 2024.

6   'Their campaigns remain ongoing...' For more information on Tate's acquisitions process and collections strategy, please visit: https://tate.org.uk/about-us/collection/acquisitions.

7   'In my view, after countless...' See Liz Rideal and Kathleen Soriano, *Madam & Eve: Women Portraying Women*, London 2018, and Katy Hessel, *The Story of Art Without Men*, London 2023.

8   'As one of the organisers...' Clean Clothes Campaign, 'News: Projection on Tate Modern Calling Attention to UNIQLO's Disdain for Garment Workers', 23 Feb. 2018, https://cleanclothes.org/news/2018/02/23/projection-on-tate-modern-calling-attention-to-uniqlo2019s-disdain-for-garment-workers, accessed 22 Feb. 2024. It is worthy of note

that Uniqlo have continued to sponsor Tate since the Clean Clothes protest; in recent times, indeed, the company have deepened their support for our free family programme, which has itself addressed the climate emergency through the work of artists like Cecilia Vicuna, who engaged a very wide range of the public through her Turbine Hall commission *Brain Forest Quipu* 2022.

9   'This was Tate Modern, on the eve...' 'Tackling the Climate Emergency', Tate, 2023, https://www.tate.org.uk/about-us/tate-and-climate-change, accessed 22 Feb. 2024.

10 'The best example I can point...' I use this example because it paved the way for many of the forms of protest we now see as commonplace in museums, especially in terms of campaigning in relation to the climate crisis. I also use it because speculating on the reputational battles and activism experienced by other institutions is unfair. My own experience tells me that any situation like this is nearly always more nuanced and complex than it appears from the outside.

11 '10 performers (myself included)...' 'Activists arrested in the Louvre secretly sent this message from jail', New Internationalist, 10 Dec. 2015, https://www.youtube.com/watch?v=1CzlKwR7C_0, accessed 22 Feb. 2024; Anna Sansom, 'Activists protest Louvre's oil ties', *The Art Newspaper*, 13 March 2018, https://www.theartnewspaper.com/2018/03/13/activists-protest-louvres-oil-ties, accessed 22 Feb. 2024.

12 'In her book of essays *Duty Free Art*...' Hito Steyerl, *Duty Free Art: Art in the Age of Planetary Civil War*, London 2017.

13 'We should not have been that surprised...' Black Obsidian Sound System, 'A public statement regarding the 2021 Turner Prize nominations', May 2021, https://docs.google.com/document/d/1l8Cl9Iiyt6h-gaumbXP8xdlJojIonFjriwzF_ynUK_bU/edit, accessed 28 Feb. 2024.

14 'As my colleague Michael Govan...' Michael Govan, speaking at 'Roundtable 1 – From acquisition to storytelling: what does the future

hold for museums?', Reframing Museums, 16 Nov. 2020, https://www.youtube.com/watch?v=niklf-mFX38, accessed 28 Feb. 2024. See also Alexandra Chaves, 'Reframing Museums symposium: what role do cultural institutions play in the pandemic?', The National News, 16 Nov. 2020, https://cimam.org/news-archive/reframing-museums-symposium-what-role-do-cultural-institutions-play-pandemic, accessed 28 Feb. 2024.

15 'This challenge to museums...' See, for example, an anonymously authored publication 'written by people who have experienced racism at the Barbican', *Barbican Stories: Everything You Need to Know About the Barbican*, London 2021, https://issuu.com/barbicanstories/docs/barbican_stories_digital_pdf_june_2021, accessed 28 Feb. 2024; Colin Moynihan, 'Protests at the Whitney Over a Board Member Whose Company Sells Tear Gas', *New York Times*, May 2019, https://www.nytimes.com/2019/05/18/arts/whitney-protests.html, accessed 28 Feb. 2024.

16 To use the US terminology...' See, for example, 'Pamela Joyner's Art as Social Change', First Republic, February 2021 https://www.firstrepublic.com/insights-education/art-collecting-with-purpose-pamela-joyners-mission-to-elevate-african-american-artists, accessed April 2024

17 'The Ford and Mellon...' See Darren Walker, 'Repeal of Affirmative Action Is Only the Beginning', *New York Times*, 30 June 2023, https://www.nytimes.com/2023/06/30/opinion/affirmative-action-supreme-court-repeal.html, accessed 28 Feb. 2024; Darren Walker, 'The Founders Bequeathed Us Something Radical', *New York Times*, 4 July 2022, https://www.nytimes.com/2022/07/04/opinion/these-truths-we-holdand-share.html, accessed 28 Feb. 2024; Elizabeth Alexander, *The Trayvon Generation: Yesterday, Today, Tomorrow*, New York 2022; Sanford School of Public Policy, 'Stand for Equity with Mellon Foun-

dation President Elizabeth Alexander', 24 Oct. 2020, https://sanford. duke.edu/story/stand-equity-mellon-foundation-president-elizabeth-alexander, accessed 28 Feb. 2024.

18   'At the Mellon Foundation...' See Mellon Foundation, 'The Monuments Project', https://www.mellon.org/article/the-monuments-project-initiative, accessed 28 Feb. 2024.

19   'These have brilliantly brought...' 14th Gwangju Biennial: *Soft and Weak like Water*, Gwangju 2023, curated by Sook-Kyung Lee; Liverpool Biennial: *uMoya – The Sacred Return of Lost Things*, Liverpool 2023, curated by Khanyisile Mbongwa.

20   'Keith's own work...' 'Keith Piper to create new work at Tate Britain in response to Rex Whistler Mural', Tate, 13 Dec. 2022, https://www. tate.org.uk/press/press-releases/keith-piper-to-create-new-work-at-tate-britain-in-response-to-rex-whistler-mural, accessed 28 Feb. 2024. At the time of writing, Piper's work, *Viva Voce*, is due to be unveiled in 2024. Relevant here, too, is Audre Lorde, *The Master's Tools Will Never Dismantle the Master's House* 1980, London 2018.

Chapter 4: Living with the Past

1   'For historians such as Dan Hicks...' See Hicks 2020.

2   'I have some sympathy...' This, as we shall see below, is now changing more rapidly, with museums across Europe beginning the process of returning legal title in these objects to Nigeria.

3   'It took nearly thirty-five...' Lubaina Himid, *The Thin Black Line*, Institute for Contemporary Arts, London 1985; Lubaina Himid, *Thin Black Line(s)*, Tate Britain, London 2011–12.

4   'This does not mean...' A brilliant BBC documentary by David Harewood demonstrates both the long-standing, pernicious nature of the racist impersonation of Black subjects in British culture and the evidence that its intrinsic racism was much more widely recognised

at the time and afterwards than is generally acknowledged. David Harewood, *Blackface*, BBC, London July 2023, https://www.bbc.co.uk/programmes/m001p474, accessed 28 Feb. 2024.

5 'This is particularly vexing...' For context, several thousand objects across the four Tate galleries are changed in any normal year.

6 'Against this, the pithy...' Oliver Dowden, 'We won't allow Britain's history to be cancelled', *Telegraph*, 5 May 2021, https://www.telegraph.co.uk/news/2021/05/15/wont-allow-britains-history-cancelled, accessed 28 Feb. 2024; Ministry of Housing, Communities and Local Government, Oliver Dowden and Robert Jenrick, 'New legal protection for England's heritage', 17 Jan. 2021, https://www.gov.uk/government/news/new-legal-protection-for-england-s-heritage, accessed 28 Feb. 2024.

7 'The Design Museum curator...' Quoted in Tristram Hunt, 'How museums can help end the culture wars', *Prospect*, Oct. 2020, https://www.prospectmagazine.co.uk/culture/40651/how-museums-can-help-end-the-culture-wars, accessed 29 Feb. 2024.

8 'Historian David Olusoga argued...' David Olusoga, 'The Toppling of Edward Colston's statue is not an attack on history. It is history', *Guardian*, 8 June 2020, https://www.theguardian.com/commentisfree/2020/jun/08/edward-colston-statue-history-slave-trader-bristol-protest, accessed 28 Feb. 2024.

9 'In February 2022...' Tim Cole, Joanna Burch-Brown et al, 'The Colston Statue: What Next? – We Are Bristol History Commission Full Report', Bristol 2022, https://www.bristol.gov.uk/files/documents/1825-history-commission-full-report-final/file, accessed 18 Feb. 2024.

10 'Some very interesting work is currently...' See 'Provisional Semantics', Tate, 2020, https://www.tate.org.uk/about-us/projects/provisional-semantics, accessed 28. Feb. 2024. For more on this initiative – part of the AHRC-funded research project Towards a National Collection –

Notes

see Tehmina Goskar, 'Ananda Rutherford on Provisional Semantics, documentation and decolonising collections management', Curatorial Research Centre, 28 Jan. 2021, https://curatorialresearch.com/decolonising-practice/ananda-rutherford-on-provisional-semantics-documentation-and-decolonising-collections-management, accessed 28 Feb. 2024.

11 'In an interview ahead of the performance...' 'After #MeToo, UK Gallery Removes Nymphs Painting, Denies Censorship', *Frieze*, 2 Feb. 2018, https://www.frieze.com/article/after-metoo-uk-gallery-removes-nymphs-painting-denies-censorship, accessed 28 Feb. 2024.

12 'As Boyce herself...' Sonia Boyce, 'Our removal of Waterhouse's naked nymphs painting was art in action', *Guardian*, 6 Feb. 2018, https://www.theguardian.com/commentisfree/2018/feb/06/takedown-waterhouse-naked-nymphs-art-action-manchester-art-gallery-sonia-boyce, accessed 28 Feb. 2024.

13 'A recent furore...' See Sally-Anne Huxtable, Corinne Fowler, Christo Kefalas and Emma Slocombe (eds.) et al, 'Interim Report on the Connections between Colonialism and Properties now in the Care of the National Trust, Including Links with Historic Slavery', National Trust, Swindon 2020.

14 'Whether or not Churchill...' 'The Art of Fiction: Chinua Achebe', *Paris Review*, no.133, Winter 1994, https://www.theparisreview.org/interviews/1720/the-art-of-fiction-no-139-chinua-achebe, accessed 28 Feb. 2024.

15 'The writer Afua Hirsch...' Afua Hirsch, *Look Again: Empire*, London 2021.

16 'In the past few years there have been some brilliant...' See *Slavery*, exh. cat., Rijksmuseum, Amsterdam 2021; *Colony: Australia 1770–1861 / Frontier Wars*, exh. cat., National Gallery of Victoria, Melbourne 2018; *Afro-Atlantic Histories*, exh. cat. MASP, São Paulo 2018.

17   'The foreword to the exhibition...' Aunty Joy Murphy Wandin AO, 'Foreword', in *Colony: Australia* 2018.

18   'Featuring over 450 works...' '*Afro-Atlantic Histories* 6.29–10.21.2018', Museo de Arte de São Paulo (2018), https://masp.org.br/en/exhibitions/afro-atlantic-histories, accessed 28 Feb. 2024.

19   'Art historian David Dibosa...' See David Dibosa, 'Colonial Fantasia in a Woke World: Rex Whistler's mural at Tate Britain', Tate Britain Ethics Committee Report, Aug. 2020, p.25.

20   'Certainly, I share David's...' In the interest of balance, I should note that a small number of writers argue that Whistler is, in fact, giving us imperial fantasy that critiques the whole enterprise: see, for example, Alastair Sooke, 'Tate Britain's "racist" mural is nothing of the sort – have we lost all sense of nuance?', *Telegraph*, 8 Dec. 2020, https://www.telegraph.co.uk/art/artists/tate-britains-racist-mural-nothing-sort-have-lost-sense-nuance, accessed 28 Feb. 2024. I should say, too, that I am unconvinced by the logic of this argument.

21   'Conversations about the mural...' Quoted in 'Tate announces next steps for Rex Whistler mural', Tate, 16 Feb. 2022, https://www.tate.org.uk/press/press-releases/tate-announces-next-steps-rex-whistler-mural, accessed 28 Feb. 2024.

22   'But then I look at the sensitive...' See, for instance, Paul Gilroy, *The Black Atlantic: Modernity and Double Consciousness*, Cambridge, MA 1995; Paul Gilroy, *After Empire: Melancholia or Convivial Culture?*, New York and London 2004; Stuart Hall, *Familiar Stranger: A Life Between Two Islands*, ed. Bill Schwarz, London and Durham, NC 2017; Stuart Hall, 'Cultural Identity and Diaspora', in *Essential Essays, Vol. 2: Identity and Diaspora*, ed. David Morley, Durham, NC 2019.

Notes

Chapter 5: New Models for Museums

1   'There are oppositions…' One could point to those formative critiques of the construction of greatness, including Linda Nochlin's 'Why Have There Been No Great Women Artists?' *ArtNews*, Jan. 1971; Edward Said, *Orientalism*, New York 1978; Richard Dyer's brilliant dissection of the construction of racial bodies, *White*, London 1997; and many other foundational texts.

2   'This means the museum should strive…' Monica Narula, Nataša Petrešin-Bachelez and Corina Oprea, 'Conversation: Where Are We Going? – Degrowth and Arts Ecosystem', SALT Galata, Istanbul, 4 Nov. 2020.

3   'In using the terms "positive"…' Kate Raworth, *Doughnut Economics: Seven Ways to Think Like a 21st-Century Economist*, London and Vermont 2017; Mariana Mazzucato, *The Value of Everything*, London 2018.

4   'In the UK, museums exist…' For more information, please see the Department for Digital, Culture, Media and Sport's headline release, 'Total income of DCMS-funded cultural institutions 2020/21' https://www.gov.uk/government/statistics/total-income-of-dcms-funded-cultural-organisations-202021/total-income-of-dcms-funded-cultural-institutions-202021, accessed 21 Feb. 2024.

5   'This is only exacerbated…' See Kavita Singh, in Grau, p.181.

6   'We are now twenty…' This expansion was largely funded in the UK by the creation of the National Lottery. This money was much to be welcomed – though was itself, of course, the proceeds of gambling.

7   'In the words of economist…' Edward D. Hess, *Grow to Greatness: Smart Growth for Entrepreneurial Business*, Stanford, CA 2012, p.29.

8   'In a conversation at Art Basel…' Frances Morris, Beatrix Ruf and Nina Siegal, 'Conversations: Reconsidering Museum Growth', Art Basel, Basel, 15 June 2017.

9   'The focus on the visitor...' Max Hollein, quoted in Gareth Harris and Hannah McGivern, 'Where next for museums? Four key takeaways from Louvre Abu Dhabi symposium on the post-pandemic future', *The Art Newspaper*, 20 Nov 2020, https://www.theartnewspaper. com/2020/11/20/where-next-for-museums-four-key-takeaways-from-louvre-abu-dhabi-symposium-on-the-post-pandemic-future, accessed 2 Apr. 2024.

10   'However committed to the artists...' See Gallery Climate Coalition, 'Our Story', 2023, https://galleryclimatecoalition.org/story, accessed 29 Feb. 2024.

11   'As their website explains...' Schaulager, 'Concept', https://schaulager. org/en/schaulager/concept, accessed 29 Feb. 2024.

12   'The V&A East Storehouse...' Victoria and Albert Museum, 'V&A East', https://www.vam.ac.uk/info/va-east, accessed 29 Feb. 2024.

13   'An incident is a fold...' Monica Narula, Nataša Petrešin-Bachelez and Corina Oprea, 'Conversation: Where Are We Going? – Degrowth and Arts Ecosystem', SALT Galata, Istanbul, 4 Nov. 2020.

14   'The creation of institutions such as...' For more information, please see https://guestartistsspace.com.

15   'At the core of MOWAA's vision...' MOWAA *Know Who We Are* publication, released to coincide with the launch of the Nigerian Pavilion at the Venice Biennale, April 2024.

16   'As former Tate Director...' Anna Cutler, 'What Is To Be Done, Sandra? Learning in Cultural Institutions of the Twenty-First Century', Tate Papers, no.13, Spring 2010, https://www.tate.org.uk/research/tate-papers/13/what-is-to-be-done-sandra-learning-in-cultural-institutions-of-the-twenty-first-century, accessed 29 Feb. 2024.

17   'At the time of writing...' Nick Merriman, *Returning the Benin Bronzes: The Story of the Horniman's Restitution* Palgrave, 2024.

18   'The 2024 Venice Biennale...' 'The Benin Artworks, Significance

and Return' Nick Merriman in *Nigeria Imaginary,* Nigeria Pavilion Exhibition, 60th International Art La Biennale Di Venezia, MOWAA Publishing.

19   'Picture a dashboard...' At Tate we already use this happiness measure to monitor colleagues' professional needs (having stolen the idea from the family company Timpsons, run by one of our former trustees).

20   'Here I try to bear in mind...' Homi K. Bhabha, 'Global Pathways', in Erika Fischer-Lichte, Torsten Jost and Saskya Iris Jain (eds.), *The Politics of Interweaving Performance Cultures: Beyond Postcolonialism,* London 2018, pp.259–75.

21   'Such 'blockbusters' do not...' On reparative readings, see Olivia Laing, *Funny Weather: Art in an Emergency,* London 2020, p.3.

Chapter 6: The 100 Year Future

1   'In subsequent years, global awareness...' 'UK Museum COP', National Museums Directors' Council, 6 Nov. 2023, http://nationalmuseums. org.uk, accessed 29 Feb. 2024.

2   'Our report clearly...' 'Climate Change: IPCC report warns of "irreversible" impacts of global warming', BBC News, 28 Feb. 2022, https:// www.bbc.co.uk/news/science-environment-60525591, accessed 29 Feb. 2024.

3   The era of global warming...' 'Secretary-General's opening remarks at press conference on climate', United Nations, 27 July 2023, https:// www.un.org/sg/en/content/sg/speeches/2023-07-27/secretary-generals-opening-remarks-press-conference-climate, accessed 29 Feb. 2024.

4   'Colleagues at the Lismore...' Eileen Kinsella, 'Devastating Floods in Eastern Australia Have Cost Galleries and Artists "Incomprehensible" Losses of Art and Property', *Artnet,* 9 March 2022, https://news.artnet. com/art-world/floods-eastern-australia-galleries-artists-2082704, accessed 29 Feb. 2024.

5   'But as museum sustainable...' Henry McGhie, 'Climate Action is Not Just for COP', keynote presentation at the National Museum Directors' Council conference Museums and Galleries Responding to the Climate and Ecological Crisis, Whitworth Art Gallery, Manchester, 7 March 2022.

6   'There is now excellent...' *The Theatre Green Book*, developed in 2022 through collaboration across UK theatres and with the support of consultants Buro Happold, the engineers leading the field in greening arts infrastructure, offers comprehensive guidance and practical support: *Theatre Green Book* (2022), https://theatregreenbook.com, accessed 29 Feb. 2024. Its buildings section has now been expanded to include all arts buildings: see *Arts Green Book* (2022), https://artsgreenbook.com/sustainablebuildings, accessed 29 Feb. 2024.

7   'The issue is that many institutions...' See International Committee for Museums and Collections of Modern Art (CIMA), 'Bizot's refreshed Green Protocol 2023', Dec. 2023, https://www.cimam.org/sustainability-and-ecology-museum-practice/bizot-green-protocol, accessed 29 Feb. 2024.

8   'Advocacy from Bizot...' For more information on the Bizot Group and the Bizot Green Protocol, please see https://www.nationalmuseums. org.uk/what-we-do/contributing-sector/environmental-conditions/.

9   'As critic Jerry...' Jerry Saltz, 'Andreas Gursky Predicted the Future – and Present', *Vulture*, 6 Dec. 2016, https://www.vulture.com/2016/12/andreas-gursky-predicted-the-futureand-present.html, accessed 29 Feb. 2024.

10 'The work spoke of mismanagement...' *The New York Times*, 2 August 1982, C. Haberman and L. Johnston, https://www.nytimes.com/1982/08/02/nyregion/new-york-day-by-day-057239.html, accessed 21 Feb. 2024.

11 'In 2014 Olafur...' Olafur Eliasson, *Ice Watch, 2014* 2021, https://

olafureliasson.net/artwork/ice-watch-2014, accessed 29 Feb. 2024.

12 'We have to find a new art...' Ben Okri, 'Artists must confront the climate crisis – we must write as if these are the last days', *Guardian*, 12 Nov. 2021, https://www.theguardian.com/commentisfree/2021/nov/12/artists-climate-crisis-write-creativity-imagination, accessed 29 Feb. 2024.

13 'As the paintings started...' 'Q&A: Vivian Suter', *Tate Etc.*, no.48, Spring 2020, https://www.tate.org.uk/tate-etc/issue-48-spring-2020/wild-art, accessed 29 Feb. 2024.

14 'To a large extent...' Foekja Boersma, Kathleen Dardes and James Druzik, 'Precaution, Proof and Pragmatism: Evolving Perspectives on the Museum Environment', *Conservation Perspectives: Collection Environments*, vol.29, no.2, Fall 2014, pp.4–9, archived at http://web.archive.org/web/20220705151233/https://www.getty.edu/conservation/publications_resources/newsletters/29_2/evolving_perspectives.html, accessed 29 Feb. 2024.

15 With great thanks, and in sad remembrance, of Achim Borchardt-Hume, at Tate Modern, who is sadly no longer with us. Also thanks to the work of his colleague Rachel Kent.

16 'The powerful letter...' Horniman Museum & Gardens, 'Horniman Aquarium's Beat Plastic Pollution display inspires young visitors', 6 July 2019, https://www.horniman.ac.uk/wp-content/uploads/2020/03/6.-beatplasticpollution-final.pdf, accessed 29 Feb. 2024.

17 'In a state of emergency...' Gillian Taylor PR, '20,000 moths to form creative call for change at COP26 in Glasgow', 8 Sept. 2021, https://gilliantaylorpr.com/2021/09/08/20000-moths-to-form-creative-call-for-change-at-cop26-in-glasgow, accessed 29 Feb. 2024.

18 'The message from this younger...' Speaking at National Museum Directors' Council conference Museums and Galleries Responding to

the Climate and Ecological Crisis, Whitworth Art Gallery, Manchester, 7 March 2022, https://www.nationalmuseums.org.uk/climate-crisis/nmdc-environment-conference-2022, accessed 29 Feb. 2024.

19   'The Tyndall Centre...' Chris Jones, Carly McLachlan and Sarah Mander, *Super-Low Carbon Live Music: A roadmap for the UK live music sector to play its part in tackling the climate crisis*, Manchester 2021, https://documents.manchester.ac.uk/display.aspx?DocID=56701, accessed 29 Feb. 2024.

20   'In 2019 we held an extremely memorable...' For more on this group and its work, see The Elders, https://theelders.org, accessed 29 Feb. 2024.

21   'This, she argued...' The video of this debate, which took place on 8 July 2019, can be seen at 'Art in Real Life: Addressing the Sustainability Challenge', Tate, https://www.tate.org.uk/whats-on/tate-modern/olafur-eliasson/art-real-life-addressing-sustainability-challenge, accessed 29 Feb. 2024.

Chapter 7: Where Now? The Museum of the Future

1   'Although the museum does hold...' For more information, please see https://museumofthefuture.ae/en.

2   'Nor do they usually...' We should note that not all privately funded museums work in this manner, and the two important Global South examples I cited earlier in the book were funded through a philanthropy that is interested in growing public engagement as well as a locally rooted artist ecology.

3   'It is a relaxed space...' Paul Gilroy, *After Empire: Melancholia or Convivial Culture?*, New York and London 2004.

4   'It recently occurred to me that art objects...' Souleymane Bachir Diagne, quoted in Grau 2021, p.225.

5   'Artist Tino Sehgal...' Tino Sehgal, *Artforum*, summer 2010: https://

Notes

www.artforum.com/features/tino-sehgal-194569/.

6 'That it was created...' See John Akomfrah, *Listening All Night to the Rain*, British Pavilion, 60th International Art Exhibition – La Biennale Di Venezia, April 2024.

7 'Furthermore, I believe we need to...' Manthia Diawara, 'Édouard Glissant's Worldmentality: An Introduction to One World in Relation', Documenta 14 https://www.documenta14.de/en/south/34_edouard_glissant_s_worldmentality_an_introduction_to_one_world_in_relation.

8 'To enact the work...' Edgar Calel, quoted in 'Tate Liverpool exhibition showcases radical new approach to collecting art', Tate, 13 June 2023, https://www.tate.org.uk/press/press-releases/tate-liverpool-exhibition-showcases-radical-new-approach-to-collecting-art, accessed 27 Feb. 2024. With many thanks to Gregor Muir and Michael Wellen for their sensitive exploration of Edgar Calel's work.

9 'This could include an attitude...' Josh Cohen, *Losers*, London 2023.

10 'That way, by resisting...' I am indebted to the brilliant artist Richard Wentworth for his idea of teaching the good manners we need if we are to disagree constructively and collaborate well, and with cultural and artistic purpose.

11 'These adventures started with...' Cornelia Parker, *Cold Dark Matter* 1991; Rachel Whiteread, *House* 1993; Jeremy Deller, *The Battle of Orgreave* 2001; Franko B, *I Miss You*, Fierce Festival, Birmingham 2000; *Anya Gallaccio*, Ikon Gallery, Birmingham 2003 and Turner Prize, Tate Britain, London 2003–4; *Rhapsodies in Black: Art of the Harlem Renaissance*, Hayward Gallery, London 1997.

12 'I saw On Kawara...' On Kawara's Date Paintings at *On Kawara: Consciousness. Meditation. Watcher on the Hills.*, Ikon Gallery, Birmingham, 1999–2000.

13 'As Josh Cohen...' Josh Cohen, *Not Working: Why We Have to Stop*, London 2018.

14   'I type these...' Isaac Julien, *What Freedom Is to Me*, Tate Britain, London 2023.

15   'As Cohen says...' Cohen 2018.